HENRY VIII'S
CONTROVERSIAL AUNT,
HONOR LISLE

Mine own sweetheart, even with my whole heart root, I have me most heartily recommended unto you... I can neither eat, sleep nor drink, my heart is so heavy, and it will never be light till I am with you.

Honor to Arthur, November 1539

HENRY VIII'S
CONTROVERSIAL AUNT,
HONOR LISLE

Her Life, Letters and influence
on The Tudor Court

AMY LICENCE

PEN & SWORD
HISTORY

AN IMPRINT OF PEN & SWORD BOOKS LTD
YORKSHIRE - PHILADELPHIA

First published in Great Britain in 2025 by
PEN AND SWORD HISTORY
An imprint of
Pen & Sword Books Ltd
Yorkshire – Philadelphia

ISBN 978 1 39905 215 3

A CIP catalogue record for this book is available from the British Library.

Typeset in Times New Roman 11/13.5 by
SJmagic DESIGN SERVICES, India.
Printed and bound in the UK by CPI Group (UK) Ltd.

The Publisher's authorised representative in the EU for product safety is
Authorised Rep Compliance Ltd., Ground Floor, 71 Lower Baggot Street,
Dublin D02 P593, Ireland.
www.arccompliance.com

For a complete list of Pen & Sword titles please contact
PEN & SWORD BOOKS LIMITED
George House, Units 12 & 13, Beevor Street, Off Pontefract Road,
Barnsley, South Yorkshire, S71 1HN, England
E-mail: enquiries@pen-and-sword.co.uk
Website: www.pen-and-sword.co.uk

or

PEN AND SWORD BOOKS
1950 Lawrence Rd, Havertown, PA 19083, USA
E-mail: uspen-and-sword@casematepublishers.com
Website: www.penandswordbooks.com

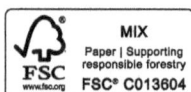

MIX
Paper | Supporting
responsible forestry
FSC
www.fsc.org FSC® C013604

Praise for *Honor, Lady Lisle*:

'Impressively researched and engagingly written, this excellent biography sheds light on one of the great chroniclers of Henry VIII's reign: Honor Grenville, Lady Lisle, whose letters are among the most important sources for the period. With a wealth of fascinating detail and evocative descriptions, Amy Licence has crafted a compelling portrait of a woman who lived under the shadow of the Tudors and suffered terrible tragedy as a result.' – Alison Weir

'What a history this is – stretching from the personal life of a lesser-known woman of the Tudor court to the opening of a global world of trade. Honor, Lady Lisle is the heart at the centre of this story and around her are the famous and notorious actors of the Tudor drama that was the death of so many innocent men and women charged with heresy, with treason and wrongly and unjustly accused. Amy Licence gives us an intimate glimpse into the household at Calais with its cages of quail and its kennels of spaniels, and even into the glorious wardrobe of the fashionable woman who commanded, through her adoring husband, a border garrison at a time of war.' – Philippa Gregory

'Yet another riveting and impassioned study from Amy Licence, for so long an admirable champion of history's neglected women. A probing account into a time of colossal religious and political change, deftly executed with commendable empathy and expertise. When it comes to delving deep into the sixteenth-century female experience, few can rival Licence's masterly skill.' – Nathen Amin

'Historians have long used the rich and illuminating Lisle letters to better understand the notable characters at the Henrician court. Now, for the first time, we can fully appreciate the life of the woman who wrote and received those letters. Thick with detail and sharp on analysis, Amy Licence has made vivid the previously opaque world of the often controversial Honor, Lady Lisle – a triumph.' – Owen Emmerson

'Honor Plantagenet was an important, fascinating, and flawed member of Tudor high society. Using Honor's own words and a wealth of information, Amy Licence has restored her in this fascinating biography, where fans of Tudor history will find a fresh portrait of power, privilege, and terror in the age of Henry VIII.' – Gareth Russell

'After the Pastons came the Lisles – a pair of impassioned letter writers whose missives give us a similarly invaluable insight into their age. Honor Plantagenet – married to Lord Lisle, illegitimate uncle of Henry VIII – is a Tudor powerhouse to stand comparison with the better known Bess of Hardwick. All credit to Amy Licence for bringing her neglected figure into the light. But Licence also immerses the reader in the daily world of this sixteenth-century outpost of empire and in doing so gives a wonderfully fresh perspective on the Tudor court back home.' – Sarah Gristwood

Contents

Dramatis Personae

Honor Grenville, Lady Basset, Lady Lisle, Plantagenet 1493–1566.

Family

Thomas Grenville II, Honor's father, d.1513.

Isabel Grenville (née Gilbert), wife of the above, Honor's mother, d.1494.

Roger and Richard Grenville, Honor's brothers; Jane, Mary, Agnes, Philippa and Katherine Basset, Honor's sisters.

Diggory and John Grenville, Honor's nephews.

John Basset of Umberleigh, Honor's first husband, 1462–1528.

Anne, Jane, Mary and Thomasine Basset, Honor's stepdaughters.

John Basset, Honor's eldest son, 1518–1541.

Philippa Basset, Honor's eldest daughter, 1516–?

Katherine Basset, Honor's daughter, 1517–1558.

Anne Basset, Honor's daughter, 1520–1557.

George Basset, Honor's son, 1522-?

Mary Basset, Honor's daughter, 1522/4–1557.

James Basset, Honor's son, 1526–1558.

John Worth, Honor's cousin, John Basset's guardian.

Thomas St Aubyn, Honor's brother-in-law, overseeing Tehidy.

Arthur Plantagenet, Lord Lisle, ?–1542.

Bridget, Elizabeth and Frances Plantagenet, Honor's stepdaughters.

John Dudley, later Lord Lisle, Earl of Warwick, Duke of Northumberland, Arthur's stepson, 1504–1553.

John, Anthony and William Wayte, maternal relatives of Arthur Plantagenet.

Court

Henry VII 1457–1509.

Henry VIII, Honor's nephew by marriage, 1491–1547.

Catherine of Aragon, Queen of England, first wife to Henry VIII, 1485–1536.

Mary Tudor, Queen of England, Honor's great-niece by marriage, 1516–1558.

Anne Boleyn, Queen of England, second wife to Henry VIII, *c*.1501–1536.

Elizabeth Tudor, Queen of England, Honor's great-niece by marriage, 1533–1603.

Henry Fitzroy, Duke of Richmond and Somerset, illegitimate son of Henry VIII, Honor's great-nephew by marriage, visitor to Calais, 1519–1536.

Jane Seymour, Queen of England, third wife to Henry VIII, 1507–1537.

Anne of Cleves, Queen of England, fourth wife to Henry VIII, visitor to Calais, 1515–1557.

Catherine Howard, Queen of England, fifth wife to Henry VIII, *c*.1523–1542.

Katherine Parr, Queen of England, sixth wife to Henry VIII, 1512–1548.

Thomas Howard, Duke of Norfolk, Lord Treasurer, uncle to Anne Boleyn and Catherine Howard, 1473–1554.

Charles Brandon, Duke of Suffolk 1484–1545.

Katherine, née Willoughby, Duchess of Suffolk, wife of the above, correspondent of Honor, 1519–1580.

Thomas More, Chancellor, executed for his beliefs, 1478–1535.

Thomas Cranmer, reformist Archbishop of Canterbury, 1489–1556.

Thomas Wolsey, Cardinal, Archbishop of York, Lord Chancellor, 1473–1530.

Thomas Cromwell, Chancellor of the Exchequer, Earl of Essex, 1485–1540.

Gregory Cromwell, son of Thomas, 1520–1551.

Edward Seymour, Earl of Hertford, Duke of Somerset, Lord Protector, 1500–1552.

William Fitzwilliam, Earl of Southampton, Lord Admiral, Treasurer, Captain of Guisnes, visitor to Calais, 1490–1542.

Stephen Gardiner, Bishop of Winchester, King's Secretary, patron of James Basset, 1483–1555.

John Russell, Earl of Bedford, Baron Russell, Comptroller of the Household, 1485–1555.

George Boleyn, brother to Anne, visitor to Calais, *c*.1503/5–1536.

Francis Bryan, correspondent of Honor, Chief Gentleman of the Privy Chamber, 1490–1550.

Henry Norris, correspondent of Honor, *c*.1482–1536.

Richard Page, correspondent of Honor, d.1548.

Anthony Browne, Master of the Horse, correspondent of Arthur, 1500–1548.

Thomas Culpeper, correspondent of Honor, d.1541.

Thomas Legh, Richard Layton and Richard Pollard, agents of Thomas Cromwell and Ecclesiastical Visitors, 1530s.

Eleanor Manners, née Paston, Countess of Rutland, friend of Honor, guardian of Katherine Basset, 1491–1551.

Mary Arundell, Countess of Sussex, Honor's niece, d.1557.

Margaret Pole, Countess of Salisbury, cousin of Arthur, d.1541.

Reginald Pole, son of the above, Cardinal and exile, cousin of Arthur, d.1558.

William Kingston, Keeper of the Tower of London, 1476–1540.

Mary Kingston, wife of the above, friend of Honor, d.1548.

Brian Tuke, secretary to Henry VIII, d.1545.

John Gage, Vice-Chamberlain, Comptroller of the Household, 1479–1556.

Perkin Warbeck, Yorkist pretender to the throne, d.1499.

Calais and the Pale

John Berners, Lord Bourchier, Lieutenant of Calais until his death in 1533.

Robert Wingfield, former Lieutenant of Calais, later Lord Mayor, adversary of Arthur, d.1539.

Jane Wingfield, wife of the above, later friend of Honor.

Richard Whethill, Mayor of Calais, adversary of Arthur.

Elizabeth Whethill, wife of the above, correspondent of Honor.

William Sandys, Baron Sandys, Lieutenant of Guisnes, d.1540.

John Wallop, Lieutenant of Calais Castle, 1490–1551.

Elizabeth Wallop, wife of the above, correspondent of Honor.

Edmund Howard, Lord Comptroller of Calais, correspondent of Honor, father of Queen Catherine Howard, 1478–1539.

John Rokewood, Councillor of Calais.

Edward Ringley, Comptroller of Calais.

Jane Ringely, née Peyton, wife of the above, correspondent of Honor.

Richard Grenville, Honor's nephew, High Marshall of Calais.

Margaret (or Maud) Grenville, wife of the above, Honor's niece by marriage.

Thomas Scriven, Mayor of Calais.

John Butler, Commissary of Calais, reformer.

Francis Hall, Spear of Calais, Honor's jailer 1540–2.

John Atkinson, chaplain and steward to Arthur.

Thomas Warley, agent of the Lisles.

Edward Corbet, servant to the Lisles.

Ralph Hare and Thomas Broke, Sacramentarians who did penance in Calais.

Dr Le Coop of Paris, Honor's physician.

John Dove, Prior of the Calais White Friars.

Adam Damplip, reformist preacher.

Gregory Botolf, chaplain to Arthur and conspirator.

Clement Philpot, servant to the Lisles and conspirator.

Henry FitzAlan, Lord Maltravers, Earl of Arundel, Deputy of Calais, Lord Chamberlain 1512–1580.

France

Francis I, King of France, 1494–1547.

Oudart du Bies, Seneschal of Boulogne, correspondent of Arthur and Honor, 1475–1553.

Jeanne du Bies, wife of the above, and daughter Ysabeau, correspondents of Honor.

Philippe de Chabot, Seigneur de Brion, Admiral of France, friend and correspondent of Arthur, visitor to Calais.

Thybalt Rouault, Seigneur de Riou, of Pont-Remy, guardian of Anne Basset.

Jeanne de Saveuses, Madame de Rouault, also Riou, of Pont-Remy, wife of the above, guardian of Anne Basset, correspondent of Honor.

Sister Anthoinette de Saveuses, cousin of Jeanne, nun at the convent of Bourbourch, Dunkirk, correspondent of Honor.

Anne de Bours, née Rouault, sister-in-law of Jeanne, of Abbeville, guardian of Mary Basset, correspondent of Honor.

Anthoine de Noyelle, Abbess of Bourbourg, St Omer, correspondent of Honor.

Ysabeau de Morbecque, correspondent of Honor.

Jehan de Gardins, priest of la Heuze, St Omer, guardian of George and James Basset

Jenne de Quierete, at the Lisle's Landreteun farm, correspondent of Honor.

Anthoine Brusset, of St Beze, Gravelines, correspondent of Arthur and Honor.

Guillaume le Gras, agent for the Lisles.

Others

Charles V, Holy Roman Emperor, 1500–1558.

John Husee, agent of the Lisles in London.

John Bonde, Honor's priest at Umberleigh.

William Bremelcum, clerk to John Basset.

Richard Norton of East Tisted, servant of John Basset.

Abbess Elizabeth Shelley, of St Mary's, Winchester, guardian to Bridget Plantagenet.

Hugh Cook, Abbot of Reading, guardian of James Basset.

John Bekynsaw, guardian to James Basset in Paris.

Sir Giles Daubeney, Baron Daubeney, Privy Councillor, Esquire of the Body and Master of the Mint, guardian to Anne and Thomasine Basset, 1451–1508

Henry Daubeney, Earl of Bridgewater, challenger to John Basset's maternal inheritance, 1493–1548.

Mr Scott and Richard Kyrton, Honor's tailors in England.

Leonard Smyth, Arthur's agent in England.

John Cheriton, merchant and agent to the Lisles.

Robert Action, Honor's saddler in Southwark.

Richard Blount, Honor's agent in Bruges.

John Smytt, goldsmith in Bruges.

Antony Baker, the Lisles' agent in Paris.

Edward Hall, Raphael Holinshed, Elis Gruffydd, chroniclers of the era.

John Foxe, Protestant author of *Foxe's Book of Martyrs*, 1517–1587.

Martin Luther, German monk turned reformer and instigator of the Reformation, 1483–1546.

Introduction

In 1493, the Tudor dynasty was entering its eighth year. The red and white paint on the union roses carved above the palace doors was still comparatively fresh and coins exchanged in the marketplace bore a slightly different face. Should any Englishman or woman have been lucky enough to get their hands on a gold sovereign, and paused about their business to examine it, they would have seen a mournful looking man seated upon a throne, smothered in rich robes, weighed down by the immense weight of his office: the heavy crown, orb and sceptre.

England's ruler, Henry VII, was a comparative outsider returned from exile, fighting to rebuild a land riven by dynastic disputes and rival claimants. His subjects had witnessed friends and relatives clashing on the battlefield, and blood spilled in the streets, as the royal houses of York and Lancaster played out their desperate struggle for the crown. Such a state of affairs could not be allowed to continue, and Henry's unexpected victory on the battlefield at Bosworth in 1485 offered the opportunity to embrace peace and move towards a new century. It was imperative that the Tudors retained control and produced heirs to secure their line.

In their grand palaces at Westminster and Windsor, Greenwich and Eltham, Henry and his wife, Elizabeth of York, raised a young family in hope of peace and prosperity. In 1493, this comprised Arthur, Prince of Wales, Princesses Margaret and Elizabeth, and a young Prince Henry (the future Henry VIII), then a sturdy toddler of 2 years old. While the queen was teaching the young red-haired prince to read his letters, a baby girl was born into a gentry family in the West Country, who would become one of the best documenters of the future king's reign. Honor Grenville is known for a collection of colourful, intimate letters detailing her domestic life in the 1530s, the exploits of her extended family, and her role as hostess and patroness. Her accounts are full of shopping and visits, pets and pleasures. In addition, she offers a perspective on tumultuous events including the systematic erosion of Catholicism, England's break with Rome, the dissolution of the monasteries, Henry VIII's colourful marital history and the births of future monarchs Elizabeth and Edward. Born just before the onset of the remarkable sixteenth century, Honor is a key primary witness of this critical decade.

Yet Honor also has a darker reputation. Through her second marriage, to Henry VIII's illegitimate uncle Arthur Plantagenet, she gained the privileged position of aunt to the king himself, bearing an ancient surname that had been held by a line of kings since 1154. Dangerous Plantagenets, survivors of the previous era, still lurked in the countryside, at court, in exile and, notoriously, in the Tower. When Henry VII had seized the throne in 1485, the family still had eighteen living descendants, most with stronger claims to the throne than he, but Honor and Arthur had the king's confidence. Their life in Calais kept Honor at one remove from Henry's VIII's court, busy as a representative of his dynasty, a minor royal who would welcome and entertain foreign dignitaries and maintain the Tudor foothold across the Channel. However, the distance also worked against them. This book will explore how Henry's paranoia about his real and perceived enemies intensified as the 1530s progressed, during which time many of his former advisers and relatives suffered the ultimate price, often on completely fabricated 'evidence'. Henry's doubts about Arthur and Honor were one element of this wider witch hunt.

After the fall of the Boleyns and his significant head injury following a fall from his horse, Henry's suspicious nature intensified. He found enemies all around him, whether as challengers to his throne or as heretics who resisted his religious changes. After the Lisles had weathered many storms, the mounting questions and criticisms aimed at Calais from the mainland suddenly snowballed. Calais was apathetic to reform, disorganised, expensive, and the Lisles found themselves in the firing line. Even the good relationships Arthur and Honor worked to establish with the French gave cause for concern – were they inviting the enemy into their home? Did the poor defences of Calais leave the town vulnerable to attack? Intrigues among the Lisles' household servants propelled the family into one of the most heartbreaking scandals of the Tudor era. After eleven happy years of marriage, Arthur's establishment was broken up and its members incarcerated and scattered.

However, it was religious reform that brought the Lisles down. The 1530s saw immense change sweep through England's churches and monasteries, destroying centuries of ritual and practice. The Henrician Reformation, urged through by Thomas Cromwell's hands, unfolded so swiftly that it created uncertainty, even confusion, about what was expected from those unwillingly appointed as its agents. Arthur was left to interpret and implement reform in a town resistant to change, which was certainly not in accordance with Honor's conscience. Subsequent historians blamed Honor's love of 'superstition' and 'papistry'. Is this another case of that familiar misogynistic malaise 'cherche la femme', or is there any truth to it? As a long-standing Catholic in a post-Reformation Europe, the question of just how far Honor was responsible for her fate has divided historians since. Predictably, Protestant martyr-collector, John Foxe, described her as 'the wicked Lady Honor ... an utter enemy to God's honour, and in idolatry, hypocrisy and pride, incomparably evil'.[1] Yet Honor's own voice, and other contemporary sources, suggest she was charming, strong-willed, industrious and loyal. Victorian biographers were slightly more circumspect, judging her case to be morally complex, from it was 'difficult to judge what Honor's religious character really was',[2] as 'she did evil that good might come: and the evil came after all',[3] to the more overt 'papist tendencies of Lisle and his wife'.[4] The religious reforms of the late 1530s provide direct context for Honor's life and their contribution to her fate is undeniable. For this first time, this book will explore Honor's faith in unprecedented detail and the impact of the Reformation upon the Lisles in Calais.

Another of Honor's alleged crimes was to be too outspoken in the patriarchal sixteenth century, especially when it came to advising her husband. Henry VIII's chief minister, Thomas Cromwell, wrote to Arthur, warning him about being governed by his wife, 'for although ... my lady might be right honourable and wise, yet in such causes as longeth to your authority, her advice and discretion can little prevail'.[5] Clearly, he thought her guilty of transgressing that most cherished of Tudor gender taboos, by interfering in her husband's business, while Arthur was too uxorious to restrain her. Such harsh censure cannot help but intrigue the historian, and demands a fresh look, five centuries after her controversial life. Was Honor Lisle wicked or devout? Devoted or controlling? How have the patriarchal pens of history interpreted, or misinterpreted her words, actions and motivation? As the king's aunt and a potential Catholic and traitor, her story embraces many ambiguities. As far as possible, this book will tell her story in her own words.

However, there is so much more to Honor than her faith and her fate, and I do not want the end of the story to spoil the telling of it. In researching Honor's life, I have drawn heavily from the domestic details of her day-to-day experience in Calais, to give a real deep-dive into the fabric of her world.

This is as much a book about the Tudor experience, from the colour of the gowns she wore, the spices she flavoured her food with, and the furnishings of her home. It aims to recreate a holistic sense of Honor as mother, wife, friend, hostess, patron, Catholic and aunt, in a thriving enclave of Tudor England that followed its own unique set of rules.

Amy Licence, Canterbury,
August 2024

One

Heritage, Birth and Childhood
1493–1513

Bideford, Devon. A fine morning in early summer at the end of the fifteenth century. Sunlight sparkles on the blue waters of the River Torridge, bringing its high tide in from the Atlantic. A wooden carrack with full, billowing sails is drawn upstream by the tide, to join the many vessels that cluster at the dock. Spilling outside from the taverns, shading their eyes from the light, sailors and merchants hurry to unload exotic cargoes from the New World. Imposing houses line the waterfront, and gently slope up the hill behind, in a mixture of smoking chimneys, gable roof ends and the odd church spire. Beyond lies the deep greenness of woods and hillsides. Bells begin to toll, drifting through the mild air, summoning the inhabitants to worship amid flickering candles and the painted statues of saints.

By the end of the fifteenth century, Bideford was one of the most important ports on the north Devon coast. Its fishermen loaded their sacks with an abundance of eels, cockles, mussels, bass and salmon that supplied the local market stalls and were traded across the county. Merchant ships, large ocean-going carracks, could sail out along the Torridge, past Appledore to the picturesque Crow Point and Westward Ho, with their long sandbanks, through the mouth of the Bristol Channel and into the choppy waves of the North Atlantic. A straight line past Lundy and round the tip of Ireland would have taken them directly to the treasures of the Eastern Seaboard, or south down to the Bahamas, newly discovered by Christopher Columbus. Although Bristol had the monopoly on New World goods, sailors and travellers would have visited Bideford spreading tales of indigenous people, strange creatures and exotic fruits and plants. These regular reminders of adventures beyond the sea, no doubt embedded themselves in the imagination of a girl destined to spend the most significant decade of her life on the other side of the English Channel.

This idyllic Devon port is where Honor's story unfolds, 200 miles away from the glamour and drama of the Tudor court. By that time, the Grenville family had become synonymous with Bideford, established there for at least three centuries before Honor's birth, lending their name and wealth to its architecture and the implementation of local justice. As their name suggests, the Grenvilles, or de Grenvilles as they were at first, originated from France, from another coastal town in the Manche district of Normandy, facing the south Devon coastline. This picturesque ancient settlement is perched high on a rocky promontory in the Bay of Mont Saint Michel, known as 'Grandivillia', in 1045/6 and by 1175, its modern name of 'Granville'. In 1066, the inhabitants were vassals of William the Conqueror, so it is no surprise that the first de Grenville sailed to England to participate in the Battle of Hastings, as part of the entourage of Walter Giffard, Earl of Longueville, later first Earl of Buckingham.

Either this Richard de Grenville, or his son of the same name, married Giffard's daughter Isabel and inherited land in Buckingham and Devon, initiating two separate branches of the family. Either they, or one of their descendants, settled in the well-located port of Bideford. Subsequent generations of de Grenvilles served the king as sheriffs, made prestigious marriages to local heiresses and achieved high office. One relative, who further anglicised his name into Walter 'Greenfield', became Bishop of York and Lord Chancellor to Edward I, while in the following century, a Theobald de Grenville II married a granddaughter of that king.

The Grenville or 'Graynfeld' manor house overlooked the western end of Bideford Bridge, with a view across the River Torridge to the less developed east bank. It would have been a substantial building, with its own hall, family accommodation, domestic wings and stables, probably improved and modernised by each generation. The house occupied a central position, on the site where numbers 1–3 Bridge Street stand today, bearing a plaque with the family name. Immediately beside the Grenville manor stood St Mary's Church, with its seventy-foot tower, where Honor's uncle John was rector between 1504 and 1509, and which the family would have attended regularly. It had been built by another Sir Richard de Grenville in the middle of the thirteenth century to replace the original Saxon church, which had fallen into disrepair. Its aisles, walls and niches would have been decorated with dedications, memorials and other reminders of the family's important role and, no doubt, their generous bequests. The statues and images of saints would be adorned with offerings, from the flowers and catch of humble fishermen to the jewels and coins of the wealthy. In the family pew, Honor would have listened to the pre-Reformation practice of honouring her ancestors in prayer, for the salvation of their souls; the name of Grenville would have rung out down the aisles many times a year. The church she knew is gone now; little of the original building remains beyond the tower, water stoop and font, perhaps the very font which was used for her christening. The Victorians completely reconstructed the main body of the church and built the ornate library which now sits squarely below the site of the Grenville house and the river, blocking the view.

Right outside Honor's front door, the famous Bideford Bridge stretched away across the feisty Torridge. The Grenville house was perfectly placed for the family to observe the daily comings and goings of townsfolk over the river, perhaps deliberately so. The largest such crossing in Devon at 678 feet long, with twenty-four archways, the first bridge had been built by a fourteenth-century ancestor named Sir Theobald de Granville I,[1] after he had been inspired by a religious vision. A papal letter of 1459 describes the bridge as sitting over a 'very rapid and dangerous river, in which, on account of the faulty structure of the said bridge, which is of wood, many persons have been drowned'.[2] The river was tidal at Bideford, with large fluctuations in the rise and fall of the waters, and the bridge's archways were uneven, perhaps as the result of being maintained by different town guilds. At some point before the 1530s, significant repairs had been made, or else it had been entirely reconstructed, being listed as the stone edifice that stands presently.[3] As was common at the time, small chapels were situated at either end of the bridge, with St Mary the Virgin's on the eastern side, and All Saints opposite, ready for the prayers and offerings of sailors and travellers.

Honor's father, Thomas Grenville II, had been born in Bideford in the 1450s, around the time that concerns were being raised about the safety of his ancestor's bridge. He was the eldest son of Thomas Grenville I (1432–83) who had decided to drop the original 'de' prefix in their name, perhaps because England was then engaged in the Hundred Years War, and the family had no desire to continue sounding French. As a young man, Honor's father had supported the Lancastrian King Henry VI during the Wars of the Roses and served as a local sheriff. In 1483, he had joined the ill-fated uprising led by the Duke of Buckingham against the Yorkist Richard III, joining his cousins, Sir Edward Courtenay, Earl of Devon and Peter, Bishop of Exeter, in raising troops to support the invasion of Henry Tudor. To do so was to risk life and limb, as well as a family's entire wealth, possessions and reputation, so Thomas must have felt strongly where his duty lay. However, adverse weather conditions scattered Tudor's fleet in the Channel and prevented Buckingham's troops from crossing the River Severn, dooming the attempt to failure. Grenville went into hiding afterwards, along with another local man, Sir Robert Edgecombe of Cothele, both of whom were subsequently fortunate enough to receive a pardon. Thomas' father, Sir Thomas Grenville the elder, had just died at the age of 51, and given his recent activity, Thomas junior was lucky to retain the Grenville inheritance intact.

Thomas was aged around 20 in the mid-1470s, when he married Isabel, formally christened Elizabeth. His wife was the daughter of Sir Otes, or Otis, Gilbert and his wife Elizabeth, née Hill, of Compton Castle, a fortified manor house fifty miles to the south-east, across Dartmoor. How Thomas and Isabel met is unknown, but the limited social circle of the landed gentry in a county as remote as Devon suggests the usual practice of arranged matches. As George Grenville of Stowe explained to his nephew in 1711: 'your ancestors for at least five hundred years never made any alliances, male or female, out of the Western counties: thus there is hardly a gentleman either in Cornwall or Devon but has some of your blood, as you of theirs'.[4]

Over the course of two decades, Isabel bore Thomas eight surviving children: two sons and six daughters. Their eldest, Roger, arrived in 1477 or 8, and was married at the age of 14 or 15 to Margaret Whiteley of Efford, soon after their covenant, or marital agreement, was signed on 11 January 1492. Roger was granted land in Kilkhampton and continued his father and grandfather's tradition of holding office locally, acting as sheriff and receiving musters for troops in times of need. The Grenville's second son, Richard, died without issue, but all six of their daughters achieved marriageable age: Jane, Mary, Agnes, Philippa, Honor and Katherine. No definite records remain to indicate the exact date of the girls' arrival, as names were only occasionally recorded by literate parents in the family Bible, and parish records were not held until after the Reformation, starting in 1538.

The first decisive event of young Honor's life was the death of her mother on 2 February 1494.[5] Isabel Grenville is likely to only have been in her mid to late thirties, but she had spent most of her married life – the entirety of her adult life – carrying and bearing children. The date of her demise raises questions about the birth order of her final two children, Honor and Katherine, who have both been variously listed as arriving in 1493. It is possible that Honor was born very early in the year, and her sister conceived straight after, with an arrival date in December, which is supported by the Victorian *History of the Granville Family*'s[6] claim that

Katherine was the youngest daughter. A potential problem with this, though, is that Katherine's marriage was planned from at least 1503, as the Pope issued a dispensation for it that year, and it took place in 1507, when the bride was potentially 13 or 14. Royal women had set a precedent for this, with Henry VII's mother, Margaret Beaufort, and his daughter Margaret Tudor being married at 13, although it was unusual for such matches to be consummated so early. Additionally, elder daughters tended to be provided for first, so Honor should have been wed before her sister, although in practice, marriages were made as they came, for any number of reasons. However, none of these problems would exist if the girls were twins. A difficult double birth at the end of 1493, might have resulted in injury or weakness that let to Isabel's death a few weeks later.

The Devon Grenvilles hadn't been content to just remain in Bideford. They had spread their empire wider, across the border into Cornwall, giving themselves a foothold in the administration of two counties. Honor may well have visited the great rural estate at Stowe, sitting twenty miles down the coast, amid fields of wandering sheep and weather-sculpted trees. The first stones of Stowe House, and its accompanying chapel, had been laid in the fourteenth century near Kilkhampton, a village listed in the Domesday Book as prestigious farmland. Isabel's death at Kilkhampton suggests the family were in the habit of visiting, and her burial in the chapel makes it more likely that Honor and her siblings returned on her memorial day, which also fell upon the Feast of Candlemas. The medieval building known to the Grenvilles was replaced in the 1670s by a larger, more impressive edifice that swiftly proved too expensive to maintain, being demolished in 1739 after that branch of the family became extinct. All that remains today of its structure is a faint outline on the ground beside Stowe Barton Farm, where the three clarions of the Grenville family arms are carved above the main door.

Thomas Grenville's career took off with the arrival of the Tudors. Given his Devon location, and former support for Buckingham's rebellion, it is highly likely that he joined the swell of men marching north-east in the wake of Henry Tudor's landing at Milford Haven. He may have fought at Bosworth although his name does not appear among the men listed in the contemporary ballads that recount the battle. Yet promotion came swiftly after. As early as 12 September 1485, three weeks after Bosworth, 'Thomas Graynfeld' was appointed Sheriff of Cornwall and returned 40s to the Crown from his region the following Easter, with a further 6s 8d in the Michaelmas receipts.[7] At the end of 1488, he was included as 'Thomas Greynvile' along with his friend, Robert Edgecombe, in instructions to 'examine how many archers each is bound to find for the king's army and to take muster of those archers preparatory to the expedition for the relief of Brittany'.[8] The following March, as 'Thomas Graynvile', he benefited from the release and quitclaim from certain manors in Devon and Dorset, which would have been a welcome contribution to his income.[9]

Further ties brought Thomas even closer to the Tudor family into which his daughter would later marry. Henry VII appointed him to the prestigious role of Esquire of the Body, an honour defined in the royal household book the *Liber Niger* as being 'attendant upon the king's person, to array and unray (*sic*) him, and to watch day and night'.[10] This meant it was his responsibility to dress the king and be a watchful presence in his bedchamber at all hours, a role that was given as a reward to only a trusted few. To fulfil his duties, Thomas would have had to attend court in London regularly, spending periods of weeks there depending upon the rota, returning to regale his Devon household with tales of life at the palaces of Richmond, Greenwich and Westminster. The role may have brought him into contact with the royal children, the eldest of whom was Arthur, Prince of Wales, who turned 11 in 1497, but was frequently away from court in his own establishment in Ludlow. Thomas is more likely to have seen Princess Margaret who was 9, Prince Henry aged 6 and the new arrival, Mary, born in 1495, the same year that her elder sister Elizabeth had died.

Thomas Grenville also served the king closer to home. Despite Henry VII's firm grasp upon the throne, the nature of his succession invited challenges from those still loyal to the former regime. In 1497, the Yorkist pretender to the throne, Perkin Warbeck, landed on the tip of Cornwall and proclaimed himself as Richard IV upon Bodmin Moor, using the identity of the younger of the two Princes in the Tower. Warbeck, who was probably a merchant born in Tournai, marched his 6000-strong army of rebels through Exeter to Taunton, 60 miles east of Bideford. Grenville would have been summoned to assist Henry VII, swelling the king's forces in Taunton on 4 October, leading the crowd to disperse. It may have been on this occasion, three years after being widowed, that Thomas connected with his second wife, the widow of a Hill de Taunton, who bore him two further children, John and Jane.

If Honor had not yet heard of the name Plantagenet – her future married name – the chances are that events of 1499 raised it in the Bideford streets. The troublesome brother of Edward IV and Richard III, George, Duke of Clarence, had left behind two children, both born in nearby Somerset;

Margaret who had been married off to a de la Pole cousin of Henry VII, and Edward, Earl of Warwick, by all accounts a gentle soul who had been incarcerated in the Tower of London since 1485, and as a result 'could not discern a goose from a capon'.[11] Amid Henry VII's negotiations for a Spanish bride for his eldest son, the question of national security had arisen, prompting a show trial for potential claimant-to-the-throne, Edward. Questionably linked to the uprising of Perkin Warbeck, Edward Plantagenet was nevertheless beheaded in late 1499, sending a bleak reminder of the dangers of bearing that illustrious name.

In October 1501, Catherine of Aragon landed at Plymouth on the south coast of Devon, ahead of her marriage to Prince Arthur. From there, her colourful entourage began their slow journey along the bottom of Dartmoor to Exeter, where she was welcomed by a delegation sent by Henry VII, led by the Earl of Surrey, with a 'goodly company' of the nobility of the south west, who had travelled 'with godly manner and haste with right honourable gifts to repair to that noble princess'.[12] As local sheriffs, it is inconceivable that Thomas and his eldest son Roger Grenville, did not rush to join the welcome party if they were able. This was not just duty, but wise forward planning. Catherine represented a new regime, a future queen of England, whose favour was worth courting from the first. Leland cites a contemporary account describing how she was saluted 'with all required points and feats of courtesy… entertaining her with her pleasures, presents and attendances, waiting and guiding her' upon her journey.[13] From Exeter, Catherine progressed to Honiton and over the Somerset border to Crewkerne and on towards London. The Grenvilles may have accompanied her all, or part, of the way.

Thomas' involvement in Catherine's arrival is confirmed by Henry VII conferring upon him the prestigious honour of becoming a Knight of the Bath just weeks later. On the eve of Arthur and Catherine's wedding, which took place on 14 November 1501, Thomas was initiated into the order alongside his son-in-law, Sir John Arundell of Trerice, husband of Honor's sister Jane, and Sir John Basset, a north Devon knight who would become Honor's first husband. The initiates took a ritual, purifying bath in the Tower of London, after which they were dressed in special robes and kept vigil until dawn. Then, Thomas would have made confession, heard Mass and been brought before Henry, who dubbed him with a ceremonial sword. Attendance at the wedding followed, and with it the possibility of service in the household of the future king. However, the promise of Arthur was short-lived, as he died unexpectedly in April 1502, passing the royal mantle to his brother, Prince Henry. Catherine of Aragon, however, remained at court, and Honor would later witness her unfolding story.

At court, Thomas Grenville is likely to have encountered the most significant person in Honor's story, her future husband, Arthur Plantagenet, a throwback to the Yorkist years. However, unlike his de la Pole and Warwick cousins, or the various pretenders of the 1490s, Arthur was not considered dangerous, and was welcomed into the fold, probably because he displayed no pretensions to the throne. An illegitimate son of Edward IV, probably by his mistress Elizabeth Wayte, sometimes known as Elizabeth Lucy, Arthur is estimated to have been born at some point between 1461 and 1480, perhaps in Calais, perhaps on the Wayte's Hampshire estates. The range of possible birth dates is problematic when trying to estimate Arthur's age, and subsequently, the nature of his relationships. He was a child at his father's court, then lived with his mother's family in Hampshire, before joining the household of his half-sister Queen Elizabeth in 1501. Two years later, though, the queen died in childbirth, and Arthur passed into the household of King Henry VII, where Honor's father would have had ample opportunity to know him further. Arthur was a companion of the adolescent Prince Henry, who respected and admired his half-uncle, their closeness and shared pursuits suggesting a man in his twenties, rather than his forties. Thus, Thomas Grenville may have unwittingly sown the seeds for his daughter's future marriage.

As the future king grew into a headstrong and exuberant youth, Honor experienced a childhood which was far quieter, and more typical of a girl of her class and location. Bideford was considered a healthy atmosphere to raise children despite its Atlantic climate, as a later historian of the town noted, due to its 'current of salubrious marine air in the summer' and the winter mildness, which prevented the inhabitants from 'suffering the inconvenience of intense frosts or lying snow'.[14] Honor's letters reveal that she was raised a Catholic and imply primarily domestic concerns; hospitality, patronage, friendship, the importance of material comforts, clothing, stocking the larder, pets, gardens, saddles, falcons, plate, furnishings, illnesses and cures, and all the things required to keep the household of her future husband running according to its estate. She would also be expected to develop high-class domestic skills such as embroidery, and the creation of culinary treats and remedies in the dairy and distilling room. Above all, though, her role was to provide children. Honor was able to read both print and handwriting but she could not write. Her letters were dictated, and she only put pen to paper shakily, when it came to adding her own name. The clerk she later employed was 'a priest, a very honest man, [who] would gladly do service to my lord and your ladyship' and who was particularly prized for his ability to write 'a very fair secretary hand and text hand and Roman' as well as being able to sing, play 'cunningly' upon the organ and being skilled in the cultivation of vegetables, of 'cocomers' (cucumbers) 'and other yerbs' (herbs).[15]

Honor and her siblings missed out on the Humanist educational wave sweeping Europe that benefited the upper-class women of their daughters' generation. Their early years were shaped more by the gendered advice of *The Book of the Knight of La Tour-Landry*,[16] a fourteenth-century manual republished in English by Caxton in 1484, than by Juan Luis Vives' *The Education of a Christian Woman*,[17] written for Princess Mary Tudor in 1523. Landry's advice included the importance and power of prayer, obedience, fasting, humility and good manners, with chapters titled 'How the king of Spain chose of the daughters of Aragon the humblest, most courteous and gentlest of speech, rather than the most beautiful; and that gentlewomen should have gentle hearts', and 'Of the woman who stole her husband's eel, ate it and lied about it', and 'How a magpie told the husband of the deception, and of the wife's revenge on the bird'. In other chapters, a 'foolish wife' publicly insulted her husband and was punished and disfigured by him as a result; another was also disfigured, but by fighting with her husband's female friend, and so lost his love, while elsewhere in the text, three merchants wagered how obedient their wives were, and put them to trial. Landry's resounding message is that of wifely obedience, coupled with a possibly unintentional subtext of the superficiality of male love.

The Grenvilles may have followed the middle-class custom of finding placements for their adolescent children in noble households. This could be among the children of another local family, or in a semi-service capacity, or in a local religious establishment. As a mother, Honor kept her children close during their early years but placed them out with trusted others, especially after her move to Calais. Her stepdaughter, Bridget, was raised by nuns from the age of 7 or 8, being taught reading and writing, religious instruction, needlework and good manners. Katherine was placed with a countess, while two of Honor's Basset daughters lodged with French families, learning good manners and social skills for the later court positions she was zealous in seeking for them.[18] Honor's early years, in the 1490s and 1500s, probably combined elements of these experiences – religious teaching and practice, reading improving books, sewing, games, behavioural and cultural lessons – designed to equip her with skills to make a good marriage. One after the other, she watched her sisters marry, all within the Devon and Cornwall network.

The Grenville family's royal favour continued into the reign of Henry VIII. Thomas received commissions of the peace for Devon between 1509 and 1513, as did his son Roger, who took over as Sheriff of Cornwall in his father's declining years.[19] This period reveals Thomas' connections to the sea and the preservation of Devon's waterways, for varied reasons. In June 1511, he received a commission from the king to assist in the maintenance of sewers 'for the district extending from Michellis Bourgh to Lyng, thence to Bokeland, thence to Bridgewater, and thence to the sea'.[20] Thomas had also invested in the industry that surrounded his Bideford base, being listed in the naval exchequer accounts for February 1513 as the master of a ship called *The Second New Spaniard*, captained by Edward Etchingham of Suffolk.[21] An experienced naval officer, Etchingham had supplied boats and soldiers for Henry VIII's engagement with France in 1512, being appointed to man Grenville's 280-tonne ship the following year, which he filled with sailors from Coventry. In May 1513, Etchingham sailed the ship to harry the French a second time, this time under the direction of Charles Brandon, Duke of Suffolk, although by this time, Thomas' association with the vessel had already ended.

Honor was aged around 20 when her father Thomas died on 18 March 1513. His will[22] was written on 9 March, nine days before his death, suggestive of a short illness or the acceleration of an existing one, and was proved the following May. Firstly, he made arrangements for his burial, specifying his desire to be buried 'in the church erthe of Bedyford, in the south est Parte of the Chancell dore … to make an Alterie and a Preste to sing there to pray for me and all my auncestors and heires forever'. He wished his chapel to contain 'my Cope of tissue and my vestiment of the same, and a suet [suit] of black velvet to be made of such velvet gowns as I have'. He bequeathed £6 1s 4d to the church and bridge at Bideford and £4 to St James' Church, Kilkhampton. Of all his daughters, he was most concerned for Honor, whom he provided for first, instructing her older brother Roger to arrange her match: 'I wille that my Sonne Roger shall marry my daughter Onor, and to gyve her in marriage CCC [300] markes to be leveyed of my landes and goodis'. The much younger Jane Grenville, Thomas' youngest child by his second marriage, 'which I had by my last wyff', was also unwed, but received only CC (200) marks towards her dowry. Thomas added that 'yf the saide Onor and

Jane fortune to dye or ever they be maryed', then Roger was to dispose of the money as he saw fit.[23]

In accordance with his wishes, Thomas was buried in St Mary's Church, Bideford, beside the family home. His monument was created on the south side of the chancel near the altar, featuring a recumbent figure on an ornately carved stone table with an arch and screen above, decorated with quatrefoils, heraldic devices and coats of arms. The Grenville arms impale those of his first wife, Isabel Gilbert, of three roses upon a golden chevron. Thomas reclines in the typical fashion of the final pre-Reformation years, his feet resting on a dog, his hair shoulder-length, his neck hung with the heavy gold chains of office, his armour fashionably riveted, although, unusually, a carved item clasped in his hand may be his heart.[24] His head tilts slightly to the left, and he has the appearance of having been a strongly-featured man, although time has worn his features down. The Latin inscription reads: 'Here lies Thomas Grenville, knight, patron of this church who died on the 18th day of March in the Year of Our Lord 1513, to whose soul may God look on with favour Amen'.

Two

Lady Basset
1513–1529

Between the years of Honor's birth in 1493 and Thomas' death in 1513, the western world embarked upon a trajectory of immense cultural change. Christopher Columbus' accounts of parrots and gold across the Atlantic were reaching the remote villages of Devon, and sailors heading along the Torridge into the Bristol Channel in May 1497 might have caught sight of John Cabot's fleet laden with goods to trade in the New World. Cabot's crew returned with tales of an 'excellent and temperate' country where silk and Brazil wood, source of the red dye brazilin, could be found, and the seas were 'swarming with fish'.[1]

As Honor grew from childhood into adolescence, the world was being recorded in more accessible forms. From the Mappa Mundi which depicted the American coastline surrounded by sea monsters, to the first globe or 'earth-apple', cartography was moving into the third dimension. Clocks were already widespread in city centres but a Nuremberg watchmaker, Peter Henlein, had created a portable timepiece, or pomander watch, by miniaturising the pendulum and coil spring mechanism, so that it could be carried about in the hand. Thus, the wealthy were gaining greater precision and autonomy over how they spent their time. In Poland, the mathematician and astronomer, Nicolaus Copernicus, had begun work on his thesis arguing for a heliocentric view of the solar system, challenging the traditional belief that the sun orbited the earth. Yet, natural occurrences were still met with superstition and fear, such as when a comet blazed across the West Country, four days before Christmas 1472, with a white flame 'fervently' burning. When an exceptionally high tide rose in 1483, preventing the rebellious Duke of Buckingham from crossing the Severn, resulting in his capture and execution, this would have been seen as propitious. Unusual phenomena such as storms, floods and comets were considered to be divine commentary upon the sins of mankind and omens of future disaster.

Art was undergoing a revolution too. A great wave of Renaissance style was sweeping north from Italy, permeating the European courts with its canvases, architectural features and Humanist thought. The Florentine artist, Leonardo da Vinci, had produced his most famous works, *The Last Supper*, *Lady with an Ermine* and the *Mona Lisa*. Michaelangelo had sculpted his 'David' and, shortly before Thomas Grenville's death, finally finished painting the Vatican's Sistine Chapel, with its famous scene 'The Creation of Adam'. German artist Albrecht Durer had created his *Adam and Eve* and his Christ-like *Self-Portrait at Twenty-Eight*, while in the Netherlands, Hieronymus Bosch had spent ten years working on his famous triptych *The Garden of Earthly Delights*. Honor would never see these images, but in later life she would come into contact with those who had. Fulfilling his duties as Esquire of the Body to the king, Thomas Grenville would have passed through the new Renaissance galleries and gardens Henry VII was building at Richmond, with their statues, friezes and rondels. The frenzied cultural output concurrent with Honor's childhood represented a shift which laid the foundations for great change, which she would sometimes embrace, sometimes reject.

Honor's life unfolded in the immediately pre-Reformation period, which shaped her lasting Catholicism. St Mary's Church towered over her Bideford home, summoning her with its bells, with its scent of incense, to listen to the sermons of her uncle, with prayers and religious readings central to her daily routine. Along with her sisters, she may have laid some of the traditional, simple offerings of flowers, coins, fruit or symbolic items before the carved statues of Mary and Jesus, on special holy days, and asked for guidance. Saints were considered a real, active presence in late medieval life, interceding for those in need, and strong ties of devotion were established based on geographic location, especially in rural communities. Right beside Honor's future marital home at Umberleigh was the twelfth-century shrine of St Urith, a martyr whose popularity as a focus of pilgrimage grew stronger during the period of her residence there, with a fraternity founded nearby in 1508. She may also have been aware of the cult of St Rumon of Tavistock, relics of whom were visited by pilgrims at Tavistock Abbey in south Devon, and in whose honour a three-day fair was held annually. More than this, Honor's Catholicism embedded a belief system which would define her lifelong practices and thinking, her very relationship with God. It was also a guarantee of everlasting bliss and the salvation of her soul for eternity. This was a definitive, powerful credo that helps us understand who she was.

Yet, this centuries-old way of life was already under threat. Even during Honor's childhood, questions of reform were being voiced at home and abroad. A more ascetic life was advocated by friar Girolamo Savonarola, who staged a burning of luxury items in the Bonfire of the Vanities in Florence, in 1497, before finding himself immolated in the same location a year later. German law student, Martin Luther, had become a monk after being struck by a bolt of lightning and was already formulating his objections to certain ecclesiastical practices which he would nail upon the church door at Wittenburg in 1517. In England, centuries-old traditions of pilgrimage and saints' cults came under scrutiny from figures of the European Renaissance, like Desiderius Erasmus, in a scathing satire upon shrines and Church wealth. For now, though, the king and his court clung to their Catholic beliefs.

The young Honor may have been more aware of these dramatic changes than her remote location suggests. Early Tudor Devon was insular, almost a backwater, in comparison with the rapidly evolving London court, but it had coastlines, and coastlines allowed for traffic. Foreigners visited Devon and Cornwall regularly, swelling their ports, bringing news and trade, genes and germs. Only a hundred miles east from Bideford lay the port of Melcombe Regis, where the dreaded black death had first arrived on English soil in 1348, and those locals in sight of the Channel were attuned to the appearance of potential French and Spanish raiders on the horizon. Cornish MPs complained to parliament of 'great disruption and damage' caused by 'the enemy' and 'the burning of all the ships, boats and towns which are in the ports and along the coast of the sea'.[2] By 1437, the alien subsidy returns[3] indicate that a Cornish port like Fowey, thirty-five miles from Honor's future manor of Tehidy, contained Irish, Dutch, Flemish, French and Breton residents, most of whom were servants or made a living on the sea. In the early years of Henry VIII's reign, 23 Bretons lived in St Ives, just round the bay from Tehidy, and there were over 300 in the county by 1523.[4]

Honor's native Devon seemed to attract more foreigners than Cornwall. In 1440, her home county recorded 675 resident foreigners, of whom only 436 paid tax and although full returns do not survive from 1483, they indicate the presence of Flemings, French, Scots, Germans, Portuguese and a 'Jacobus Black' who was a servant in Dartmouth, originating from either Indea (*sic*, India) or Judea.[5] Honor would have seen their ships arrive in Bideford, sailing down the river, but as a knight's daughter, the extent of her interactions with them would have been limited. Foreigners came and went, sometimes even residing in the town, but the high tax levied upon their subsidies expose just how far they were classified as competitors. Devon's leading families were insular-looking, socialising with those of similar status within the Cornish-Devon network, which had supplied spouses to the Grenville family for ten generations.[6] As Honor approached her late teens, she would have been looking for a husband closer to home.

In the 1510s, no one would have dreamed that a Grenville daughter might marry into the royal family. It was about as absurd as a Boleyn becoming queen. When it came to the marriages of Honor's sisters, potential husbands were knights and gentry, selected from within a maximum radius of seventy miles from Bideford. The eldest, Jane, moved furthest away from home, having been married in the year of Honor's birth, to Sir John Arundell of Trerice, near Newquay in Cornwall. There was already an existing family connection, as Honor's great-great-grandmother, Margaret, had survived Sir John Grenville upon his death in 1412 and remarried into the Arundell family, bringing her new husband to live at Bideford. It was a prestigious match socially, as Sir John was Sheriff of Cornwall, appearing in the rolls for November 1510,[7] and receiving commissions of array in 1511,[8] but he was also Vice-Admiral of the West. This made John responsible for controlling shipping and piracy, defending the coast and fulfilling his local duties as a Justice of the Peace. Jane bore their first child in 1495, when Honor was 2, and went on to deliver five more, so it unlikely that Honor had much contact with her while she was growing up in the Grenville's Devon home.

Jane's match paved the way for Katherine, possibly the youngest Grenville daughter if not Honor's twin, who married another Sir John Arundell. However, this Sir John came from Lanherne, a junior branch of the family, based sixty miles from Bideford, just a short ride from Trerice, allowing these two Grenville sisters to establish a closer connection. Katherine's John became a Knight of the Bath in 1494 and was made Receiver General of the Duchy of Cornwall in 1506. He had previously made a prestigious first marriage to Eleanor Grey, granddaughter of Queen Elizabeth Woodville, wife of Edward IV, making Katherine stepmother to his four children. Katherine became his second wife in around 1507, when she was in her early teens and he was 33, bearing him a girl named Mary, who would later encounter Honor's daughters at the Tudor court. In 1513, John accompanied Henry VIII on expedition to France, where he was made Knight Banneret for fighting at the Battle of Spurs, where Thérouanne fell to the English.

The third Grenville daughter, Agnes, was not too far away from her sisters, marrying John Roscarrock, of Roscarrock near Port Isaac, where the grey stone house still stands in an idyllic location in sight of the sea. Twenty-three miles north of Trerice and eighteen north of Lanherne, it forms the third corner in the triangle of the Cornish Grenville marriages.

The marriages of Mary and Philippa Grenville took them in the opposite direction, east into Devon and Somerset. Second daughter Mary became the wife of Richard Bluett of Holcombe Rogus, fifty miles east of Bideford. However, as a younger son, Richard took his wife to reside at Cothay Manor, a further three miles to the north-east, across the border into Somerset, spending years expanding the house. Local legend states that he planted red and white roses in the newly created gardens to mark the end of civil conflict in 1485,[9] although the lack of contemporary use of those symbols gives this anecdote the feel of romance and hindsight. As the fourth Grenville daughter, Philippa's marriage to Francis Harris took her sixty miles south of Bideford to Radford in Plymstock, now a suburb of Plymouth, where the Harris family had established their seat during the reign of Henry VI.

According to the terms of Thomas Grenville's will, his eldest son Roger was charged with arranging the marriage of his sister Honor, but the process of selecting her spouse may have begun earlier. Sir Thomas had already come into contact with his contemporary, Sir John Basset, as part of the Cornish network and can be placed in the same room on at least one occasion. Basset, of Tehidy in Cornwall and Umberleigh in Devon, had been born in 1462, into a family of Norman settlers from Montreuil-au-Houlme. The Bassets had arrived in Cornwall in the twelfth century, when Baron Thomas married Adeliza de Dunstanville, acquiring the manor at Tehidy, situated on the north Cornish coast between St Ives and Newquay.[10] Honor's future husband was a reliable, loyal servant of the Crown, filling the family role of Sheriff of Cornwall in 1497, when the Cornish rebels, enraged by high taxes, gave support to Perkin Warbeck's invasion and marched to Taunton, where Sir Thomas Grenville awaited them. While Basset was absent from home, possibly assisting in Taunton, the rebels turned upon his Tehidy home and dismantled it, piece by piece. The house was being rebuilt when John became a Knight of the Bath in 1501, an experience he shared with Thomas.

John Basset had already been married once, in a union arranged in 1474, to Elizabeth Denys, daughter of John Denys of Orleigh, just south of Bideford. Basset was only 12 at the time, and Elizabeth's age is unknown, so the couple would have waited until at least their middle, or late, teens before consummating the match. Their only son died young, but four daughters survived, born between the late 1470s into the 1490s, making them contemporaries of, if not actually older than, their new stepmother Honor. By this point, Basset had despaired of fathering a son, so settled his inheritance upon a local dignitary, Sir Giles Daubeney, Baron Daubeney, Privy Councillor, Esquire of the Body and Master of the Mint, in the expectation that he would marry his son and heir, Henry, to one of the Basset girls. In 1504, an official agreement, the Great Indenture, was drawn up and two of Basset's daughters, Anne and Thomasine, were sent to join the Daubeney household at South Petherton in Somerset.

Living on the site of an old royal palace, in a town significant enough to have once contained a mint, in a family with royal connections, the two Basset girls would have had expectations of grand futures. As the heir's potential bride, Anne and Thomasine acquired the status of other daughters in the family, rather than carrying out the light servant duties of some displaced adolescents. However, the indenture did not outlive Giles' death in 1508. For some reason, the proposed match did not go ahead, and Anne married James Courtenay instead, from a junior line of the Earls of Devon. Thomasine does not appear to have married and is likely to have returned in 1515 to the family home of Umberleigh, where her sister Jane dwelled, also unwed. They were probably in their thirties at the time of Honor's arrival, deep into the socially ambiguous territory of spinstership. Margery, or Mary, Basset, is likely to have already been married by the time Honor arrived, to William Marrys of Marhayes Manor, just south of Kilkhampton, and therefore was not the new stepmother's responsibility.

In 1515, at the age of 22, Honor married the 53-year-old John Basset. The groom might have travelled to Bideford and said his vows in St Mary's before carrying his bride home, or else Roger escorted his sister eleven miles east to the parish of Umberleigh. Set on the old A337 to Exeter, with a modern population of 360, the village overlooks the flat green plain bisected by the river, with scattered houses spread along wooded lanes. The Basset manor overlooked the River Taw, a mile from its bridge on the western bank, on a site where the palace of King Athelstan is reputed to have stood,[11] two miles from Chittlehampton's St Urith's shrine. The house originally had a chapel attached, founded in the thirteenth century, of which a single wall remains as part of later farm buildings. Dedicated to the Holy Trinity, with pointed gothic doorways and lancet windows in the Romanesque style, it contains tombs of three knights in full armour.

Surviving architectural fragments display elaborately carved and moulded designs of quatrefoils, shields and perpendicular lines. If this was the location where Honor and John exchanged their vows, it would have neatly echoed the ceremony of her own grandfather, Thomas, who had married his first wife, Anne Courtenay, in the chapel in 1447. Honor received the manors of Tehidy and Umberleigh, and lands in Bickington and Atherington as her marriage settlement.

Little is known about Honor's first marriage. It represents a considerable silence in the life of a woman who later proved to be such a regular, thorough and efficient communicator, yet in her silence, Honor is more typical of her peers, and it is actually her hoard of later letters that are the historical anomaly. A generation separated husband and wife, but to the patriarchal nature of rural society, when spouses were legally, culturally and morally unequal, this was considered an advantage. Honor had been passed from the care of one father into that of another, experienced, older man, who would guide and protect her.

Judging from the evidence of her letters, it is not difficult to imagine Honor as a busy and engaged wife, seeing to the needs of her new family, running the household, active in the community, in charity work, and bustling about the parish. If she was in line with contemporary advice echoed in the 1484 translation of *La Tour-Landry*, Honor would have been respectful in company, yet counselled her husband in private 'with goodlie words' and 'not cause striff between them ... in especial before folk', and 'chastised herself with kindness' in order to learn. This image is far removed from the admonishment Cromwell gave Lord Lisle in the 1530s, about Honor being too free with her advice. Landry was adamant that 'the pleasaunce of all good women ought to be to visite and to fede the poor and fatherless children, and to norshe and clothe yong litelle children'.[12] Honor had to adapt to the demands of her new role, but large families were common, with remarriages among the gentry blending potentially several households into one, at a time when 'until death do us part' might realistically represent only a handful of years. The kindness and diligence Honor displays in her later letters regarding her stepchildren began with her residence at Umberleigh, with John, Thomasine and Jane Basset.

Honor and John's marriage swiftly proved fruitful. She bore him seven, maybe eight, children within the space of twelve years. Although the brass on John Basset's tomb shows seven figures, these represent live births and a stillbirth might not have been included. Muriel St Clare Byrne, editor of the Lisle Letters, refers to an additional, short-lived first daughter named

Honor. Arriving in the same year as the marriage, 1515, the new mother's little namesake may have been premature, or else the full-term child of a wedding ceremony which had taken place between January and March. Honor appears to have been christened,[13] although this could have been by a midwife summoned to a difficult birth, rather than a celebration of her safe arrival in the Umberleigh chapel. When a newborn was understood to be in difficulty, it was customary to baptise the crown of the head, or foot, or whatever body part first protruded from the mother's body, in order to ensure the child's passage to heaven. Honor's first experience of delivery ended in loss, but she conceived again soon after, bearing Philippa in 1516. The dates of all her children's arrivals cannot be stated with certainty, but it appears that Katherine was born in 1517 and John followed a year later, giving the family the longed-for son.

As his family grew, John Basset continued his service to the Crown. On 26 June 1515, he received a commission of the peace for Devon, along with Honor's brother Roger Grenville, and Devon neighbours John Gilbert, Thomas Denys, William Courtenay and Piers Edgecombe.[14] Similar instructions were issued to him for Devon in July 1517[15] but that November, he was also one of three men named as Sheriffs of Cornwall,[16] continuing to exert significant influence in both counties. Although his appointments were indicative of his property, and presence, in Devon and Cornwall, they occur more frequently in Devon, as his family's main base.

In the summer of 1520, when Henry VIII transported his court across the Channel to meet King Francis I at the Field of Cloth of Gold, John Basset and Roger Grenville were among the contingent in attendance upon the king.[17] John was one of six knights representing Devonshire, along with William Courtenay, brother of Anne's husband, James. The five knights from Cornwall included Sir Roger Grenville, Piers Edgecombe (son of Robert of Cothele), Baron Broke and Sir John Arundell,[18] while Henry Daubeney, son of Giles, represented Somerset. Daubeney took his wife Elizabeth Neville with him, as did Robert Willougby, Lord Broke, both of which ladies were allocated two waiting women, three servants and six horses.[19] Honor's name does not appear among the lists, so it must be assumed that she remained at home, to oversee the estate and growing family; she may possibly have been pregnant at the time with her daughter Anne. For the month of June, the English king and his 5804-strong[20] entourage met, jousted, wrestled, feasted, drank, danced and prayed with the court of Francis I, staying in the temporary village with its decorated pavilion, gold tents and fountains running with wine. When the men returned home that July, no doubt Honor heard tales of the feats and marvels performed in golden valley and the knights dressed in silk and velvet, decked with gold chains. Honor may previously have heard her father speak of the king and court, but this event marked a new aesthetic, an ideal of Renaissance chivalry, 'the last golden hurrah of the pre-Reformation world'.[21] It was also her first awareness of the area of France that was later to become her home.

After John Basset's return, Honor bore four more children. Anne appears to have arrived first, in around 1520, followed by George and Mary in the next four years, with James, definitely the youngest, born in 1526–7. John continued to receive commissions for the peace for Devon in November 1520,[22] June 1521,[23] and July 1522.[24] In November 1523, he was called upon, along with his brothers-in-law, John Arundell of Trerice and John Arundell of Lanherne, to assist with the collection in Cornwall of a subsidy to assist the Duke of Suffolk in his support of the Duke of Bourbon against Francis I.[25] He was sheriff for Devon again in November 1523[26] and November 1524,[27] and representing Somerset and Dorset in November 1526[28]; he received a commission for the peace in Devon in 1524[29] and further instructions to collect the subsidy that August.[30] In March 1527, John was at Westminster Palace to witness a grant made in advance of a marriage between his associate Sir Piers Edgecombe and Lady Katherine ap Rice, who became his second wife.[31]

This record suggests Sir John was continually active in his home counties, mostly Devon, until the first quarter of 1527. Illness intervened, however, and on 6 November that year he completed his will. In it, he appealed to his brother-in-law Roger Grenville, to ensure that every year upon the anniversary of his death, he would keep 'a solemn dirige (*sic*) and the morrow upon three masses for the good estate of the said Sir John Basset and Honor his wife'.[32] Honor was left all the rents and profits from six manors, until she remarried, with which she was to pay his debts and provide dowries for her unmarried stepdaughters, Jane and Thomasine, and her own daughters, Philippa, Katherine, Anne and Mary. John Basset died in January 1528 at the age of 66, probably at Umberleigh. He was initially buried in the chapel there, although in 1818 his remains were relocated to St Mary's Church, Atherington.

John and Honor's eldest son and heir, John, was only 9 or 10 at the time of his father's death. In such circumstances, it was customary for the appointment of a male guardian, to have legal responsibility for a ward's upbringing, finances and properties until they came of age. In April 1529, John's wardship was purchased jointly from the king by Honor and John

Worth of Compton Pole, a distant cousin with connections to Umberleigh. Worth was a sewer (server at table) in the chamber of Henry VIII, whose family home was based fifty miles south of Honor's, across Dartmoor. He was granted 'custody of the possessions of Sir John Basset, deceased, during the minority of John Basset, son and heir of the said John, with wardship of the said heir' for the cost of 200 marks.[33] His partnership with Honor, and his proximity, suggests a mutually beneficial relationship, and John is likely to have continued to reside with his mother at Umberleigh for a while, or at least divided his time between her and Worth, until she remarried.

In 1533, Honor arranged for funereal brasses to be created and fixed to her husband's box tomb. Among her correspondence are the details supplied by a Richard Kyrton, updating her on their progress:

> *The plattes for the town are sent home by the carrier, and for the gilting, they must dyscrye all the arms by the reason of colours. They ask £5 for the doing of it, and George Rolle has laid out 33s. 4d. till Candlemas, which Burye then must pay him.*[34]

The brasses had been affixed to the tomb by 30 April 1534, when Honor's priest at Umberleigh, John Bonde, wrote to her about them, confirming they had been set in place by an Oliver Tomlyng, incurring a cost of £4, although the repair of the chapel would 'be a great charge'.[35] That July, George Rolle wrote to Honor that he had 'been paid for the images and scripture I bought for Mr. Bassett',[36] indicating that there was once an inscription upon the tomb, which has now been lost. The final tomb, still present in St Mary's, shows the brass image of Sir John, in traditional armour and pose, his features generic, his hair fashionably shoulder-length. He is flanked by his wives, almost identical in appearance, with their French gable hoods, sleeves trimmed in wide fur, and the long pomander on a chain hanging from a girdle decorated with a single flower. Beneath each are the small brasses of the children they bore and the wives' coats of arms. In her mid-thirties, with responsibility for four young adults and seven children, Honor found herself a widow.

Three

Lady Lisle
1529–32

1529 was an awkward year for a royal wedding. The most important marriage in England was unravelling, with Henry VIII hell-bent on proving that he was not legally united to his wife and queen of twenty years, Catherine of Aragon. Hoping to annul this first match, he would then be free to marry Anne Boleyn and father a legitimate son. That summer, the Palace of Blackfriars hosted a Legatine court, presided over by Cardinals Wolsey and Campeggio, who scrutinised the validity of the union and questioned witnesses, including the king and queen themselves. All through the spring, tension hung over the city, as legal answers were sought, arguments rehearsed, bishops and witnesses prepared their statements. The case would drag on into July, without reaching any conclusion, until it was finally, frustratingly, referred back to Rome. Yet, at some point in this difficult year, Honor married into Henry's troubled family, becoming the king's aunt.

Exactly when, where and how Honor Basset met Arthur Plantagenet, Lord Lisle, is unknown. It might have been in her home county of Devon, for although her future husband was based in Portsmouth, his duties as Vice Admiral of the West required him to oversee locations that Honor knew well. Whether he ever visited the old Basset property at Umberleigh, though, is dubious. It is more likely that they met in a town like Bideford, still a significant port, or at the Devonshire home of Sir John Worth, guardian of Honor's son John, who was based at Compton Pole, five miles from Torquay. Worth had also been serving in Henry VIII's household, offering a London connection, but in November 1529, he entered the retinue of Sir Robert Wingfield at Windsor Castle.[1] It is possible that Worth brought his young ward with him at some point to see the court, with Honor accompanying him, meeting Arthur at some royal occasion, but this can only be speculation.

However their meeting and courtship unfolded, Honor and Arthur were married before the end of the year. Remarriages among maturer bereaved spouses were common, when life expectancy, childbirth and plagues regularly cut first marriages short. Arthur was older, potentially as old as his sixties, although he may have been as young as his late forties, depending upon his birth date. Honor was then 34, and might anticipate living for decades, even bearing more children. She was already used to an older husband. Given the affection that is conveyed in their later letters, it may well have been motivated by genuine feeling and attraction. Whatever the cause, Honor had struck gold – it was an ambitious, prestigious match for a woman of the gentry class, who might easily have slipped back into Devonshire life, rejoined her extended family and lived out her days on the rural coast. Despite his illegitimacy, Arthur was significantly higher in status than the Grenvilles or Bassets, and his first wife had also had royal blood running in her veins, being a niece of Queen Elizabeth Woodville's first marriage. Yet Elizabeth Grey and Arthur had produced no surviving son; perhaps it was Honor's proven fecundity as well as her physical charm that drew the tall, mature man to the younger, diminutive widow.

Honor's new husband had been by the king's side since before his accession. In their younger days, he had jousted and feasted at his nephew's court, enforced his laws as an Esquire of the Body since 1509, served as a Justice of the Peace, a law student at Lincoln's Inn in 1511, survived a terrifying shipwreck, accompanied the king to fight in France at the Siege of Tournai and Battle of the Spurs, and been knighted in Tournai Cathedral for his efforts. His salary in that important year of 1513 had been an impressive £60 16s 8d, made to cover his expenses abroad[2] and in 1519 it had been supplemented by grants of land in England, Wales and Calais, through his wife's claim.[3] In 1518, he was recorded as living in Drayton, Hampshire, a village just to the north of the main city of Portsmouth, probably with an existing connection to his maternal family, as Drayton Manor would be leased to a William Wayte in the 1540s.[4] Arthur also owned land in Harting, an area in East Sussex, twenty miles to the north-east of Portsmouth, where he arranged for a Thomas Suffcote to carry out the harvest in 1520, for a sum of £4.[5]

Arthur had a good reason not to be present in Harting in the summer of 1520. He had accompanied the king to the Field of Cloth of Gold, along with John Basset and Roger Grenville, his name listed among the attendees. The royal favour continued at Christmas 1521, when Arthur was a carver at the king's table, sometimes when Henry dined in his privy chamber, sometimes in the great hall. When a French invasion was feared in 1522, Arthur received the commission to all ports to ensure all dwellers on the seacoast between 16 and 60 to prepare beacons to be lit and be ready to defend themselves against an invading army. Fortunately, the army did not materialise and on April 23, 1523, at Bridewell Palace, Arthur was created Viscount Lisle, a title which came to him through his wife following the death of her brother's heir. It brought a grant of 20 marks a year, which was welcome to a young family, now including three Plantagenet daughters as well as Elizabeth's three Dudley sons, who were then in their teens. Although Elizabeth herself died two or three years later, in 1525 or 1526, Arthur was to retain the viscountcy for the duration of his life.

Arthur had a life-long connection with Portsmouth and its surrounding area. The city had been an important port for centuries, witnessing the departure of many kings' invasion fleets and suffering attacks from foreign ships. Henry VII had invested in the harbour, rebuilding it in stone, creating the defensive Square Tower, creating a new dry dock and giving it royal status. In 1497, Portsmouth produced its first English warship, the *Sweepstake*, followed by the *Mary Fortune*. As the centre of trade, the navy and shipbuilding, it was the place to be for a High Sheriff of Hampshire and Vice-Admiral of England, but the necessary funds were not always forthcoming. By the 1520s, the eleventh-century castle was falling into disrepair and needed attention, and the town maintained a huge, costly presence of sailors and maritime workers. In January 1525, Arthur visited five of the king's beer houses to make an inventory of their stores, including items such as buckets, kettles, tubs, rakes etc. present at the Rose, the Lion, the Dragon, the White Hart and Anchor, followed by visits to their mills, recommending that repairs take place.[6] The following month he received a commission for the peace in Hampshire, and Henry VIII recommended his 'trusty and well beloved cousin' to William Parr – Henry's own future brother-in-law – who was seeking the promotion of a clerk.[7] Arthur was overseeing more work at Portchester Castle in December 1526, where a storehouse was being built[8] and the following summer, he was corresponding with a Robert Thorne, whom he offered to send the 'Book of Hampton', probably the town book containing legal matters to assist Thorne with establishing the release of a portion of his farm.

Arthur was also a trusted ambassador. In May 1527, on a special commission from Henry VIII, he was charged with delivering the Order of the Garter to Francis I in Paris. Arthur described his meeting with the king of France as taking place in a great hall hung with fleur-de-lys, where the king sat on a raised chair, dressed in purple velvet furred with sable, and white hose and doublet, surrounded by his court, bishops and ambassadors. The following day, Arthur witnessed Francis swear his oath in Notre Dame Cathedral, splendidly dressed, before processing to music, to the house of a nearby canon for a great feast. Arthur's attention to detail, listing the numbers of the servers and their specific roles, was no doubt sharpened by his own duties as a carver at Henry's table. A masque followed, in a palace hung with antique garlands bearing the arms of England and France, with dancers dressed in Turkish costume, followed by a pastoral story and more dramatic displays, until two in the morning.[9]

When he returned to England, Arthur's work as Vice-Admiral continued, with naval warrants, grants and payments listed for repairs carried out on the king's ships, including the *Mary Rose*. He dealt with thieves, pirates, received more commissions for the peace and assisted with the collection of taxes and subsidies. One little detail, typical of the Lisle letters, emerges in Arthur's correspondence with Cardinal Thomas Wolsey in March 1528, when he described the encounter of his ship with a Spanish pirate vessel, one of the crew whom he had taken prisoner and was keeping in the King's Tower at Portchester. Lisle then followed his account with an apology for the delay, as he had 'been ill since mid-Lent Sunday, of a surfeit, taken by eating Frydstoke fish',[10] reminding us of his humanity.

In November 1529, Arthur attended Henry VIII's fifth parliament, also now known as the Reformation Parliament, which assembled at Blackfriars early in the month, before adjourning to Westminster. It would sit for the next seven years, passing some of the most significant legislation of the century which separated the English Church from Rome and reformed religious practices in England. Arthur would only be present for a few of its subsequent years, but within its sights in 1529 were the privileges of the clergy and the reintroduction of the crime of praemunire, an old law forbidding any foreign claims of supremacy in England, which would be used to bring down Cardinal Wolsey in 1530. If Arthur's devout Catholicism caused him to privately question or doubt these changes, he was first and foremost a devout servant of the Crown, and loyal to his nephew.

Honor would have accompanied her new husband into Hampshire, where she had her first taste of his world, and met her new extended family. Between 1528 and 1530, Arthur leased two properties owned by his relation John Wayte, twelve miles apart. First, the Manor of Lee, or Lee-on-the-Solent, in Gosport, had been in the Wayte family since 1310,[11] and conceivably lies under or near the largely eighteenth-century farmhouse to the east of the River Test on Lee Lane, between Southampton and Portsmouth, in the parish of Romsey, operating as a hotel in 2024. Positioned right on the edge of the coast, it overlooked the bend in the Solent above the Isle of Wight. Second, Wayte leased him the Manor of Soberton, further inland on the River Meon, formerly owned by Titchfield Abbey. This was probably the first country home that Honor lived in as Lady Lisle, and where she began to juggle the needs of the huge extended family she had married into.

Arthur's own stepchildren, from Elizabeth Grey's first marriage, were grown men now and no longer needed a new maternal figure. John Dudley was 25, married, and a Knight of the Body, later to rise to prominence as Duke of Northumberland; Andrew, probably 22, had been placed in the household of the Duke of Norfolk, leaving only Jerome, whose biography is curiously quiet until the 1550s, by which point he was described as being infirm. Arthur's three daughters by Elizabeth, though, could not have been more than 17 at the oldest. The youngest, Bridget, attended the convent school at St Mary's Abbey, in Winchester, but the elder two girls, Frances and Elizabeth, may have been at home. Honor had inherited four more daughters from John Basset's first marriage, closer to her own age, of whom Anne and Margery were already married, and although Jane and Thomasine later lived permanently at Umberleigh, they may also have visited Soberton. Honor's own children by John Basset were all under the age of 14. Arthur purchased young John's wardship from Worth, and the boy took Latin lessons, in anticipation of a future in law. After Philippa, who was the eldest at 13, Katherine was aged 12, while Anne, George, Mary and James were between 8 and 2 years old.

The first surviving letter that mentions Arthur and Honor together dates to June 1530, when Arthur's chaplain, Oliver Browne, opened with compliments to his Lordship and Lady. His letter was directed to their Soberton home, bringing news of Arthur's impending bill about the royal parks, and the gathering of twenty-four university doctors at Westminster, no doubt to discuss the king's marriage further, although Browne coyly added, 'but what it is, I cannot certify'.[12]

Honor also kept in touch with her brother-in-law, Thomas St Aubyn, husband of her sister Mary Grenville, who was watching over Tehidy, the Cornish house she had received in her jointure from John Basset. He wrote in October 1530 that he had been attending her local courts, and watching over her businesses, to see that she lost no profit, referring to various practices of her late husband. He thanked her for a gift of rabbits, as his own warren was 'decayed', requested a new coat to replace the threadbare one and promised to send her a dish of puffins at Lent. Later, when he sent the puffins, Thomas thanked Honor for a string of beads she had sent to Mary, as 'there is none such in Cornwall, as far as he knows' and promised to send some 'fat conger' eel for her Lent table.[13] As devout Catholics, the Lisles would have been observing the strict regulations about fasting during Lent, omitting meat, eggs and dairy products, although any creatures that dwelled in or around the sea were considered exempt.

The Lisles were dividing their time between Hampshire and London. A letter Arthur wrote to Thomas Cromwell, either in 1529 or 1530, reveals that he had recently been in Winchester, but was soon due in London, typical of their movements during the early years of marriage. By November 1530, the Lisles were at court again, probably resident at Blackfriars Priory, or in the district nearby, which was situated between Baynard's Castle and Bridewell, with a set of river steps that made it convenient for court. It fell within Farringdon Within ward, lying just within the city walls as the name suggests, containing Newgate market, St Nicholas Shambles, Butchers' Alley, Bladder Street and Stinking Lane, indicative of the local meat trade, set alongside the more refined Old Exchange. If they weren't given lodgings in the Friary, as many court members were, the Lisles would have had a grand London house on somewhere like Water Lane or Knightrider Street. Honor may have worshiped at St Peter's, St Augustine's or St Martin's churches, unless she favoured the nearby cathedral, St Paul's, towering over the city at its highest point. Years later, Honor would be thanked in a letter from a Felicia Hertford, 'for your manifold goodness when I was your poor neighbour at the Blackfriars in London, when it pleased you to have me often in your company'.[14]

While the Lisles settled into married life, things at court were dramatically imploding. In the late autumn of 1530, the net closed in around Cardinal Thomas Wolsey, previously the king's closest friend and advisor, and Lord High Chancellor. Wolsey had failed to grasp the true nature of Henry's intentions towards Anne Boleyn and had persisted in trying to negotiate a French match, only to return home and find that Anne had replaced him in the king's confidence. Wolsey's failure to secure the result Henry desired during the Blackfriars Court of summer 1529 began a spiral of descent that not even the Cardinal's desperate pleas and gifts to the king could halt. That December, he was charged with the freshly resurrected crime of praemunire, (serving the Pope above the King), stripped of his properties and goods, and banished to his Archbishopric of York. For the following twelve months, Wolsey was in a state of limbo, hoping to regain favour, while Henry hesitated. It was a flood of desperate letters to the Pope that reached the ears of Henry's Orator in Rome,[15] which finally sealed the Cardinal's fate. On 4 November, he was arrested and began the journey south, no doubt anticipating his trial and execution. However, he never made it to London, dying at Leicester, which prevented the dramatic finale anticipated at court.

The Boleyn faction had gained the upper hand over one rival, but another more significant one remained. 1530 was the final Christmas that Henry, Catherine and Princess Mary would spend together under one roof. It is very likely that Arthur and Honor accompanied the king to Greenwich, for what proved to be a 'solemn'[16] festive season, when tensions were high over the unresolved divorce. Honor would have found the palace at Greenwich spectacular, with its beautiful riverside location, fountain courts and gardens, with the season marked in feasting, entertainments and devotions in chapel, and her status as part of Henry's extended family allowed her a pleasing degree of precedence. The girl from Bideford was seated close to the royal dais as her husband served the king and knew her new position in line. However, the atmosphere in those short winter days was heavy with pain. Catherine and Anne tried to avoid each other as much as possible, but their unhappy situation was plain for all to see. Early in the new year, Imperial Ambassador Chapuys reported that Anne was assured of her future, 'braver than a lion', and had wished 'all the Spaniards in the world were in the sea', including the queen, 'and would see her hanged rather than acknowledge her as her mistress'.[17] Such unpleasant sentiments must have overshadowed Greenwich, to which Honor would have been witness.

As soon as the festivities were over, Henry hastened to Wolsey's London residence of York Place, taking Anne with him, to pick over the dead man's belongings. He then set about transforming it into the new Renaissance-style palace of Whitehall that was intended to be his future home with Anne. Arthur, and perhaps Honor, visited York Place a few weeks later, where the Privy Purse accounts list one of Lord Lisle's servants as receiving 10s for giving assistance.[18]

In February 1531, Henry rejected the Pope's authority and made himself Supreme Head of the Church in England and Wales, severing centuries of English practices and allegiances to Rome. Such a bold, dramatic step was shocking, even blasphemous, for many of his subjects, who had to rapidly adjust their thinking. As deeply traditional Catholics, the Lisles would have found it politic to bite their tongues, especially when Henry displayed such contradictory behaviour by continuing to visit the shrines of High

Catholicism, leaving an offering of 7s 6d to the Holy Blood at Ashridge Priory[19] and 4s 8d to the Lady of the Rock at Dover soon after.[20] What the Lisles discussed in private, and what they thought of Henry's brazen step, went unrecorded. Perhaps Honor mentioned him in her prayers, asking for God to guide him.

From this point, events seemed to speed up. The Reformation Parliament reconvened in March, to discuss the judgements given by the great universities of Europe upon the royal marriage. Arthur would have attended, dressed in his formal black robes. April saw the court at Greenwich again, where Arthur was listed among the attendees of the traditional Order of the Garter service. Then, in the summer of 1531, Henry decided he had had enough, and rode away with Anne, leaving Catherine behind at Windsor. She would never see her husband again. Taking her place at Henry's side, Anne left no one in any doubt that she was the rising star at court, resplendent in the authority gifted to her by the king, relentless in demanding the obedience and respect of the court.

A letter written in April 1532 indicates that Honor paid a visit to Henry and Catherine's only daughter, Princess Mary. Sir Richard Hart, Canon of Bruton, who was scheduled to visit Honor, wrote that he 'would have come by her Ladyship but my Lord informed him that she was with my Lady Princess, and ordered him home by the nearest way'.[21] Mary was then 16, suffering intensely at the breach between her parents, experiencing ill health and soon to be separated from her mother forever. She was passionately opposed to the rise of Anne, marginalised by the changes to her household and now distanced from her once-devoted father. The troubled girl had become Honor's great-niece through her connection to Arthur and was probably resident at Hatfield or Eltham. With the deepening tensions between the Boleyn faction and Catherine and her daughter, it is interesting to see Honor's awareness of the difficult situation her new family faced, and perhaps extending kindness to the lonely child.

Other than this, Honor never recorded what she thought of Anne's rise. Like many of her generation, her life had unfolded quietly, with royal events and characters being little more than exciting stories in the background. Until recently, Catherine of Aragon had been a distant, romantic and tragic figure. Honor had heard tales from her father of the Spanish princess landing at Portsmouth and making the long journey to London to marry Prince Arthur, followed by her tragic widowhood, her struggle for recognition, her fairy-tale marriage to Henry, and their happiness marred by the loss of children. The adult Honor joined the king's family to find this significant figure of her childhood had been displaced by a former lady-in-waiting, of far less social standing than was usually required of a queen. What did she make of Anne? She was wise enough to court the favour of Henry's chosen one, and would later exchange greetings and gifts with Anne, but none of her letters reveal quite how close they were or whether Honor expressed any personal views about her.

Anne and Honor may have been close in age. With various estimations placing Anne's birth date between 1500 and 1507, there could have only been seven years between Honor and the queen-in-waiting, but the age gap may been as much as fourteen years. However, experience mattered, and the two women were at very different stages of their lives, with Honor managing a large stepfamily, while the childless Anne impatiently waited to be married, aware of her dwindling fertility. As a mature woman, formerly a widow, a Catholic and a mother, Honor had more in common with the cast-aside Catherine, but she was wise enough not to commit this to paper, and pragmatic enough to see that the future lay with Anne, whose new position opened up a swathe of possibilities for the Lisles. Yet Honor also shared similarities with Anne, with love bringing her from the obscurity of a provincial home into the heart of the court, mirroring the trajectory of her mistress' rise. Above all, Arthur was Henry's family, his flesh and blood, beholden to the king for his position. Whatever sympathies he and Honor felt for the rejected queen, their loyalty to Henry was beyond doubt.

Honor and Arthur are likely to have been at Windsor Castle when Anne Boleyn was created Marchioness of Pembroke on 1 September 1532. The significance of the moment was inescapable, as it elevated Anne's status ahead of the impending royal visit to Calais, where Henry intended to gain the approval of his fellow king, Francis I, for their impending marriage. And Arthur and Honor were invited to the party.

Four

Calais and Ceremony
1532–3

In October 1532, Honor first visited the town that was to become her home. Nestled on the north French coastline, Calais was all that remained in English hands of the one-great Angevin empire, a bitter-sweet reminder of the old affectation by which its kings also titled themselves King of France. The town had a long and controversial history, and a marginal, border status like no other Honor would have experienced.

Previously lost to the French during the Hundred Years' War, Calais was regained in 1437 by Edward III in a dramatic piece of theatre when the lives of six condemned burghers were spared after the intervention of the queen, becoming the stuff of legend. Yorkist rebels of the 1460s had exploited its marginal status to lurk in exile, forging forbidden marriages and planning invasions. One of them had been Arthur's own father, Edward IV, who used the town as a base to launch his campaign against Henry VI, with whom Honor's father had sided. More recently, Calais had been a conduit for Henry VIII's army in 1513, ahead of the siege of Tournai and Battle of the Spurs, and a gateway to international friendship at the Field of Cloth of Gold. Since then, Calais had retained its status of being 'other'; a piece of England across the sea, English in style and rule, yet closer to Catholic France with the constant threat of invasion hanging over its gabled roofs.

Calais' geographical location intensified its isolation. The inhospitable marshes, or Pale, spread around it in an oval shape of approximately twenty miles to the east, south and west between Gravelines and Wissant, including the outlying villages of Guisnes, Oye and Hammes, making a land buffer with northern France. And yet it was these surrounding areas, and the potential enemies beyond them, that the town relied upon for trade. In past centuries, Calais had grown wealthy on its profits as a Staple Port: a designated trading spot with accredited merchants, protected by law. From 1363, it had been the centre of trade for the Staple, an English company named after the staple or fixed market, encompassing twenty-six traders with a monopoly on wool. Seventy miles separated the town from the European economic hubs of Lille, Arras and Bruges, with Ghent at ninety miles and Antwerp and Brussels a little further afield at one hundred and twenty. A former mayor of the Calais Staple had been Richard Whittington, or *the* Dick Whittington of the well-known fairy tale, although there is no evidence that he owned a cat in Calais, or elsewhere. However, recent changes in trade and the rise of domestic wool produce had diminished the company. In recent years, this 'brightest jewel in the English crown' had fallen into decline, clinging to its former glory, which was echoed in its grand buildings and fortifications. Yet there was still enough history and the former trappings of wealth left in the town in order to put on an impressive show, a temporary façade of its former self, for the royal visitors. Calais typified all the paradoxes of a frontier town.

In October 1532, Calais was to play a strategic role in the king's great matter. After breaking with the Pope, and alienating Catherine's nephew, Emperor Charles V, Henry needed support, and turned to his former ally and rival, Francis I. It was not just desperation; Henry had good reason to think that his fellow king would be well-disposed towards the woman he wanted to marry. In her youth, Anne Boleyn had served in the household of Francis' first wife, Claude, and had frequently been at court, shaped by French manners and fashions. So in the summer of 1532, Henry planned a trip to Calais, officially to discuss the threat posed by the infidel Turks under Suleiman I, but the real business would take place during the feasting and dancing. Henry would re-introduce his intended bride and gain French approval for the immense step he planned in marrying Anne. Arthur was among those chosen to travel in the royal retinue, and Honor found herself promoted to serve in Anne's household for the duration of the visit. It was a step that brought Honor right into the heart of the king's great matter, to Anne's side, crossing the Channel, as the most dramatic months of the royal love triangle unfolded.

Henry and Anne departed from Dover aboard the *Swallow* at around three in the morning on Friday 11 October, arriving at Calais seven hours later. A small fleet was required to ferry over the numbers of men, women, horses, clothing and provisions necessary to maintain the court on a grand scale. Henry's scouts had estimated that the town and surrounding villages could accommodate 2400 visitors and 2000 horses,[1] often displacing the townsfolk, whose homes were temporarily requisitioned in exchange for a fee. Arthur was allowed twenty-four men in his retinue, not as many as a duke, who had forty or a marquis who had thirty-five, but the same as the earls and bishops.[2] As she was part of Anne's retinue, Honor may have travelled with her mistress on the *Swallow*, but upon her return from Calais, repairs and payments were made to use the Lisles' balinger from Portsmouth called *Sunday*,[3] a small, swift sea-going vessel without a forecastle, usually weighing less than a hundred tonnes but able to transport around forty people. Accounts were also settled later for meat, herring and barrels that the Lisles brought across from Soberton and Portchester Castle. The crew of the *Sunday* – Thomas Persey, master, and John Morres, pilot, along with other mariners – were also paid for the voyage.[4] This was probably the first sea voyage of a woman who had grown up watching the fishermen land their catch and the carracks sail out into the Atlantic.

As her ship approached, Honor had no idea that she was seeing her future home for the first time. Any land she could glimpse was gently sloping, sweeping back from the waves, in contrast with the dramatic white cliffs of Dover which were receding behind them. The town sat on the water's edge, showing its gabled roofs and church spires, where lookouts were watching for their approach. Calais harbour was dominated on one side by the Rysbank Tower and on the other by the old castle, a square fort of six towers surrounding a donjon. Between and behind them, spread huge defensive walls, a reminder of its martial past. Posterity has made the Lisles synonymous with the town, but Honor cannot have known then that these were the landmarks that were to define her life, through such highs and lows to come.

Calais must have looked a lot like any English port of the time. Great ships lay in the harbour, waves buffeted the jetties and sea wall, with the spray, mist and wind a constant reminder of the might of the Channel and its changing moods. Disembarking, the royal party were welcomed by two formidable figures dressed in their ceremonial robes: John Berners, Lord Bourchier, as Calais' Lord Deputy, and the former deputy turned Lord Mayor, Sir Robert Wingfield, in whose household Honor's cousin, John Worth, had served. The welcome committee, complete with ranks of town dignitaries and cheering citizens, conducted the king and Anne in a procession[5] through the Lantern Gate, connecting harbour and town. Above the gate were engraved the prophetic words, 'then shalle the Frenchman Calais winne, when iron and leade like cork shall swimme', and to reinforce the precarious town's status, the gate was ceremonially locked and unlocked, morning and night.

Tall, narrow houses lined the medieval streets on each side, leaning inwards, timber-framed. The streets would have been swept, prominent objects like statues, conduits or fountains given a fresh coat of paint and any undesirables removed. Berners led the party ahead into the marketplace, the civic and economic heart of the town where the Staple Hall and larger Town Hall were located, standing shoulder to shoulder on the far side. Taking a right turn, and passing along four blocks in the western quarter, they saw first the spire, then the medieval edifice of St Nicholas' Church on the left. Here, Henry and Anne paused to hear mass, and give thanks for their safe arrival. Immediately opposite the church stood the vast sprawling complex of the Exchequer, the town's largest building, where Henry and Anne were to stay. Beside Honor, Anne had thirty ladies in her retinue, many of whom were to be lodged in the seven rooms allocated to Anne, while others may have been accommodated nearby. Also present in the party was Henry's illegitimate son, Henry Fitzroy, Duke of Richmond and Somerset, then aged 13. Honor would have the opportunity to get to know her new great-nephew by marriage.

The Exchequer had palatial dimensions, recently refurbished and all spruced up for the royal visit. Local memories were long and by 1556, after the Lisles' time, it was still being listed in official documents as 'Henry VIII's Palace'.[6] The main entrance on the High Street, opposite the church, led into buildings situated around a pair of courtyards, bookended by gardens. The complex sprawled beyond this, arranged around a smaller court and yards, including tennis courts and stables. For a week, Anne and Henry enjoyed these luxury surroundings and ventured out to discover what the Pale of Calais had to offer, riding, hawking, hunting and feasting, before returning to spend their evenings together, sleeping in connecting rooms. Honor was witnessing their relationship grow closer; if this was the moment they consummated their love, then Anne's ladies would have known.

The Privy Purse accounts reveal just what an expensive, exciting time the stay in Calais was. The royal party dined well, although much of their food was brought in from outside, with payments made to servants who supplied them with carp and porpoises, pasties of red deer, and a special 46s 8d given to the servant bringing grapes and pears to Anne.[7] Henry also made some significant purchases from the Calais goldsmiths and jewellers, paying vast sums to at least six different craftsmen, ranging from 450 crowns to 7496 cr, 3s, 4d to an Alart Plumer for jewels.[8] He also bought furs and a hat with a plume. Henry also liked to be entertained, paying 7s 6d for his fool's lodgings, who was probably Will Somers, and later gave 40 crowns to the French king's jester, Triboulet.[9] A hundred crowns was paid to a French servant for bringing hawks to Henry.

During this waiting time, a few other payments give insight into the king and his circle, of which Honor experienced a microcosm in Calais. Henry's intense concern about his own security was reflected in the removal of his locks, the large metal contraptions that moved with him from property to property. A smith was paid 7s 6d to transport, and presumably attach, the royal locks to the doors of chambers in the Exchequer. Henry's more charitable side was apparent too; in walking about the town, he gave 4s 8d in alms to a poor woman begging on the walls.[10] Her marginal position is significant, as all vagrants, beggars, poor and needy would have been cleared from the town centre in order to preserve appearances. The king may have seen her when he went to make his 5s offering to Our Lady in the Wall,[11] a shrine which would prove significant for the Lisles later, probably strategically placed to bless the civic defences or assist fisherman. Henry also gave 7s 6d to a local child he had apparently healed, through divine intervention.[12] A further 10s was also paid to a servant of Lord Lisle, and although the task he had fulfilled was not specified, it serves as a reminder that Arthur and Honor were at the heart of this visit, in close proximity to Henry and Anne.[13]

This was probably the first time that Honor was drawn into Anne's inner circle for any sustained period of time. As part of Anne's entourage, she would have passed the days with some of the key players of the coming years, although the surviving sources make it difficult to pinpoint exactly who was there. The Lisle letters list six by name: Anne's own sister, the widowed Mary Carey, who was Henry's former mistress; Anne's sister-in-law Jane Boleyn, née Parker, Lady Rochford, wife of George Boleyn; Dorothy Stanley, Countess of Derby, half-sister of the Duke of Norfolk; Margaret Radcliffe, née Stanley; Lady Fitzwalter; and Honor's future friend, Elizabeth, Lady Wallop. The presence of Lady Wallop was no surprise, as her own townhouse in Calais had been requisitioned for use as lodgings. All houses of the 'higher order' had been similarly commandeered by the Lord Chamberlain, Lord William Sandys, in order to make room for the additional guests.[14] A list of local houses appropriated to lodge the English includes four public buildings and thirty-nine private homes, with an additional thirty-seven set aside to house the French.[15]

The twenty-four other ladies with Anne may have included some of those known to attend her in the coming year, including Mary Howard, soon to be married to young Fitzroy; Elizabeth Howard, Duchess of Norfolk; Mary Shelton, Anne Boleyn's first cousin; Anne 'Nan' Gainsford, who was in her company by 1528; Margaret Gamage who had served Catherine of Aragon; Jane Ashley; and the wives of the many noblemen who are listed by name. There is a slim chance that Anne was accompanied by her future sister-in-law, Mary Brandon, Duchess of Suffolk, née Tudor, and former Queen of France, but the ill health that led to her death the following June probably prevented her from travelling, and she might have been swayed by her loyalty to Catherine of Aragon, so she probably remained at home. Together, this group of women formed a queen's household, suitable for Anne's projected status.

There was one setback to the plan, though. The corresponding French queen's household had elected to stay at home. Eleanor Hapsburg, Queen of France since 1530, was a niece of Catherine of Aragon, and refused to attend and welcome the woman who had displaced her aunt. If that wasn't damning enough, Francis' sister, Marguerite of Navarre, formerly a friend to Anne, had also declined to attend, without giving her reasons. These were deliberate slights, meaning there was no female counterpart to Anne's retinue which protocol required, ruling her out of much of the planned activities. Chafing at the rejection, Anne was forced to remain behind, playing dominoes and dice with Honor and her ladies, while the two kings met.

Arthur was among the 'diverse viscounts'[16] who left Calais with Henry on 20 October and rode south-west, crossing the border at Wimereux and entering France. Francis awaited them in a valley at Sandingfield, outside Boulogne, where the two kings 'with all lovely honour met with bare heads', and embraced, so that all who saw them rejoiced.[17] With Henry in russet velvet adorned with gold and pearls, and Francis in crimson with cloth of gold pulled through his slashed sleeves, their gentlemen were also 'richly apparelled'.[18] No doubt Arthur was wearing his best clothes for the occasion, perhaps guided by Honor's hand, as he hawked, drank and fired artillery, before being conducted to Francis' lodgings at the nearby Abbey of Boulogne. Henry was offered a suite of rooms adjoining those of the French king, the walls hung with arras and green velvet, and embroidered with silver and gold, where panels told the story of Ovid's Metamorphosis, with its scenes of love, transformation and violence. Did Arthur admire these, lingering over the rich colours and tiny stitches, unaware that such themes would come to apply to the lives of the Lisles?

Once again, Henry's expenses reveal the entertainments and losses of his stay with Francis. He paid £4 13s 4d to the singers of the French king's privy chamber, and 44s 8d to John Parker, Yeoman of the Robes, for a number of doublets that the guards wore to wrestle in before the two kings. Henry also found himself beaten in a game of tennis by the Cardinal of Lorraine, for which he forfeit £46, and later put himself in debt for over £116 in a game of cards with the Cardinal of Guise and Dukes of Norfolk and Suffolk.[19]

Five days later, Henry returned to Calais, bringing the French party with him. They re-entered through the Mill Gate, where the soldiers stood lined up in red and blue, with the serving men in tawny gowns, with scarlet caps and white feathers. Honor would have heard the cannons fired from the tower and the ships in the harbour to announce their arrival. It was so loud that the French commented that they had never heard such shot.[20] Henry conducted Francis to the Staple Inn, a luxurious building set on the south side of the town, two blocks behind the Staple Hall, which would later become the Lisles' home. The preparations began in earnest for the masque and dances that were to reintroduce Anne as Henry's intended queen.

On Sunday, October 27, Honor was one of six women selected by Anne to accompany her on a visit to Francis at the Staple Inn. The women were led into the chamber where Henry and Francis had dined, hung with cloth of tissue of silver and gold, embroidered with wreaths and embellished with gold and pearls. That ultimate display of Tudor wealth – a cupboard – was prominently displayed, bearing nothing but plates of gold on its seven shelves, reflecting the light of dozens of candles set in silver branches. Looking around at the splendour inside, Honor had no idea that soon these chambers would house her, for better and worse. The women were masked and dressed in crimson tinsel satin and cloth of silver, tied with gold laces, as each selected a male partner, with Anne choosing Francis, and dancing until the moment came to reveal their identities. A huge £11 13s 1d was later paid in recompense to Richard Gibson, Yeoman of the Great Wardrobe and Tents, for supplying 'masking gear' for the occasion.[21]

After gaining the French king's approval for his new wife, Henry's intention had been to exchange gifts and return to England on October 29. However, stormy conditions made the Channel unsuitable for sailing, forcing the party to remain for two weeks at the Exchequer, whiling away the time by playing cards. On November 1, Honor and Arthur dined with rising Privy Councillor, Thomas Cromwell, the capable former servant of Cardinal Wolsey, who did them 'many other kindnesses' whilst in the town, establishing a connection that was to carry through the coming years.

The royal party finally sailed out of Calais harbour on 12 November, but their smooth voyage out was not to be repeated; after being battered by wind and rain, the ships limped home on the morning of St Erkenwald's Day, November 14. It is possible that Anne and Henry had not only consummated their relationship, but had undergone some form of marriage service, either in Calais, or in the chapel or royal apartments at Dover Castle. If this was the case, it was done in great secrecy, before limited witnesses, and Honor may not have been aware, or even present at Dover. The Lisles travelled back together aboard the *Sunday*, perhaps heading for Portsmouth rather than the Kent port, with Honor revealing that their journey was dangerous, as 'my lord and I were in great peril for lack of a good pilot'.[22]

By November 22, though, Honor was safely back home at Soberton, writing to Thomas Cromwell, to thank him for their dinner and sending him a gift of some cheeses.[23] With a mysterious, lower-class background, about whom rumours and speculation swirled, Henry's new chief minister was to prove inexhaustible in his pursuit of the king's wishes. Having survived the fall of his former master, Cardinal Wolsey, Cromwell had already demonstrated his abilities but was yet to reveal his ruthless streak. It was essential for Honor to court his favour, as a direct conduit to the king, but also as another marginal figure on the rise. Honor, like Cromwell, was balanced on the verge of an upwards trajectory, and the coming months would see both their lives embrace powerful new challenges. She had no way of knowing, though, just how fate would conspire to bind them together.

Five

The New Constable's Wife
1533

Back in Calais, John Bourchier, Baron Berners lay dying. Having just hosted the king and his entourage, his health had taken a sharp, sudden decline. Now in his sixties, and a descendant of Edward III, he had a long association with the town, first serving as its Lieutenant in 1520, acting as Lord Chancellor since 1524 and translating *Froissart's Chronicles* and other texts from the French. A portrait in the Netherlands style, painted during the 1520s, shows a solid, sombre, clean-shaven man with watchful eyes, clasping an apple. He made his will on 3 March 1533, appointing his half-brother, Edmund Howard, as his executor, and died on the sixteenth. According to his wishes, he was buried in the choir of the Église Notre Dame de Calais.

This left a prestigious vacancy across the Channel. However, Henry had already decided that Arthur was the man to fill it, appointing him Captain of Calais, or alternatively, Lieutenant or Deputy. The question is: 'why?' Arthur is reputed to have been born in Calais, which might have recommended him for the job, and his father had spent time there, albeit in rebellious activities. Arthur was mature in years, had travelled frequently and knew something of the place. He was a member of Henry's extended family, and therefore, presumably, trustworthy. Yet, through all his years at court, even as Vice-Admiral, server and in various other roles, Arthur had remained something of a background figure, displaying no huge talent, never achieving great success, or fame, or even notoriety. His presence is easy to miss, and has been, in many accounts. Historians have judged Arthur's abilities harshly over the years: to Geoffrey Elton, he was 'the most touchingly idiotic figure of his day' while C.S.L. Davis considered it a 'mystery' as to why he was given the Calais post.[1] Arthur didn't appear to be fulfilling all of his many responsibilities either. In February, Henry had warned him that he was falling short in his duties as Keeper of Claryngton

Park, leaving the role to others, so that 'the king's deer and game are much decayed'. If he did 'not take better care of them', Henry warned, Arthur would be 'discharged' from the role.[2] Perhaps Calais was the place to better focus his skills. Perhaps Arthur volunteered. Perhaps it was a convenient place to remove an older conservative relative to.

Yet Calais was expecting Arthur. On the day of Lord Berners' death, John Rokewood, a Calais councillor, wrote a no-nonsense business letter to his replacement, recommending a beer supplier. It was clearly well-known in the town who would be taking over, and those who relied upon the constable's patronage were keen to ensure their future smooth relations. Normal life had to continue:

> *My Lord Deputy is dead. I understand that your Lordship comes to supply his place. I beg you to allow Robt. Donnyngton, one of the soldiers of the retinue, who keeps a beerhouse and brews, and has served the late Lord Deputy ever since he came into Calais, to supply you also with beer.*[3]

While Arthur tried to get to grip with this complex and demanding legacy, Honor was faced with the task of packing up their Hampshire household, ready to ship over to Calais. When it came to the king's wishes, Honor had little or no say in the path of her husband's career and had to swiftly adjust her expectations. She had recently found Calais to be a place of pageantry and feasting at the splendid Exchequer and Staple Inn, a town putting on its best face, cleaned and decorated, to welcome its king for a few weeks. The reality, though, was vastly different. Calais was something of a poisoned chalice. Maintaining the splendid short-term edifice of October 1532 had proved costly, compounding the long-standing debts Berners had accrued, and the deficit experienced by the Merchant Staplers, whose immense debt of £22,000 had seen their trade suspended that March, overseen by Thomas Cromwell. Berners' large house on the south of the town was in a state of disarray, and now needed to be furnished and provisioned. Upon his death, Henry had ordered the place to be guarded until Berners' relative, Lord Edmund Howard, could arrive and seize what was owed, in repayment.

Lord Berners' will indicates that he had little to leave. He opened with a lengthy apology to the king for his debts, asking for his indulgence and offering several manors in recompense, to be given to the Crown after the death of his wife. His daughter Ursula and son George received £40 each, with a further £10 going to each of his executors and a silver cup to his half-brother Edmund, but the remaining items are a few items of clothing and non-specified goods. The tawny damask gown and black velvet coat furred with marten indicate his status, but there is little besides this to show for a man who had been ruler of Calais.[4] As a result of his debts to the Crown, nothing else from inside his 'great tenement' was mentioned in the will; no picture emerges of the house and furnishings that the Lisles were about to call home. However, a subsequent inventory of his goods tells a different story, as Honor was about to discover.

The letters of Arthur's chaplain and steward in Calais, John Atkinson, spoke of privation. There was some difficulty in getting hold of Lord Berners' plate, which was stored in the treasury, and Arthur would need to speak to the king in order to release it, especially as Berners' illegitimate son, Francis Hastings, was attempting to claim the property and goods for himself.[5] Also on the same day as Berners' death, another household member, John Knolles, wrote that he had 'stayed all things that Master Hastings can do for you, and all things in his keeping shall be at your commandment'. He also clarified the debts Berners had left, writing that it was 'reported here that my Lord was indebted to the King, and that the goods are to be seized for payment. If so, a word from you to the King, or to my lord of Norfolk, will suffice to have the house, with all implements, as it stands. If not, you shall be sure of it from Hastings'. Another portend of future difficulty came in Atkinson's warning to Arthur concerning the scarcity of fuel to be found in the surrounding Pale: 'You had better send from Hampshire two or three hoys for provision of wood, for that is costly here'.[6]

Atkinson wrote again, dispatching a servant to England with beef and mutton for the Lisles, although he was concerned about restrictions on its import and warned that an urgent pardon was required from the king, or else they would be 'shrewdly served' for the coming months and all through the winter, and there was no fish to be purchased yet. This situation was far removed from the carp, porpoises, deer and fruit that had furnished the Calais tables the previous autumn. Arthur had recently dispatched the balinger *Sunday* again, carrying goods and furniture supervised by his porter, with instructions from both Arthur and Honor. Its cargo was 'well delivered' and the empty vessel dispatched back to England within twenty-four hours.

The arrival of the Lisles was keenly anticipated in Calais. As early as 18 March, two days after Berners' death, Sir Edward Ringley was writing that he and 'Lisle's other friends', were 'desirous to hear of [your] coming' and hoped it would be before 6 April.[7] By June 1, after the arrival of more furniture, Atkinson confirmed that the Lisles could arrive as soon as they like, as the house would be ready for them; he only required two days' warning from when they set out to Dover.[8] The correspondence reveals that Arthur was already well-known and popular in Calais, which is likely to have influenced Henry during their stay in town the previous autumn. Therefore, Arthur was probably appointed as constable due to his existing connections, his knowledge of the town and his ability to speak French.

However keen they might have been to depart for Calais, and despite the encouragement of friends and connections, the Lisles could not leave at once. The delay was necessary in order to attend a very important event. Soon after returning from Calais, Anne Boleyn realised she was pregnant. Her child was probably conceived at some point in late November or early December 1532, and it acted as the spur Henry needed for action. With Catherine of Aragon languishing in the countryside, insisting that she was still Henry's lawful wife, Anne and Henry were married on 25 January 1533, in the king's chapel at Whitehall, in a service presided over by Rowland Lee, Bishop of Coventry and Lichfield. On April 12, Anne attended mass for the first time as queen, perhaps with her ladies in attendance, which may have included Honor. Just days later, as Anne's increasing belly could no longer be ignored, Thomas Cranmer, the newly appointed Archbishop of Canterbury, pronounced Henry's marriage to Catherine null and void. All that remained was for Anne to be crowned in a lavish ceremony and publicly take her place at the king's side; the mother of his future son.

Anne Boleyn's coronation was symbolic; to attend was not just an honour, but a validation of Henry's choice. Those who made their excuses, according to their conscience, such as Thomas More, could not have known that they were foreshadowing their own fates. As members of the king's extended family, Honor and Arthur played significant roles in publicly supporting the heavily-pregnant queen, aware of the narratives of discontent that rumbled against her.

Given Honor's status and her recent trip to Calais in Anne's entourage, there is no doubt that she attended Anne's coronation. As a royal relation, she would have been among the ladies who accompanied the new queen on a warm day in late May, as she sailed from Greenwich to the Tower of London. The royal barge was topped by Anne's device of a white falcon, surrounded by the red and white roses of the Tudor union, around which sat maidens singing and playing. It was followed by a flotilla of fifty ships, so that the 'whole river was covered' with banners and flags, playing music, saluted by cannon as they drew near.[9] The ships were draped in Arras and hung with cloth of gold, their flags fluttering in the breeze that caught the numerous strings of silver bells and set them tinkling. One bore the head of a dragon, breathing out real fire across the waves, while others fired guns in salute. As they approached the Tower, its mighty cannon rang out in response.[10]

That night, after dining with Henry, Anne and her ladies rested at the Tower, in a suite of rooms that had been refurbished especially for the occasion, with classical and 'antique' motifs. The following day, a number of new Knights of the Bath were created, following the same ritual that Thomas Grenville and John Basset had undergone in 1501. Waiting in those rooms, the atmosphere must have been one of excitement, as after years of setbacks, the fulfilment of Anne's dreams was finally within reach. The women would have celebrated, looking to the coming months as Anne would deliver her child and establish herself as queen. Honor would have been conscious of witnessing a moment in history of intense importance.

On 31 May, Anne emerged dressed in her royal robes of silver tissue, a coronet placed on her long, loose hair, and was borne through the streets of London in a white satin litter under a canopy of gold. Honor took her place among the ladies following, seated either in one of three gilded coaches or on horseback, dressed in black or crimson velvet. It's not impossible that she was one of the 'two other ladies' riding alongside the procession, in the company of Jane Rochford, Anne's sister-in-law, and Mary Howard, Anne's young cousin. Behind them marched dukes and constables, archbishops and ambassadors, and then between 200–300 of the 'great lords of the realm', including Arthur, dressed as befitted his role as Vice Admiral. They paused at intervals along the street to watch mystery plays performed, hear speeches, and refresh themselves from fountains flowing with wine, in a lavish and colourful display. The figures of Apollo and Calliope awaited them, along with the nine muses, declaring their admiration for Anne, and their hopes for her reign. An actor playing St Anne sat beside another falcon, while honorific verses by John Leland and Nicholas Udall were declaimed to the new queen. Beyond that, the procession was greeted by three graces, rode under painted banners and were showered by wafers inscribed with greetings while the boys' choir of St Paul's sang.

In the London streets, with onlookers thronging on both sides, the procession was more vulnerable. In many places, the crowd was held back, heavily guarded, behind ropes and railings, and the royal entourage was surrounded by soldiers. What carried, though, were voices. People crowded into the buildings on either side, hanging out of windows, even paying to rent rooms in the closest houses, to get the best view of the procession. Depending upon which source you read, the crowds were either jubilant or subdued, delighted or sullen[11] – it is a measure of the controversy of the match, and the popularity of Catherine of Aragon, that such dichotomic accounts exist. In previous years, there had been incidents of individuals speaking against Anne; a drawing of her decapitated had been discovered at court, and on one occasion in 1531, a group of women had verbally abused her in public, forcing her to flee. Although the perpetrators had been severely punished, the procession through the city streets may have been tinged with uncertainty. As it transpired, to Anne's relief, they reached Westminster Palace without incident.

The following day, 1 June, Honor dressed herself in the aristocratic robes of scarlet with a furred collar, to follow Anne the short distance into Westminster Abbey. The new queen wore purple velvet and a jewelled circlet, her long train carried by the Duchess of Norfolk. They processed through the main entrance into the nave, with its vaulted ceiling and hangings of cloth of gold, before heading slowly down the aisle. Honor watched Anne take her seat and hear mass, witnessed her make her oath and be anointed, before retiring in procession for a feast in the palace's vast great hall. The new queen was seated on the king's throne, on the dais at the front, before a marble table. Two senior ladies, the Countesses of Oxford and Worcester, stood at her side and two others sat at her feet throughout the duration of the meal, but Honor was among the women on the side tables, where she was served from what was estimated by an Italian visitor as the hundreds of dishes on offer. Gentlemen of the aristocracy acted as bare-headed servers, including Arthur who took the role of Chief Panter, responsible for distributing the bread.

With the narrative of Henry's great matter apparently having reached its conclusion, and the long-anticipated heir soon to arrive, the Lisles could now depart for Calais. They sailed into the town harbour on 10 June, 1533.

Six

The Calais Inheritance:
People and Places
1533

The Calais which welcomed the Lisles in the summer of 1533, was not the glittering, ceremonial town they had visited the previous autumn. After the spectacular ceremonies of the royal visit, followed by Anne's coronation, it proved something of a comedown. With the flags and banners removed, the streets unswept, the lines of aldermen in red disbanded, the residents going about their business, the veil of pageantry had lifted to reveal a dilapidated, impoverished town whose lifeblood – trade with the Low Countries – had been suspended. Surveys conducted in 1531 and 1532 detailed thousands of pounds of necessary repairs to buildings, walls, bridges, dykes, towers and the harbour.[1] It was not altogether a surprise, but the extent of the town's ruin meant that the new Lieutenant and his wife had a formidable task ahead.

Honor settled her children into Lord Berners' old house on the south side of the town, located somewhere behind the Staple Hall, Staple Inn and Town Hall. According to Sir Christopher Garneys, there was 'none like it in this town',[2] and it was duly leased to the Lisle family for £10 a year. It was large enough to house four of Honor's Basset daughters: Philippa, Katherine, Mary and Anne, and Arthur's daughter Frances, and had previously housed Berners' forty servants. Honor's sons, her Basset stepdaughters and Arthur's other two daughters remained behind in England. The new house also came with a considerable garden, for which the Lisles continued to employ Berners' former gardener, and keeping three pheasant hens and a cockerel which he had raised, estimated to provide fifty or sixty eggs a year, the rest of the birds being sent back to the king to contribute towards Berners' debts.[3] Former residents had also been successful in cultivating almonds there, which had previously been sent to Catherine of Aragon, being a luxurious ingredient of many rich dishes of the era.

After the scrambling arising from his will, Lord Berners' goods and furnishings had been confiscated by the Crown in lieu of his debts. Some were distributed among his Calais connections, but the vast majority remained in the house when the Lisles arrived to take up residency. An inventory taken early in 1534 gives an indication of what greeted the new arrivals.

The house contained three main beds: a great bed of state with silk coverlets embroidered with Lord Berners' arms; a green and yellow bed, with canopy and curtains in yellow, red and green sarconet; and a third bed with iron rods, with a crimson damask and cloth of gold canopy and red and yellow curtains. Other feather beds were listed (the Tudor equivalent of mattresses), and more bedding. Berners had owned seven pieces of wall tapestry, or arras, depicting the deadly sins and seven others showing the cardinal virtues. Of the chairs, one had belonged to the Duke of Richmond, perhaps left behind when he passed through Calais for the French court the previous October. Also included were a number of stools, an old coffer banded with iron and a plain chest nailed up 'with certain books'. A great glass, or mirror, stood in the main bedroom.[4]

The chapel was full of the trappings of Berners' Catholicism: a table with two leaves painted with Our Lady, a painting of St George, two white sarcenet altar cloths edged with red velvet, and two in blue, embroidered with knots. There were special altar cloths for Lent, vestments of red, white and blue velvet, mass books and holy water stoups. The scullery was clearly accustomed to grand dining, with pans of all sizes and purposes, and two racks for drying, while the pantry held two cases of knives, towels, napkins and tablecloths. The leftover supplies included quantities of ling and white herring, oats, verjuice, vinegar and Gascon wine. In the armoury, they found headpieces, gauntlets, beaver helmets, brigadines, splints, rivets, harnesses for men at arms, halberds, equipment for horses, a small coat of armour covered in green velvet, gussets for a doublet, eighteen sheaves of arrows, a standard and three pairs of gauntlets.[5]

Berners' clothing and more personal effects had already been seized by those named in his will, or appointed to oversee the liquidation of his assets. Francis Hall had his parliamentary robes, an old grey fur, the taffeta gown edged with old velvet, a black gown lined with black satin, a jacket of tawny damask furred with black rabbit, tawny and black silk doublets and a hundred pairs of black hose. Berners' illegitimate son, Francis Hastings, had a tawny velvet gown furred with black lamb, a black velvet riding coat, a black satin gown lined with pine marten, a bed with sheets, pewter vessels, trenchers and Berners' carpet, adorned with his devices. The dead Constable's plate was being held by the Treasurer, which must have borne witness to many past feasts, comprised goblets, gilt pots, a gilt salt cellar with scutcheons hanging on it, chalices, spoons, silver flagons, silver candlesticks, basins and ewers, and standing cups with a design of the Beaufort portcullis, strawberries, roses and Berners' arms. There was also a gold chain bearing a gold cross and five pearls, all totalling £376 9s 8¾ d.[6] In addition, Jasper Bourchier held silver pots, plates, goblets, cups, candlesticks and snuffers, as well as velvet and sable gowns with gold buttons and aglets, a jacket of cloth of gold, bedding of gold and crimson velvet embroidered with gold drops and matching curtains, a huge carpet, napery and fabric sewn with the Bourchier family arms. Berners' brother, Humphrey Bourchier, had more silverware, a bed with sheets, a velvet coat and tawny damask gown.[7] As this inventory was signed nine months after her arrival in Calais, it is likely that tracking down all these items was one of Honor's first tasks. She also had to try and live among them, accommodating all the furnishings and items that she and Arthur had brought from Hampshire. The disposal of the goods was left at the discretion of Cromwell, and the Lisles negotiated well into 1534 for the use of the plate, which they were finally permitted to buy with a down payment of £110, followed by £50 yearly until the sum was complete.[8]

When she had time, Honor could explore the town and get a sense of her bearings. An inventory of its streets, compiled shortly after the Lisles left Calais, lists familiar sounding street names, indicative of landmarks, famous residents or business conducted there. The town was ringed by its gates – Boulogne Gate, Lantern Gate, Water Gate, Mill Gate – defined by its size – Little Lane – and function – Prison Lane, Sewer Street and Cow Lane where beasts were herded. Consistent with the usual method of grouping similar professionals in one district, a range of trades is indicated in the town, far more prosaic than the jewellers, goldsmiths, furriers and clothes shops that had accounted for Henry's luxurious purchases in November 1532. Some relate to shipping, such as Hemp Street, Rigging Street and Roper's Lane; others offered necessaries, like Shoe Lane, Fuller's Street, Layden (Leaden/Plumbers) Street and Mingraven (Engravers) Street. Love Lane may have housed the brothels that courtier Francis Bryan frequented, as may Cocks Lane, although that may equally have contained a pit, where bets were placed upon fighting birds. Penny Lane and Farthing Street suggest financial connotations, although there was a town mint inside the Staple Hall, and the wealthiest may have been drawn to Golden Lane. The

Catholic nature of the town is indicated by the presence of Great Friars Street and Bigging (Beguines) Street, as well as the two hospitals and the nunnery outside the Lantern Gate. The White Friars , situated on the next block to the Lisle house, would be dissolved in 1539 and its properties, gardens and valuable wool houses granted to Arthur. The main church was Notre Dame, although there was also St Nicholas, St Peter, St Mary and other private chapels. Present and former town residents – Whethill, Pickering, Brampton, Langham, James, Fisher and an unspecified 'Duke' – all gave their names to streets within the town.[9]

Honor set about equipping her new home. She would have left most of her daily shopping to her servants, drawing on the existing network of local suppliers, but there were opportunities to visit the central market square nearby. In June 1533, though, Honor would have noticed the lack of food, fuel and goods, due to restrictions being placed upon the Staple. Until the town's economic problems were sorted out, they would have to source these necessaries from the Pale or from England, while the usual Low Countries trade was forbidden. The Lisles were fortunate in their new business agent, John Husee, appointed in 1533, who was to prove invaluable over the coming years, and whose correspondence is most revealing of their lives.

Husee was the son of a Southampton wine merchant who became Master of the Vintners Guild, but after initially following his father's footsteps, he entered the service of Richard Wingfield during his tenure as Deputy of Calais. He transferred to serve the Lisles in August, soon after their arrival in the town, frequently travelling between them and England, purchasing many items for Honor in London, sending ribbons, dresses, lengths of material, food items, drink, letters, household stuff and even animals, when required. Husee would prove himself to be loyal, hardworking, patient and discreet, as well as a useful source of information about events as they unfolded at the Tudor court.

Honor and Arthur quickly established their own patterns of local patronage, gift-giving and reciprocation, sending or dispensing necessaries, from their Calais resources. One natural resource they could draw upon in these hard times was the wildlife that the surrounding marshes offered: plovers and quails particularly are mentioned in their letters, as well as the herring that were farmed from the coast. Soon after arriving, they received a gift of rhubarb and cassia, delivered by the son of Gilbert le Brun from nearby St Omer, who recommended that Arthur took it after the full moon next Friday.[10] Rhubarb was a contemporary treatment for bile and phlegm, while cassia, a form of cinnamon, was administered to sore throats, suggesting that Arthur had some kind of cold or throat infection. Honor sent to England for a 'lettice' (fine worsted) bonnet for Frances Plantagenet, and a frontispiece to be embroidered by the queen's embroiderer in time for Christmas, velvet saddles and for bolts of cloth. She gifted wine, cheeses, meat, remedies, pets, birds, fish, advancement and advice; in return, her English correspondents asked for a doe, a live wild sow and employment, and sent bloodhounds, falcons and other birds. A further source of supplies came from the travellers outside the formal remit of the Staple, who converged on Calais. Important guests stayed with the Lisles, or at the Staple, while others were catered for by a number of inns or hostelries in the town: the 'Salamander' (heraldic device of Francis I), kept by John Masters, the 'Three Heads' under Mistress Burton, the 'Balance' and the 'Red Cross'.[11]

Looking south over Calais' walls from her new home, Honor had a view across the Pale, to the little church of St Peter's that stood alone in the marshes, in the direction of the second largest settlement, Guisnes, where Henry had met Francis at the 1520 Field of Cloth of Gold. Illustrations made later in the century show this area covered with wooden windmills. Gravelines lay to the east and Sangatte to the west, but a range of scattered settlements between were peopled by English settlers. Especially as the town was experiencing such shortages, it was important for the Lisles to familiarise themselves with those English subjects living outside their walls – farmers, victuallers, fishermen and soldiers – whose assistance they might come to rely upon.

On the road out to Gravelines was a large farm run by Harry Greenwood, and the George Inn run by a man named Rickborne. At Hâmmes Castle, lived a brewer names John Hawll, whilst two 'northern' women provided victuals (food and drink) at Marck. Two brothers by the name of Vincent farmed at Guisnes, while Thomas Haines catered for travellers at Waeldame. In the direction of St Omer, in the west, where George Basset was studying French with a priest-teacher, the Lisles would have passed the houses of John King and John Slayney, the fisherman John Brown at Whitsand, the Irish Archer at Mount d'Or, and en route to Gravelines, English soldier Laurence Mintner.[12] Honor would have learned that there was a centre for the manufacture of woollen goods at Escalles, while the sandy plateaus at Marck gave a good view over the Flemish border. This area, and the people in it, was to prove important for political and practical reasons, enabling Arthur to write to Cromwell that he had 'divers folks, both east and west, to advertise me of news'.[13]

The Lisles also needed to establish positive relationships with the burgher families in the town. Perhaps by way of Honor's recommendation, her nephew, Sir Richard Graynfelde, or Grenville, son of Honor's elder brother, Sir Roger, was appointed as the new High Marshall of Calais. Roger had married Matilda Beville, sometimes known as Maud, a Cornish girl from Truro, who may have been around ten years older than Honor, and was the mother of four children, the eldest of whom was 15 in 1533, the youngest perhaps only 3. With her nephew's family close by, and plenty of young cousins to offer company to Honor's Basset brood, the Grenvilles may have been regular visitor to the Lisle home. Among them was a single son, Roger, who would later perish as the captain of the ill-fated *Mary Rose*. However, two surviving letters suggest this may not have been a straightforward relationship. Later, the Lisle agent in London, John Husee, would write that 'Mr Marshal nor his wife will not do their duty unto your lordship and my lady', expressing gratitude that the Lisles 'may live by them without their help'.[14] The following year, though, when Honor visited England, she wrote more warmly about them to Arthur, asking specifically to be 'heartily recommended unto … my nephew Graynfylde [*sic*] and his wife'.[15]

Part of Honor's duty was to befriend the wives and female relations of the leading men with whom Arthur worked, and her letters indicate that she became close to at least one of them during her tenure as the constable's wife. This was certainly the case with Arthur's comptroller, Sir Edward Ringley, who later apologised to Arthur for his bluntness. While the men often clashed, Honor became close to Edward's wife, Jane Peyton Langley Ringley, who was based in Calais but often visited England. Jane wrote in terms of affection: 'though my body be far from you, yet my heart is with you', and asking Honor to 'command' her in anything she needed doing, sending tokens of affection including capons and cheese[16] and a set of coral beads with a gold heart, which Honor wore about her wrist and loaned to Jane. In return, Jane set Honor a flat ring with a diamond. Jane also confided in Honor about her jealousy of another Calais lady, Mrs Banyster, perhaps in jest, perhaps seriously, hoping that she 'take not away all the love between my husband and me until I come home again'.[17]

Honor was already aware of Lady Sandys, née Margaret Bray, the wife of William, Lord Chamberlain, from her visit the previous autumn. Now Sandys was appointed Lieutenant of Guisnes, six miles south-west of Calais, centred around a medieval castle close to the border with France. In September, Arthur sent Sandys and his wife two hogsheads of wine, Claret and Gascon, and offered them more wine and herrings for the winter season.

Guisnes was an area currently ravaged by the sweating sickness, possibly malaria arising from the surrounding marshland, and the following month Sandys fell ill with the disease, and was still so unwell by the following spring that his life was feared for. Six months later, though, Sandys was well enough to make some unspecified complaint to Cromwell about Arthur, which Cromwell promptly dismissed. The matter was resolved, and Arthur later wrote to Honor, asking to be remembered to Sandys as a friend. His wife Margaret was the heiress of Sir John Bray, and had been married in the 1490s, so was of a generation older than Honor. She and her husband divided their time between Calais and England, so Margaret may have not been so familiar a face as others.

Also on the Calais Council were Lieutenant of the Castle, Sir John Wallop, with his second wife Elizabeth, whom Honor had met the previous autumn. The Calais Vice Marshall William Sympson's wife remains elusive through the records, although he had at least one daughter, named Alicia. The Lieutenant of Rysbank Fort was Sir George Carew, who came from a Devon family and lived with his first wife, Thomasine Pollard. Sir Edmund Howard, uncle to Anne Boleyn and father to Catherine Howard, was Lord Comptroller, then married to his second wife, Dorothy. The final council member, Sir Thomas Palmer, was Knight Porter, and possibly unmarried, or widowed, as no mention is made of him having a wife. This was the circle of men with which Arthur worked most closely, thus dictating some of Honor's social connections, but it was one of many groups that required his attention. Whether Honor made an effort to connect with Elizabeth, Thomasine and Dorothy is unrecorded, but it would have been entirely in keeping with her character to do so, and the active role she took to support her husband. While Arthur was affable and easy going, Honor was often busy behind the scenes, forging connections, organising and giving advice. After six weeks' residence, the Lisles appeared to have settled in well, with Sir John Russell writing to Arthur on August 10, that he was 'glad to hear how you are beloved, and how well you use yourself there. I would like to know how you like the air there'.[18]

Council relations were not always easy though, and Honor may have been aware of tensions arising between Arthur and two other city burgesses over questions of precedence. Richard Whethill was Mayor of Calais, a Justice and King's Lieutenant, who clashed early on with Lisle in the belief that he had seniority. Hearing of an incident when Whethill treated Lisle 'very ungoodly' (*sic*) in Lisle's own garden, Cromwell commented that the new Lieutenant should have clapped Whethill in prison. In 1534, Elizabeth Whethill went to court to complain about Lisle, but at that point she had a far better relationship with Honor, going by a letter she sent her from London that May. She thanked Honor for the great pains she took in feasting Elizabeth's guests at the Frankfurt Inn and was glad to have such a lady to furnish her room. She also enquired after Honor's daughter Anne, perhaps a favourite, but asked to be remembered to all the Basset girls.[19] The relationship would become more difficult after Arthur declined to give the Whethills son a room as a Spear, (soldier), instead offering it to another, giving rise to years of drawn-out tension between the families. In December 1534, Lisle would even write dramatically about young Whethill that 'he and his allies are my extreme enemies and I would rather be seven years in prison than he should have any room here'.[20] Later, though, their son Robert would marry Honor's niece, Jane.

Robert Wingfield's quarrel with Lisle cut even deeper. A former ambassador to France, Wingfield had been Lord Deputy of Calais immediately before Lord Berners, during which time he had drained 4000 acres worth of marshland outside the town called the Meanbroke, and built himself a house and park there. Arthur considered that the wetlands were an important part of the town's defences, so ordered the land to be reclaimed by flooding, and Wingfield's property to be destroyed. Unfortunately, a number of Wingfield's tenants were also affected, having been refused the compensation Wingfield had promised them in case of this eventuality, and petitioned Lisle in despair.[21] Honor had made attempts to befriend the second Lady Wingfield, Jane, but the complete destruction the Wingfield home can't have helped. The quarrel would rumble on over the coming years, although by 1538 the women were writing on affectionate terms. There was an added poignancy to the connection, as Wingfield's uncle and godfather, another Robert Wingfield, had been comptroller in the household of Arthur's father, Edward IV.

Arthur was also cultivating connections with their French neighbours. He sent Oudart du Bies, Seneschal of Boulogne, a gift of a gelding and cramp-rods upon arriving in Calais, and by the end of June, he added a horse and some venison, while Honor sent him some cramp-rings.[22] In return, du Bies sent Honor some artichokes from his garden, prompting the Lisles to reciprocate with some fine hunting hounds. Gift-giving was a crucial means of establishing a local network and goodwill, especially between those on opposing sides of a border, and it was an activity which Honor could participate in as the constable's wife. By arrival of September, after the pair had hunted together, du Bies was referring to Arthur as 'my good neighbour and excellent good friend'.[23] Madame du Bies, née Jeanne de Senlis, would later send Honor the gift of a monkey, while the wife of another French neighbour, Madame Ysabeau de Morbecque, offered her a piece of jewellery called a chatelaine, worn as a hook or clasp around the waist, from which useful household items could be hung, such as keys, scissors, seals, thimbles and timepieces.

The Lisles were dealing with regular diplomatic traffic through Calais, accommodating the arrivals and departures of ambassadors, travellers and others between England, France and the Low Countries. In September 1533, Arthur received a letter from Jean de Dinteville, a French diplomat, with instructions to pass on a packet of letters to a messenger to take to King Francis, and thanking him for assisting his servant with greyhounds.[24] De Dinteville is better known today as the commissioner of what is probably Hans Holbein's most famous work, *The Ambassadors*, which had been painted only that Easter, and which features the diplomat standing on the left hand side, along with George de Selve, Bishop of Lavaur. It is not impossible that the Lisles saw the picture, even during production, before they departed England two months later. This connection takes us right back to the heart of the Tudor court, where Holbein was painting the most important people in the realm, a world of which Honor had once been at the centre.

Another important visitor who passed through Calais, enjoying the Lisles' hospitality, was the king's illegitimate son, Henry Fitzroy, Duke of Richmond and Somerset, who left behind a chair at their property. Honor had previously met her new great-nephew-in-law when he accompanied them to Calais the previous autumn, but after the English party returned home, Fitzroy had proceeded to the court of Dauphin Francis, heir to the French throne. He had remained there until August 1533, when his father recalled him, passing through Calais on his way back. A short while later, he would write to Arthur and Honor, thanking them for their kindness.

Honor's position in Calais relied upon her building a successful network of social connections. In her role as wife of the Deputy, she was hostess and patron, building friendships and allegiances with those directly and indirectly involved in Arthur's world, as was appropriate to her rank and gender. In addition, she had the responsibility of overseeing their household, of furnishing and supplying the home which doubled as a reception for guests and the setting for important work. During the second half of 1533, Honor adjusted herself to the different people who had entered her world, whether as fellow wives, tradesmen, neighbours, friends, court connections, councillors or her husband's rivals, providing the necessary behind-the-scenes support to the new Deputy.

Seven

Finding Solutions
1533–4

The most pressing matter when the Lisles arrived in Calais was the trade stalemate that was crippling the Staple. With winter approaching, the markets were empty and the shortage of food and fuel in the town was worsening. The debt accrued by the guild the previous autumn, amounting to over £22,000 owed to the Crown, had led to a complete suspension of trade by England, cutting off the town's lifeblood, so one of Lisle's first tasks was to enter into negotiations with Thomas Cromwell. Luckily, he could draw on the existing relationship with Cromwell, established after the Lisles had dined with him the previous November, and which Honor had nurtured since with letters and gifts. However, the king's chief minister would not always prove so affable or easy to work with.

Arthur found himself in the middle of a delicate situation. Calais was dependent upon royal approval, but the merchants had rejected new English trading rules as excessively punitive. Cromwell was particularly critical of the Staple's former mayor from 1523, Sir Thomas Seymour of Saffron Walden, Essex, uncle of his more famous namesake, who had reputedly engaged in illegal exports, breached statues, freed prisoners on bail and other offences. Since then, he claimed, the abuses had worsened, the debts deepened unchecked. This reminds us that while Calais was an outpost, often a law unto itself and sometimes in conflict with London, it was ultimately ruled by the king's distant ministers, and could be subject to retrospective and punitive accountability.

Arthur would have attended council meetings at Staple Hall, mere steps away from his new home. This group formed the backbone of the Calais community, ensured its prosperity and represented most of the leading families of the town. In the days following his arrival, Lisle and the council sent King Henry their thoughts about comments received from Cromwell regarding trade, but received no reply. On June 21, they wrote again, explaining that the town lacked necessities and appealing for urgent remedy.[1] Wingfield added his own complaint in writing, stating he had not been paid since last Lady Day (25 March) and refused to co-operate whilst the king had withdrawn certain payments that had previously been made to himself and other burgesses. Five days later, it was Cromwell who replied, by Henry's 'express command', that he would 'do his best to bring the matters to good effect'.[2] At many times, it would feel to Arthur that Cromwell was the gatekeeper to the king, controlling the gap between court and Calais.

Calais' unique position, as a marshy enclave surrounded by France and the Channel, made it dependent upon any crops such as wheat and corn that might thrive there. When these failed, and while trade was banned with France, the town turned to England for supplies. Lisle wrote to Cromwell again, to consider the effects of the rise in wheat prices, which meant they have not received the necessary English exports. Any wheat they currently had in store was not fit to make bread, he said, being four years old, and the bakers and brewers of Calais were concerned that those Tudor essentials, bread and beer, would soon run out.[3] There were not six bullocks in the town, 'much less cheese, tallow, malt or beer' and if they could not be 'victualled from all parts of the realm, we shall be undone'.[4] The council added that the town 'has never been in such poverty as at present since it was English, and the king's servants here were never so bare or needy'.[5] This was a potential crisis.

However, Henry was not impressed. Cromwell wrote of his master's 'displeasure' and belief that 'he ought not to be importuned for such like business'. He 'marvelled' that Arthur was 'so soon inclined' to listen to what others say, including apparently, Honor. It is unclear through what channel word had reached him of her role in the crisis, but as the mistress of a large household, and the constable's wife with her responsibility for hospitality, she must have felt the shortage of supplies acutely. Perhaps she voiced her concerns to her husband, or offered advice, or expressed her opinion, which reached Cromwell's ears. The minister commented that 'although my lady be right honourable and wise, yet in such causes as (be)longeth to your authority, her advice and discretion can little prevail'.[6] Cromwell issued a definite warning to the Calais Lieutenant that Honor remain in her sphere, and not try to do Arthur's job for him. Such words from a man whose friendship she had courted, would have stung and annoyed her, if her husband ever passed them on. When Francis Bryan made similar comments to Lisle two years later, Honor would reply directly, and received reassurance from Cromwell that he meant no ill will towards her.

As Arthur and Honor moved around Calais, they noticed that significant parts of its defences had fallen into disrepair, allowing for flooding. Arthur commissioned men from the Guisnes area, led by Henry King and Henry Frowyke, to investigate an overrun area called Dykeland, near Sandgate, that had previously been used to cultivate sluice, and sent his findings to Cromwell on July 15, requesting that a strong dyke and wall be built.[7] On August 1, his name headed a list of Calais aldermen, along with Wingfield and Whethill presenting a long, thorough list of repairs for royal approval. Their picture of missing doors, broken walls, dangerous stairs, weak towers, worn leaden roofs, worn gutters and holes in walls depicts a town barely able to defend itself, in a state of pervasive ruin.[8] The shrine of Our Lady in the Wall, where Henry had made an offering the previous November, required repairs to a ground floor door, a replacement door at the leads, repairs to the mouth of the vault and a cloven door to be fixed. At Lantern Gate, where the king and Anne had been welcomed, a hole had 'fallen out in the foot of the wall'.

Finally, to the relief of all in Calais, an agreement with the Crown was reached, and trading with the Low Countries reopened for the Staple in mid-November. The town could begin rebuilding itself and supplies returned in time for the Lisles' first Christmas season in residency. Arthur entered into an agreement with Henry Bourchier, Earl of Essex, a brother of Lord Berners, who promised to ship out oxen, sheep and wood, in return for the dispatch from Calais of wine, sturgeon, salmon and barrels of cod and herring, although frustratingly, this was delayed at customs until the new year. Finally, the king approved a warrant for the Lisle household to export from England to Calais: 60 cows, 300 sheep, 60 lambs, 20 pigs and a quantity of fish, butter, cheese and tallow for candles. A grateful Arthur sent the king a New Years' gift of £20 via John Husee, who reported that Henry received it 'right lovingly'. Honor could set about making the arrangements for their first Calais Christmas, which would have included hosting feasts, and attending church services at St Nicholas, with her new circle.

While Arthur was busy improving the town, Honor was making arrangements for their extended family. Between them, Arthur and Honor had ten dependents, and both also had stepchildren from their former marriages, who were now grown up. Honor's three sons had remained behind in England to be educated; John with the Norton family at East Tisted in Hampshire, 11-year-old George with John Salcot, Abbot of Hyde, in Winchester, and the youngest, 7-year-old James, with Hugh Cook, Abbot of Reading, with the intention in 1533 of equipping him for a clerical career.

John was aged 15 when his mother went out to Calais in June 1533. He delayed a few months after her departure, perhaps being wary of the sweating sickness that had broken out, probably supervised by one of the family's Cornish servants, William Bremelcum, before heading to East Tisted. On 11 October, Richard Norton wrote to Honor that John had arrived last Friday and was merry and in good health, reassuring her that the nearest case of sickness was five miles away, and none had fallen ill in their parish in the last six weeks. Norton thanked Honor for the wine she had sent him, and for her consistent kindness and promised that John would spend each day in lessons with Peter Bentley, Parson of Colmer, who would make him a 'very good grammarian'. John later wrote to his mother in Latin, translated by Bremelcum, reassuring her of his good health and hard work, thanking her for the gifts of money, furs and clothing, for velvet for the Nortons' son and beads for Lady Norton. In July 1534, Richard Norton wrote that Honor had reason to be thankful for bearing John, 'for assuredly there is in him many good qualities, like a gentleman concerned to wisdom and learning … courtesy, gentleness and kindness'.[9] John would remain with the Nortons until going up to study law at Lincoln's Inn early in 1535, at the age of 17.

The elder Basset girls, Philippa and Katherine, now aged 17 and 15, lived in the Staple with their mother, along with Arthur's daughter, Frances Plantagenet, who would later marry John Basset. Saddles were ordered for them to ride in the area, and they would have participated in Calais society, assisting their mother as hostesses, but their principal concern would have been to find a husband. Neither Basset girl married, though, during these Calais years, finding husbands after their return to England in the 1540s. The younger two daughters, Anne and Mary also crossed the Channel in the summer of 1533, but did not remain in Calais for long. As was the custom, they were placed in local families to be educated and 'finished', although this pair of siblings appeared more ambitious and keen to advance through their mother's court connections.

In November 1533, when Anne was around 13, she was sent to Pont-Remy, six miles south of Abbeville, on the river Somme. It was seventy-five miles south-east of Calais, around the coast, well outside the Calais Pale, into French territory. But the friendships Lisle had cultivated remind us that for most of this period, working relations were friendly, and borders were frequently crossed. Six years previously, when delivering the Order of the Garter to Francis I in Paris, Arthur had met Thybalt Rouault, Sieur de Riou, a soldier from a Poitou family which had long been loyal servants of the French Crown. Thybalt's wife, Jeanne de Saveuses, was an heiress from an ancient family, with connections to the Crown; one of her daughters was then in the household of Francis' mother, Louise of Savoy. Honor sent gifts to Jeanne and her cousin, Sister Anthoinette de Saveuses, a nun at the convent of Saveuses, for whom she commissioned a statue of St George to sit in her cabinet.[10]

Honor probably accompanied Anne to the Chateau at Pont-Remy, which had been rebuilt after the Hundred Years' War. Ruins of the castle still stand, overlooking the river, with its turrets, towers and gothic windows giving an indication of their former majesty. Jeanne wrote to Arthur on 15 November, days after Anne's arrival, saying the girl was 'so much the more than very welcome to me' that she didn't know how to thank him, as Anne was 'of such good conditions that it will not be difficult to instruct her'. She would guide and cherish her, 'entreating her every way as she were my natural daughter', and requiring no recompense but the Lisles' friendship and good favour.[11]

Anne wrote to her mother the following spring, confirming that the Rouaults could not have treated her better if she was their natural daughter, and requested some demi-worsted, a velvet kirtle, linen for smocks, hose, shoes and three ells of red cloth to make a cloak, adding that if she was 'to pass the winter in France, begs she may have an every-day robe' and regrets that she costs so much, requiring 'many little trifles that she would not have required in England'.[12] When she wished very much that 'my sister might be here with me in these parts', Honor started considering Mary's future.

In May 1534, Honor went on pilgrimage to Amiens. The city lay a hundred miles south of Calais, on the Pont-Remy Road, a centre for Catholics who followed the thirteenth-century labyrinth on their knees, made offerings at the shrine of John the Baptist, and gazed in awe at the fragment of his skull on display. Honor had retained the devout Catholicism of her youth, as had Henry VIII until recent years, but her visit was possible in France in a way that would very soon become obsolete in England. Henry's Reformation Parliament had already passed acts to remove the privileges of the clergy, deprive the Pope of English revenues and remove his jurisdiction over English affairs. In July 1534, Henry would be excommunicated for his actions, but that autumn the Act of Supremacy was passed, initiating the dissolution of the monasteries and the disbanding of saints' shrines, stripping them of the relics that pilgrims had venerated for centuries. Honor would have found these moves difficult to accept, and would be later described as 'superstitious' or adhering to the old ways.

Whilst en route to Amiens, Honor paid a visit to Anne and the Rouaults at Pont-Remy. There, she discussed the possibility of Mary, then aged around 12, entering the household of Jeanne's sister, Madame Anne de Bours, who lived in the nearby city of Abbeville. Set on the River Somme to the north-west of Amiens, it had played an important strategic role during the Hundred Years' War, was alternatively owned by the French and English, and visited by Francis I as recently as 1531. With her mother's permission, Anne Basset paid a visit to the de Bours family there, chaperoned by the daughter of her hosts' family, to help smooth the path for her sister. She wrote to her mother from there on 10 June, saying the bearer would tell Honor her news, and greatly desiring to hear from home. The letter is not very forthcoming, but Anne's visit was definitely a success, because a month later, Mary had arrived in Abbeville.

Anne de Bours, née Rouault, wrote to thank Arthur for his 'honourable proposal', and describing her new charge as being of 'such an excellent disposition' that she was beloved of all, and had 'begun well with a good will'. It is clear from the letter that Mary did not yet know much French, as Madame de Bours anticipated her having 'greater pleasure' once she had learned it, but she was being praised for her beauty.[13] Mary wrote to her mother in November, asking for news of home and for her mother to recompense the bearer for a gold ornament he had sold her. She hoped to write again when time allowed, and mentioned that Madame de Bours was sending Honor some goshawks.

Anne continued to thrive with the Rouaults, with her hostess writing to thank Honor for the pins and sleeves she had sent her, adding 'I should like to find something in this country you might wish for, to make you a present'. Anne had not yet 'shown that she [was] weary of this country', but when they visited Boulogne, Madame Roualt promised they would also come to Calais. She sent Honor some cherry and prune preserves, while Anne sent a 'small remembrance' for her mother and sisters.[14]

Of Arthur's three Plantagenet children, only Frances was living with the Lisles in 1534. His youngest daughter, Bridget, had been sent to stay with Elizabeth Shelley, Abbess of St Mary's, Winchester, where she was apparently in good health but required some more clothing, as she was only 7 or 8 and growing fast. Elizabeth Plantagenet had remained in England in the household of her half-brother John, from Arthur's first wife's previous marriage to Edmund Dudley. In 1534, terms were drawn up for a marriage between her and Thomas Lovell, son of Francis, by which Lisle was to pay a dowry of 700 marks, clothe both parties for the wedding day and pay for the wedding feast, while Lovell would settle an income of £100 annually on Elizabeth.[15] For some reason, this plan came to nothing, and Elizabeth would marry later in life.

Honor also remained in touch with relatives from Cornwall. An affectionate letter arrived in September 1533, from her widowed sister-in-law Margaret Grenville, also known as Maud, mother of the Jane Grenville who married Robert Whethill. Margaret sent Honor a pair of Guernsey hose, which Jane delivered, and wished that 'I were one day with you'.[16] Honor heard regularly from her stepchildren by her marriage to John Basset, who remained in Cornwall. Jane Basset wrote that she and her sister, Thomasine, had removed from Umberleigh due to sickness, but requested that she be lodged there again, with 'such stuff as is necessary, and permission to pasture a cow'.[17] Later, she wrote about lost items at Soberton, surprised to hear anything had gone missing in Honor's absence, as it was all inventoried in a book. She thanked Honor for sending her a gown and some bucks, although they had not arrived, and wished to ask for a doe for the winter.[18] Concluding, she asked to be remembered to Frances, Philippa 'and the rest'.

It was Honor who petitioners approached when it came to matters of the family or domestic disputes. While Arthur dealt with business, Honor's role as the Lisle matriarch encouraged such approaches as that from her niece, Elizabeth (also known as Isabel) Staynings, whose husband Walter was in prison for debt. Elizabeth was possibly from the West Country, a cousin of the Cornish Arundells, as she commented upon their cruel treatment of her husband and daily troubling of their tenants, suggesting the origin of the dispute. She also requested that Honor write to Henry Norris, one of Henry VIII's closest friends, her 'special good master', to thank him for the pains he had taken in the matter, and to Cromwell, and that Honor might write to 'any lady she knows at court who is familiar with the queen, that she may resort to her sometimes'. Honor was clearly a source of comfort, as the thought of her 'goodness comforts her when she is not merry, for she is bound to none of her kin in her trouble, but her ladyship'.[19] Eventually, after much petitioning, Henry granted permission for Walter Staynings to visit his tenants in the country, and make provision for the payment of his creditors.[20]

Honor continued to deal with business relating to the Lisles' Hampshire home. John Perpowntte, their Soberton curate, wrote to assure her that he would see every bushel of the estate's wheat winnowed and that a recent payment had been spent wisely.[21] She also was in contact with Arthur's maternal Wayte relatives in the county, receiving letters from William and Anthony, his distant cousins. Both wrote to her from Wymering, a district of Portsmouth ten miles south of Soberton. William was probably the William Wayte who would lease Drayton Manor in 1540; on 7 April 1534, he thanked Honor for her continuing kindness to him in remembering him to Thomas Cromwell and asked her to remember his cousin's sister to the Abbot of Welbeck, who was then a John Maxey. William had sent Honor the gift of some saffron, then valued as a very expensive spice produced in East Anglia, and explained he hadn't wanted any money in return for it. He asked after the Basset girls and passed on the news to Honor that her eldest son, John Basset, was in good health.[22]

Anthony Wayte's letter came in October, enquiring about a recent illness that Arthur had experienced, possibly the one for which he had been taking rhubarb and cassia. Anthony expressed gratitude for the trust that Honor had put in him when leaving for Calais, and wrote about his wife's health issues, of which Honor seems to have been aware: 'she is but faintly merry, and goeth up and down but weakly, for her sustenance is but small that a man may marvel that with so little food a woman may live'.[23] Wayte mentions that he has shipping in Calais, and that his Lord, Thomas West, Baron de la Warr, a 'good lord and a just', had been ordered by King Henry to receive the French ambassador. Wayte's master was supposed to go too, but 'cannot for his age, especially at this fall of the leaf'.[24]

Perhaps as she was known for her devout faith, Honor received a number of petitions from clergymen of varying kinds. Oliver Browne, Arthur's chaplain who was now in Colchester, requested that she favour a servant of John Grenville, who had been wrongly accused of stealing a boat. If this was not bad enough, the accuser, Thomas Greenleaf, had destroyed one of Lisle's letters and 'jests in every alehouse against my Lord's honour'.[25] A priest that Honor had known during her first marriage, John Rugge of Exeter, wrote to thank her for her kind letters and offer to support him in his search for a new benefice. Honor had been touched when he commented that she would be 'as good to him as master Basset was'.[26] Her priest at the Basset home of Umberleigh, John Bonde, kept in touch to inform her that they had kept John Basset's year's mind, meaning they had remembered him in the church upon the anniversary of his death, as well as instigating repairs to the chapel. Bonde's letter also contained domestic details about the estate, including the cattle and two colts in the park, the book of fishing accounts, and the gift of twenty gulls he had sent Honor, although he had not yet heard if they had been received.[27]

Another poor cleric, Thomas Gilbert, curate of Bishop's Waltham, wrote to ask Honor for a cloth gown which she had promised to send him upon her arrival in Calais, as he had 'no other friends to turn to' and feared she must have 'so many whelps pertaining to you that poor Thomas Gilbert shall be forgotten'.[28] Gilbert later wrote to Honor with news of the Nortons, and John Basset, so he was clearly connected to the family, but adding a request for vacant parsonage of Southwark, and the unfortunate case of William Rose. Rose, he stated, required Honor's assistance, as his marriage had broken down, and he spent his time weeping as his wife could 'not suffer him in ease no manner of way ... because she is so unreasonable a woman ... more like a woman of Bedlam'.[29] However, this letter was swiftly followed by another, from Honor's own priest, Gilbert Burton, who had taken Thomas Gilbert into his service at Honor's request, stating that William Rose had, in fact, 'misconducted himself in many ways, which I will not write for the honour of priesthead'. Following an episode where Rose was verbally abusive, he had been paid his wages owing and dismissed from the house, putting the wife's reaction into quite a different context.[30]

That summer, Honor was in correspondence with Anthoine de Noyelle, the Abbess of Bourbourg, a Benedictine Abbey in St Omer. Honor had promised to source ten or twelve pieces of alabaster from England for the abbey, after which Anthoine wrote on 7 June 1534, with the 'bill of the dimensions' she required, and the 'measure of the Flemish foot', in case it differed from the English one. She needed the stone 'as soon as possible', perhaps to carry out repairs to the fabric of the nunnery, or else for use as decorative features, or even tombs.[31] Bourbourg Abbey was situated on the plains between Calais and Dunkirk, and held the significant relic of Thomas Becket's chalice, while his mitre and a piece of linen dipped in his blood resided in the church of St Bertin in St Omer. It is possible, given her recent pilgrimage to Amiens, that Honor also travelled the sixteen miles to visit Bourbourg in person, and even the twenty-seven to St Omer. Such distances would be considered nothing given the precious relics waiting at the end.

France remained a Catholic country, resistant to the religious reforms that were taking place in Germany and Switzerland under the influence of Martin Luther and Ulrich Zwingli. Honor may have felt more affinity with the old practices that she still found in the churches and monasteries on her side of the Channel, than with the dissolution of shrines and banning of rituals that the English considered superstitious. France was no less intolerant of heretics though, as Sir William Penizon wrote to Arthur from Paris, describing how as many as 200 were being held in prisons in the Capital. One had been burned two days before, another that day and 'tomorrow or shortly there will be others'.[32] By December, Penizon reported that heretics were being burned daily.[33] This news reinforced the Lisles' border status in Calais, caught between two countries displaying extreme religious differences. In England, the country of her birth, Honor's traditional Catholicism would soon be considered superstitious, but in France, and especially suspicious as foreigners, individuals classified as diverging from the national faith were suffering the most terrible deaths. Her home's marginal status may have afforded Honor some comfort, her beliefs overlooked, for now.

Even in her new role in Calais, or perhaps because of it, Honor remained the recipient of requests for assistance and patronage from her English connections. Some were already connected closely to the family, in their service, or as formal acquaintances, while others wrote asking for justice for perceived wrongs, or the advancement of their candidates. In her influential role, Honor was able to offer the female equivalent of good lordship, to be a good lady to those beneath her, dispensing the kindness that many letters thank her for. When her servants and friends travelled into England, as Francis Hall did in April 1534, she ensured they had tokens, remembrances and recommendations to dispense among her connections at home.[34]

Eight

Court News
1534–5

Across the Channel, England was beginning the process of immense cultural and religious change. Three months after the Lisles' arrival in Calais, on 7 September 1533, Anne Boleyn had given birth to a daughter, Elizabeth, instead of the male heir Henry had longed for. The king was initially disappointed, but the birth of a live heir was promising and he stated pragmatically, that by God's grace, healthy sons would follow. Had Honor's path been different, she would have been at Anne's side, in her household, as these events unfolded. The Lisles' New Year's gift for Henry of £20 in gold had been 'received right joyfully',[1] as part of the constant exchange of the tokens that kept the Lisles connected with the king and Anne. John Husee wrote that Henry had kept a 'great court' and was 'merry and lusty as ever I see',[2] but changes were afoot.

That March, the first Act of Succession had disinherited Princess Mary in favour of baby Elizabeth, requiring all the king's subjects to swear allegiance. Those who refused could be charged under the new Treasons Act that followed. No doubt news crossed the Channel that Catherine and Mary had refused the oath, as expected, but also that some high profile members of the court also resisted, including Stephen Gardiner, the king's own secretary, John Fisher, Bishop of Rochester, and the Humanist scholar Thomas More, who had resigned his position as Lord High Chancellor as a result. Gardiner also stepped aside, allowing Thomas Cromwell to step into his shoes. Presumably, as Henry's subjects, Honor and Arthur swore this oath too, choosing a form of pragmatism suggested by their closeness to Anne and her circle.

John Rokewood, a Councillor of Calais, wrote to the Lisles whilst he was on a visit to England, with details about the treatment of Catherine of Aragon. On the same day that the Act of Succession had been passed, Rome had pronounced its verdict on the royal marriage, in favour of Catherine.

This made little difference to Henry, who now considered the Pope himself to be the greatest heretic in Christendom. The former queen had been stripped of her titles and was to be referred to as the Lady Dowager, or Dowager Princess of Wales, the new Act making it a treasonable offence to refer to her as queen or offer her the appropriate deference. Her jointure had been taken away by an act of parliament, and her royal jewels removed, with all that wealth being awarded to Anne Boleyn instead. The Duke of Norfolk, Henry's treasurer, ever the bearer of bad news for Catherine, had been dispatched to her country home, to inform her of the change. As a result of her failure to acknowledge the change, she had been sent even further into the countryside, from her residence at Buckden to Kimbolton Castle in Cambridgeshire. Here, with a skeleton staff of loyal Spaniards, she kept to her rooms, in what would be her final home. Sir Brian Tuke wrote to Arthur with the information that Princess Elizabeth had been established in her own household at Hatfield, which her half-sister Mary was forced to join, now that her own home had been dissolved.[3] This meant that Mary's old servants were displaced, many after years of service, and Tuke asked whether there was a chance that Mary's usher, Richard Baker, might be offered a Spear at Calais.[4]

Rokewood also described how some figures were on the rise as Catherine, Mary, More and Fisher fell. He had observed that there were no longer any preachers other than those appointed by the king, who were sympathetic to his new reforms. These new appointees were proving popular, the letter said, drawing large audiences to see these 'most famous doctors of Oxford and Cambridge', which included Sir Hugh Latimer, soon to be appointed Bishop of Worcester. Latimer was preaching every Wednesday in Lent before the king and was 'very well liked'.[5] Standing his ground on the other side of the debate was Rowland Phillips, Vicar of Croydon, a powerful speaker who remained in favour of Rome, and would not be silenced. Rokewood could predict trouble 'when the parties are suffered to dispute',[6] and Phillips would indeed resign his position in the coming years. There had also been some concern for the Lisles that Henry wished to take their castle at Portchester and the forest of Bore and grant them to Anne, but after investigation, Rokewood had consulted with 'your friends', Cromwell, Norris and Bryan, and could reassure Arthur and Honor that 'the king is as good a lord to you as ever, and means to take nothing from you'.[7]

Another influential figure who fell foul of Henry's regime in the spring of 1534 was Elizabeth Barton, the Holy Maid of Kent. A servant in a household connected to the Archbishop of Canterbury, Barton had begun by having visions and fits in the late 1520s, during which she made predictions and spoke in favour of Rome and the practices of Catholicism, such as pilgrimage. Initially, Henry had been impressed, inviting her to court, but after she had spoken against his new marriage, predicting his imminent death, she was arrested. It is possible that Honor saw Barton at court at some point between 1529 and her departure for Calais in 1533, as the maid was championed by Thomas More and other leading figures, and periodically in the king's presence. John Husee wrote to the Lisles on the day of Barton's execution, 20 April 1534, explaining that 'this day, most part of the city was sworn to the king and his legitimate issue by the queen's grace now had, and hereafter to come'. The Bishops who had supported Barton, or had expressed doubts over Henry's path had been summoned to London, including Cuthbert Tunstall of Durham, Stephen Gardiner of Winchester and Edward Lee of York.[8] More and Fisher were already in the Tower. As Honor sat tight in Calais, it would have been concerning for her to see how the tide was turning against her faith.

Honor had remained in touch with a network of women across the Channel, either connected to her by blood or marriage, or friends she had made during her four years at court. They included Eleanor Paston, the Countess of Rutland; the king's Plantagenet aunt, Margaret Pole Countess of Salisbury, who was Arthur's cousin; and Honor's niece Mary Arundell, who became Countess of Sussex in 1535. Another of Honor's particular friends in England was Mary, Lady Kingston, née Scrope, formerly Lady Jerningham. Newly married to Sir William Kingston, Constable of the Tower, her voice can be heard in her husband's letter to Honor, who wrote 'my poor wife recommends her unto you and my lady both'. Kingston thanked the Lisles for their gift of cheese, but had little news to offer, apart from that the king and queen 'be in good health and merry'. He promised to send venison to Calais, if any was available.[9] Later, the Kingstons thanked Honor for sending Mary a token, presumably a religious symbol, which she offered to St Eloi, in the hopes that her horse would not go lame and throw her off. The same wording regarding the king was echoed by George Taylor in a letter to Honor, that Henry and Anne were 'in good health and merry', planning to leave Westminster for Windsor by water, and then on to Greenwich He also requested that the bearer of the letter, a son of Mr George Gainsford of Calais, be taken into the Lisles' service as he currently had no master.[10]

The connection between Honor and Anne Boleyn is evident through several letters relating to gifts and pets, culminating in a sad little vignette.

When the Lisles left England, it appears they found new homes for those animals they could not accommodate, or which were not suited to the transition. Sometimes, they had little choice – Anne had admired a linnet that once hung in Honor's chamber, which now made Anne 'rejoice with her pleasant song', which Francis Bryan hoped would comfort Honor for the loss of the bird.[11] Honor had taken one favourite pet with her to Calais, though, a dog, Purkoy, named for the French word 'pourquoi?' (meaning 'why'). However, the dog seemed to have been a hit with Bryan, and by early 1534, he was begging John Husee two or three times a day for the animal to be sent to him.[12] As Husee explained, 'there is no remedy, your ladyship must needs depart with your little Purquoy, the which I know well shall grieve your ladyship not a little'. Eventually, Honor relented and sent her pet to Bryan, but she would come to regret it, as Bryan did not keep him long. As soon as Anne set eyes on Purkoy, who must have been a very bewitching beast, she desired him for her own, and Bryan was powerless to resist her demands. He explained to Honor that 'it remained not above an hour in my hands but that her grace took it from me'. Sadly, though, Purkoy came to an unfortunate end. At the end of 1534, Thomas Broke wrote to Honor, seemingly unaware that she had formerly owned the dog:

> *… the Queen's Grace setteth much store by a pretty dog, and her Grace delighted so much in little Purkpy that after he was dead of a fall there durst nobody tell her Grace of it, till it pleased the King's Highness to tell her Grace of it. But her Grace setteth more store by a dog than by a bitch, she saith.*[13]

Reputedly, the dog died after a fall from a window. Honor's grief on hearing of this loss can only be imagined.

Honor clearly loved her pets, and the visit to Calais of the French High Admiral, Philippe de Chabot, Seigneur de Brion, brought some unusual creatures into her home. Arthur had probably met the Seigneur at the 1520 Field of Cloth of Gold, hosting him now as he passed to England as a formal ambassador. The visit was such a success that de Brion's man, Jehan de Moucheau, wrote thanking Honor, and sending a number of gifts which included a pair of marmosets from Brazil and a long-tailed monkey, 'a pretty beast and gentle'. Moucheau sent detailed instructions about their care, as they should only be fed apples and nuts and drink warm milk. The monkey needed to be kept close to the fire, while the marmoset cages should be hung up for the night close to the chimney, although they could tolerate being out of doors during the day. A Rouen merchant, a 'man of substance', was charged with their safe delivery.[14] There is an element of karma about this gift, after the loss of Purkoy to Anne Boleyn. The creatures had been intended to be presented at court by Francis Bryan, probably for Anne herself, but Moucheau suggested that de Brion bypassed the queen in favour of Honor:

> *Mr Bryan, who is your proper friend, was with him, to have given them to the court. But I was in presence when my lord the Admiral said that without respect of persons, none should be served by him before he had served Madame de Lisle; by the which you may perceive whether very cordially he loveth you or not.*[15]

A month after the death of Purkoy, Honor sent Anne one of the marmosets as a gift, perhaps to replace the dog. However, she was told by John Husee that 'the queen loveth no such beasts nor can scant abide the sight of them'. What happened to the offending marmoset is unknown.

Sir William Kingston, Mary's husband, wrote to update the Lisles in April 1534 after having seen Henry and Anne at Eltham Palace, with little Princess Elizabeth, just eight months old, and 'as goodly a child as hath been seen … much in the king's favour as a goodly child should be'.[16] By marriage, Elizabeth was Honor's great-niece, although she had not yet met her. Kingston thanked his friends for sending him French wine, the likes of which he had never tasted better, and commended himself to Honor, 'who binds me to her service by her good remembrance'.[17] Anne had swiftly fallen pregnant again and at the end of the month, George Taylor wrote directly to Honor that 'the king and queen are merry and in good health. The Queen hath a goodly belly, praying to our Lord to send us a prince'. This pregnancy is supported by a dispatch made by Imperial Ambassador Chapuys at the end of January, so Anne must have been at least five or six months along by April. Taylor's letter also included the gift of two gold and six silver cramp rings, which were traditionally used as a cure against cramp and epilepsy, being blessed by the king on Good Fridays. During the ceremony, prayers were said, psalms recited and holy water was poured over the rings. Such superstitious practices were about to be wiped out in the reformist waves, and would be eradicated from England forever. When Taylor added that he had no more rings 'given him this year', it may be an indication that such practices were already on the wane.[18]

In response to the news about Anne's pregnancy, Honor sent her a gift of live Calais dotterels for her table. Dotterels were small birds of the plover family, which the Lisles may have acquired from the marshes of the Pale, and much prized as a delicacy. John Atkinson was responsible for delivering them, handing them over to Anne's brother, George, along with the Lisles' good wishes and some 'images', which were 'highly accepted'.[19] These are likely to have been religious in nature. The birds had been slaughtered that day at noon when they arrived in Dover, hurried up to the royal kitchens, plucked and roasted in time for that evening's meal. Six birds were served up for supper, with another six for the following day's dinner and six more for the ensuing supper.[20] George Boleyn wrote directly to Honor, thanking her for the gift and confirming Anne's enjoyment of the birds, as they were the first she had received that year. The Lisles continued to send gifts of dotterels to the English court until they were asked to stop, as there was an abundant native supply in Lincolnshire.

In July 1534, the Lisles anticipated hosting George Boleyn and William Fitzwilliam when they crossed the Channel on business at the French court. The journey proved difficult though, with the pair blown off course by a north-east wind off the coast of Dover. Instead, they landed up the coast, near Boulogne, 'and as our journey demands haste we could not [see your] lordship at this time, but will at our return'.[21] Upon their return that July, Boleyn and Fitzwilliam did stay in Calais, and the Lisles may have taken the opportunity to show them the improvements they had been making to the town. At this point, Lord Sandys was still suffering the ill-effects of what may have been the sweating sickness or malaria he had contracted the previous autumn at Guisnes, becoming critical and endangering his life. John Husee wrote that the invalid had reached his estate in England in a horse litter, suggesting the extent of his illness, but adding that the main successor under consideration to replace him in Guisnes if he died, was George Boleyn himself.[22] In the event, Sandys recovered and returned to Calais, where he would serve until his death in 1540.

This momentary turn of fate presents a fascinating historical what-if. Had Sandys died, and George Boleyn been installed as his replacement in Guisnes, he may well have been absent from the English court during the desperate spring of 1536, when the Boleyn faction fell. Had George become Lieutenant of Guisnes, at a geographical remove, the specific, dated accusations of his incest with Anne would have been impossible, and his life might have been saved. Alternatively, as a frequent visitor to the English court, it may have made no difference whatsoever in the face of Henry's determination. When Sandys recovered, George was rewarded instead with the role of Warden of the Cinque Ports.

There had also been some suggestion of Henry and Anne returning to Calais in the summer of 1534. Sir Francis Bryan, a Boleyn cousin, who had been part of the commission surveying Calais two years earlier, asked to be recommended to Lisle's 'good lady your bedfellow' and reporting that the king told him 'in mine ear' that he would be coming to Calais before next August, and that they were to provision as they thought fit. The ever-health-conscious Henry had asked John Rokewood whether Calais was safe for his impending visit:

> *If any dangerous sickness arose in Calais, you should cause*
> *those infected to be turned out of the town, and that you should*
> *have the streets kept as clean as may be, as he intends to be*
> *there shortly to meet with the French king, but he does not wish*
> *it to be reported yet; also to have the town well victualled.*[23]

Bryan though, added that they might 'take hindrance … for ye know the minds of princes sometimes change and times appointed deferred', and indeed, this visit was still being discussed as late as April 1536, and never came to fruition.

That June, Sir Edward Ringley wrote from England to reassure Arthur that the king was satisfied with his progress in Calais. He had seen Henry at Hampton Court, where he had been invited into a new garden, freshly laid out according to the king's specifications. Henry asked him 'heartily how you did, and whether the town was free from sickness and kept clean', of which Ringley assured him. Henry was 'well contented' that 'his works go so well forward', and 'the pains you have taken about' the walls and towers and the 'conduct of his retinue'.[24] He advised Arthur to mend the gutters from the market to the church, offering to send paviours, or stoneworkers, from London if necessary. Arthur did take up the offer, and two paviours were found that June, who asked for 2d a yard of work, plus their journey costs.[25] Ringley also informed the Lisles that John Dudley, Arthur's stepson by his first marriage to Elizabeth Grey, had been made Master of the Armoury. He reported that the king and queen were in good health, and that Henry was due at York Place for supper, then Waltham Abbey, before returning to Hampton Court.[26]

Ringley wrote separately to Honor on the same day, 11 June, that he had passed on her recommendations to Anne, 'who asked heartily how she did and how she liked Calais'. Honor must have been concerned about people speaking badly of her at court, as Ringley reassured her that 'almost every gentleman and gentlewoman' of the court asked after her, speaking 'of her good and honour' and he promised to try and discover 'who they are that report about her ladyship'.[27] There was no mention of Anne's pregnancy, which should have been approaching its due date, suggesting that she had miscarried, or that it had been a case of pseudocyesis, or false pregnancy, as her predecessor Catherine of Aragon had experienced.

John Husee remained the Lisles' most constant conduit between Calais and the court. He wrote in May that Henry had a very good opinion of Arthur, which had been bolstered by Cromwell. Cromwell intended to visit the king the following day, when he planned to speak on the Lisles' behalf, both in favour of them using the plate previously owned by Berners, which Cromwell was retaining in lieu of the former constable's debts, and to try and mediate in a dispute that had arisen with Sir Edward Seymour.[28] Two days later, Husee wrote again to reassure Arthur that the matter was in hand; Henry was pleased with the sandhills Arthur had made but displeased by so many Calais spears being in England. He also added that the Duke of Richmond was observing the feast of St George and the court would not move from Hampton Court until Whitsuntide.[29]

The Lisles' dispute with Edward Seymour had arisen over the inheritance of Arthur's stepson, John Dudley. The son of Elizabeth Grey and the scapegoated minister Edmund Dudley, executed by Henry VII in 1510, John was then 30, and the estates of his mother had passed to Arthur 'except certain lordships which the said Sir John Dudley had immediately after the death of the said lady'.[30] Lately, though, Edward Seymour, brother to the Jane who would become the king's third wife, had purchased from Dudley certain manors worth the annual sum of £140. Lisle had signed the papers without giving them due consideration, but asserted his rights to other lands, only to find the documents supporting his claim had been lost. The tenants on the lands now paid their rents to Seymour, not Lisle, out of fear of him.[31]

John Husee tried pressing the matter with Cromwell, obtaining his assurance that April that Lisle 'shall sustain no loss in your difference with Mr Seymour'.[32] He delivered wine, wild swine and horses to Arthur's friends on his behalf. A neighbour living in the Pale of Calais, John of Mark, or John Bunolt, also carried letters and gifts on behalf of the Lisles in the Seymour matter. He visited Greenwich, where many court officials, including the Cofferer of the Green Cloth and Mr Clerk of the kitchen, who

Arthur would have known from his roles as sewer and pantler, 'asked after you, with many kind words'.[33] Bunolt presented Cromwell with tokens that Honor had given him and asked for his assistance in the Seymour case, 'in which he promised to satisfy her'.[34] Honor's nephew, John Grenville, who had recently become a sergeant-at-arms at court, was present when Cromwell and Seymour spoke about the matter, and added his voice to the Lisles' cause, although he asked Arthur to 'strike out this with a pen as soon as you have read it, that no man may read it'.[35] The matter would be resolved according to Lisle's satisfaction in March 1535, when Lisle's lawyers successfully argued that Dudley had not fulfilled his covenant when he came of age, and therefore did not have the right to sell, making the arrangement with Seymour null and void. By this, Arthur had 'as much money as you did before, if not more, by those lands'.[36]

Honor was drawn into a problem relating to the supply of white wine to Francis Bryan, from an Antwerp merchant, Antony Cave, who wrote directly to her. Cave explained he had written first to Bryan about the difficulties of getting a licence, and a second time in an attempt to get the matter resolved. Honor wrote to Robert Baynam, a connection in Antwerp, with Baynam replying in June, trying to unravel the miscommunication. Such letters suggest that as Arthur's wife, Honor could exercise influence over decisions and misunderstanding arising from trade passing through Calais.[37]

Occasionally, the Lisles entertained important figures from beyond their immediate European circle. In September, the secretary to the queen of Hungary, Nicholas Olahus, passed through Calais, pausing at St Omer to write and thank Honor for the kind reception she and Arthur had given him at breakfast. He reassured Honor he had passed on her commendations to the queen, as she had requested.[38] This queen of Hungary was Mary Hapsburg, sister to the Holy Roman Emperor Charles V, and thus a niece of Catherine of Aragon. Since being widowed at the age of 20, Mary had assisted Charles in the administration of his huge empire in the Netherlands, as well as acting as regent in Hungary. The Lisles' admiration of the Imperial family is evidenced by the portrait of Charles V, which hung upon the wall of their home.

By the middle of 1534, the Lisles had settled well in Calais, as hosts and leaders of a town that had its own share of problems but sat at an influential European gateway. They maintained their connections to the Tudor court, listening at a distance to the changes that were taking place there, as they went about their daily business.

Nine

Embroidery and Spices
1534–5

The Lisle letters are most revealing and personal when dealing with the domestic nature of their household. While national events, such as Henry's divorce and the Reformation, recur in correspondence of the time from witnesses far closer to the throne, Honor's arrangements for her clothing and table give a unique insight into the kind of establishment she was running. Through her, we gain an important reminder of how life continued while the drama of the king's two marriages was played out. Because Honor was based in Calais, separated from her tailors, friends and craftsmen by the English Channel, she was obliged to commit to paper such instructions as might usually have been verbal, or else recorded merely in account lists. It is also possible to get a good impression of Honor's personal tastes, as she and her representatives sought out very specific materials and styles. She was a woman of status and style and made her exacting requirements clear.

John Husee remained Honor's main agent in sourcing the kinds of clothing she chose for herself and her family. In January 1534, he sent Honor half a pound of ribbon, comprising 17 pieces, but he was still searching for other items from her shopping list, which was difficult because she had fixed a specific cost. He confessed he could not find a cap of scarlet for under 14 groats, and had no luck yet with the cloth he had ordered. Also, Honor had experienced poor workmanship from an embroiderer who worked on her gorget, which was worn to protect the throat, costing her 6s 8d, prompting Husee to show the piece to Honor's tailor, Mr Scott, 'who is sorry the obligation ever came into the lewd fellow's hands'.[1] He did manage to send Honor a satin cap and bonnet, with the promise that if the cap did not fit, he could have it changed.[2] Honor also sourced clothing from tailors she knew in Devon, as the same month, Husee was at the Bishop of Exeter's palace when he heard that Honor's kerseys were ready, and was able to inform her that a man called Kerne would be soon bringing them out to Calais. Ever the helpful servant, Husee also sourced hose and two undercaps of velvet and satin for Arthur, and a yard and a half of violet frisado for young James Basset.[3] At the time, Honor was expecting a visit from her nephew, Diggory Grenville, who was bringing her out nine silver and one gold cramp rings.[4]

Husee was shopping for Honor again in July. He bought twelve yards of satin at 8s 6d the yard, but could find no cloth of silver that he liked for the right price. The only silver he had found so far cost between 18 and 28s the yard, but wasn't suitable for Honor's tastes. He was sending three other pieces of fabric for her perusal, one plain, one violet with knots of silver and one branched, although the last one was pricey at 43s 4d a yard. In addition, he dispatched two ounces of ribbon and two thousand pins, along with a frontlet, which was the headband under a bonnet, although he feared she 'will not like it at the price for of a truth it is dear, of 11 nobles'.[5] He wrote shortly after again, reluctant to commit to a purchase whilst waiting to hear from her, as 'I know cheap silver is not for your wearing'.[6] In his next letter, after having dropped off her twelve yards of satin and furs to Mr Scott to be transformed, he added that the cloth of silver was scarce because only great personages wore it 'making it dearer'.[7] By the end of July, the satin gown was ready to be furred, but the skinner was currently away in Bristol, and Husee was sending off patterns of cloth of gold and tinsel to convince Honor that the price she was paying was reasonable by comparison.[8]

That December, Husee was still chasing ribbons and embroidery. Honor's new frontlet was complete, according to her instructions, which she had to send twice because the original letter was lost. He had also purchased her two dozen pairs of gloves, silken and ribbon points and a remnant of very good white ribbon. He had experienced difficulty securing exactly what she required, and had spoken to Honor's 'gossip, Broke's wife', a common term for a good friend, who explained to Husee that it was not possible to buy any ribbon at Mr Judd's establishment at the price Honor had hoped. He finished by asking her to make a list of how much sugar and spice she required.[9] Like Honor occasionally, Arthur's agent, Leonard Smyth, had an unrealistic expectation when it came to prices. Soon after Husee's attempt, Smyth wrote asking her 'pardon for thinking the price of a velvet gown less than it is' and assuring her 'if he had bought as many as she has worn he would know the price', but had been 'deceived therein'.[10] It must have been frustrating at times for Honor, having to rely upon men to purchase her clothing, when it must have been so much easier to have done it herself, had she been in England.

Towards the end of November, Leonard Smyth was feeling pressured for time ahead of the Christmas season. Honor's scarlet was ready, but the fur bonnet she wanted for Frances Plantagenet would cost 13s 4d and would take six days to make. He had delivered the new frontlet to Queen Anne's embroiderer, who anticipated finishing the work in the new year. Smyth told Honor he had hoped the matter dealt with sooner, but he couldn't arrange more cloth to be sent by his supplier Holt, who had promised to make the Lisle liveries back in August. Holt was now saying 'he cannot get so much cloth of one colour before Christmas without ready money. After Christmas he will send the residue to furnish the whole number'.[11]

Early in 1535, Honor sent some lengths of kersey to Anne Boleyn, via John Husee, who was able to report back that the queen had liked them 'specially well'.[12] In response, she was to have a kirtle of the queen's livery by Midsummer that year.[13] Even though Honor was in Calais, wearing such an item demonstrated her loyalty to Anne and impressed upon those around her that she was a servant of the queen, bearing her authority. Husee also told Honor that he was keeping her turquoise safe and would bring it to Calais himself. Turquoise was a highly-prized precious stone, used exclusively in the jewellery of the Catholic Church until the fourteenth century, when it found its way into secular items. It was believed to have the ability to heal and prevent riders from falling off their horses. This was a very real fear, as Honor found when her cousin Diggory was unable to visit Calais at Easter 1535, because he 'took a misfortune off my horse … and had great pain ever since' which had 'hindered me in doing divers things'.[14] She had also previously sent a token to protect Mary Kingston against this. Another little detail from the letters was the account for Arthur's shoes showing that over an eighteen month period, he spent 38s 6d on quarter shoes and black shoes with corked heels, boots and buskins, which were laced calf-length leather boots.[15]

Honor also dealt directly with Richard Kyrton, who made clothes for herself and her children. In July, she had arranged for him to make and send a velvet cap to George Basset[16] and in September, he wrote to her, also struggling to meet her requirements. Despite looking, he could 'get no cloth of gold like the pattern of her sleeve', except a piece of only three quarters of a yard, which he offered to send her. He had thirteen yards of tawny velvet, but was waiting to purchase tawny silk to go with it until he had heard from Honor. Instead, he sent her a pair of russet velvet sleeves, a gown and a kirtle of black satin, four lawn squares for her hair and a pair of sleeves 'of the best work he can get'. She had also written to him requesting a kirtle, but she would have to send more money for that.[17]

Shipping items back and forth across the Channel, with the imperfect communication that arose, could be a risky business. Merchant John Cheriton, who acted as an agent for the Lisles, wrote to Arthur in December, explaining that one of his ships carrying gall, alum and cotton had been lost between Genoa and Savona, and unfortunately also the 'silks which he had purchased for lord and lady Lisle and their daughters'.[18] Cheriton wrote again in March from Bordeaux, where he had a good deal of woad, or dark blue dye, to sell. He had sailed from England in his ship the *Portingale*, which he had filled with 'as much silk as cost me above 500 ducats beside the silks I had appointed' to replace that which had been lost, along with other merchandise for the Lisles, the total value being more than 800 ducats.[19]

Robert Action, a saddler from Southwark, received orders to make up a saddle for Honor. He wrote to her in September, asking whether she wanted both the saddle and harness fringed with silk and gold, or if she had a preference over types of velvet. He suggested that 'other lords' wives have theirs of Lewkes velvet fringed with silk and gold with buttons', following the fashion of Paris, and 'tassells quarter deep of silk and gold'. He also needed to know whether she wanted her stirrup to be gilt, or covered in leather or velvet, and what device she wanted to feature on the head of the saddle, made 'of copper and gilt'.[20]

Richard Blount was charged with sourcing Honor's jewellery and accessories, travelling to Bruges in October 1535. The city had strong trading links with Venice, and was known for its goldsmiths and jewellers, especially those handling diamonds that had been mined in India. Blount reported visiting goldsmith John Smytt with a diamond and three pearls Honor had entrusted to him, hoping to get them set in gold, at a cost of four angels and twelve styvers. He enclosed a pattern that Smytt had drawn of the final design with spots where the gems would be, but deferred agreeing to the project until Honor had approved it.[21]

Jewellery featured again in Honor's dealings with Antony Barker in Paris, who sent her a 'girdle of the best fashion' and the 'best enamel of any I could find'. He had to choose carefully, finding no other that 'would less hurt your sleeves and the wreaths upon the enamel will keep it long'.[22] In return, Honor entrusted him with several precious items from her collection, including a flower with four diamonds and a ruby, with three pearls suspended beneath, a brooch of the Salutation of Our Lady, a gold cross to be altered into a brooch and a jewelled flower, like a gillyflower (carnation) which she desired to be strengthened, 'for it breaketh oftimes because the branches be slender'. Honor instructed that these be made 'rich and goodly, and of the best and newest fashion that you can devise, [as] though it were some person being under a cloth of estate'.[23]

Honor needed to ensure that all the children were adequately provisioned, especially those who were absent from home, as well as attiring those employed to care for them. As they rapidly grew, it was difficult to keep an overview of their existing provision, and their evolving needs. The servants who cared for them also needed liveries, supplies and clothes of their own. To John at East Tisted, overseen by Justice Richard Norton and the Lisle family servant William Bremelcum, she sent a crimson velvet purse and shirt band, a pouch of russet velvet and a pair of beads for Norton's wife. Bremelcum thanked her for the gifts and requested some hose and a shirt cloth for himself, and told her that John needed crimson and black satin to provide him with two doublets.[24] The following spring, she sent a purse of crimson velvet and a shirt collar. Bremelcum requested that she send 'to his master cloth for a green coat against summer, a petticoat and cloth for hose'.[25]

On 6 February 1535, at the age of 17, John Basset was entered into the register at Lincoln's Inn and began his training as a lawyer. The largest of the four Inns of Court, it had been situated at Holborn, near the Westminster law courts, since the thirteenth century. Such a prestigious career would require John to look the part, however Husee had gone through the young man's wardrobe to find him 'all out of apparel' and never 'hath a good gown but one of chamlet, the which was very ill-fashioned', having been mended several times. He had a 'meetly' or suitable satin gown, a damask gown and two other passable ones, but needed a jacket, because his former one had been used to patch up another garment. He was also down to his last pair of white hose. To remedy this, Husee intended to make him two pairs of black hose, a new gown of damask furred with pine marten or civet cat and a study gown with fox pelts. If he was able, Husee would add a gown of fine cloth furred with white lambskin, and make his old damask gown into a jacket. With these additions and changes, John should be equipped for the next two years.[26] Honor responded by sending some pieces of red, yellow and green say (a cloth made from combed wool) to dress John's bedroom, for which Husee thanked her, and requested that she send two coffers – one to store his clothes and the other for his sheets and linen.[27] Later, she supplied John with cloth for a coat, three shirts, and yards of satin, as well as a hogshead of wine for Mr Norton.[28]

Bridget, in Winchester, was growing quickly, and needed a gown and kirtle, partlet and coif, as she had nothing else suitable. Abbess Elizabeth

Shelley had been supplying the girl from her own wardrobe, giving her four pairs of hose and four pairs of shoes, as well as paying for her gowns to be mended. Some drama arose when a bonnet ordered for her went on a wild goose chase in March, when it was supposedly delivered by a stranger who demanded more money, but did not arrive elsewhere, was searched for and promised, before finally being brought to Winchester from London.[29] George had been unwell with an ague and required money to pay his laundress, but was also to have a velvet coat ordered by Husee.[30] Hugh Cook, Abbot of Reading who had the charge of James Basset, asked to be sent four tuns of red and claret wine and a barrel of herring, if the Lisles would be so good as to keep their promise to do so.[31] By January 1535, when James was 8 or 9, he was brought over to Calais, and went from there to school in Paris, 'in good health and merry', to the Collège de Calvi. The college was part of the Sorbonne, founded in 1271, where younger students were taught grammar and philosophy, usually for nine years. It was proposed that on account of James' age, he was to have his own bedroom and to eat with the college Principal, but Honor was advised it would cost less than £20 a year to lodge him in the town. James would only remain in Paris for a year before joining his mother in Calais.

Anne Basset, still with the Rouault family at Pont-Remy since November 1533, wrote to her mother in May 1535, that she was still being treated like a daughter of the house, and asked for worsted to make a gown with a velvet side, three ells of red cloth to make a mantle with a satin hood and cloth to make smocks, some hose and shoes. She also asked her mother to procure 'une dogue' (a dog?) which she had promised to a gentleman.[32] That gentleman turned out to be Anne's host, Thybalt Rouault, who wrote to thank Arthur for his gift of dogs ten days later. Honor had also sent them some virginals to play upon, and they looked forward to her impending visit, planned for St John's day, or the midsummer feast of St John the Baptist on 24 June, when they would 'make her the best cheer they can'.[33] Anne's hostess, Jeanne, wrote that she had sent to Amiens for wools of the colours Honor had requested. It had taken a long time, as they had not yet been dyed, but she now sent 17lb of wool for Honor to choose from.[34] Honor also sent a pretty frieze of violet and learned that a red night mantle was being made for her daughter; in response, she made her host's daughter a mantle with white fur.[35]

That August, Thybalt wrote that Anne had recovered from an illness, and referred to her sister Mary Basset, staying with Anne de Bours, his sister, who was 'the prettiest girl possible'.[36] Mary's hostess had also been ill in

Bideford Bridge, built by a fourteenth-century Grenville ancestor across the River Torridge, almost to their door.

St Mary's Church, Bideford, right by the Grenville house, where Honor's uncle, John, was rector from 1504–1509.

Left: The old entrance to Umberleigh Chapel, where Honor may have married John Basset in 1515.

Below left: Tomb of John Basset at Atherington Church. Commissioned by Honor in 1533, this memorial featured herself beside John Basset and his first wife, Elizabeth. It originally stood in Umberleigh chapel but was moved in 1818.

Below right: The Basset coat of arms.

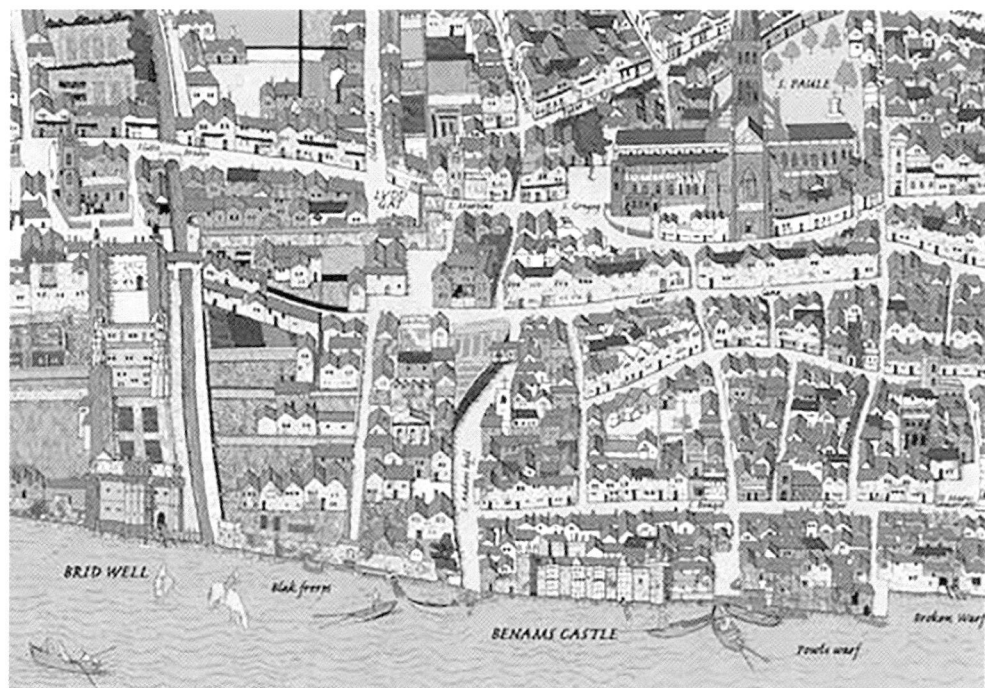

The Blackfriars district of London, where Honor stayed with her second husband, Arthur Plantagenet.

Above left: Edward IV, father of Arthur Plantagenet, grandfather to Henry VIII.

Above right: Anne Boleyn, in whose household Honor served, attending upon her in Calais in 1532 and taking part in her coronation procession.

Left: Henry VIII at the time of his marriage to Anne Boleyn.

Below: A Tudor sailing ship, depicted in the 1540s.

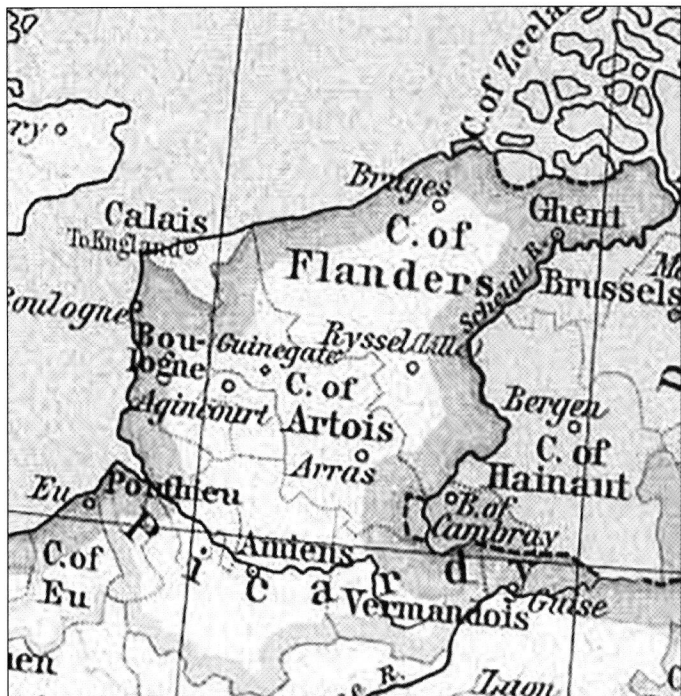

Right: The Pale of Calais at the start of the sixteenth century.

Below: An early depiction of Calais from above, probably late fifteenth century, showing the citadel, marketplace, churches and harbour.

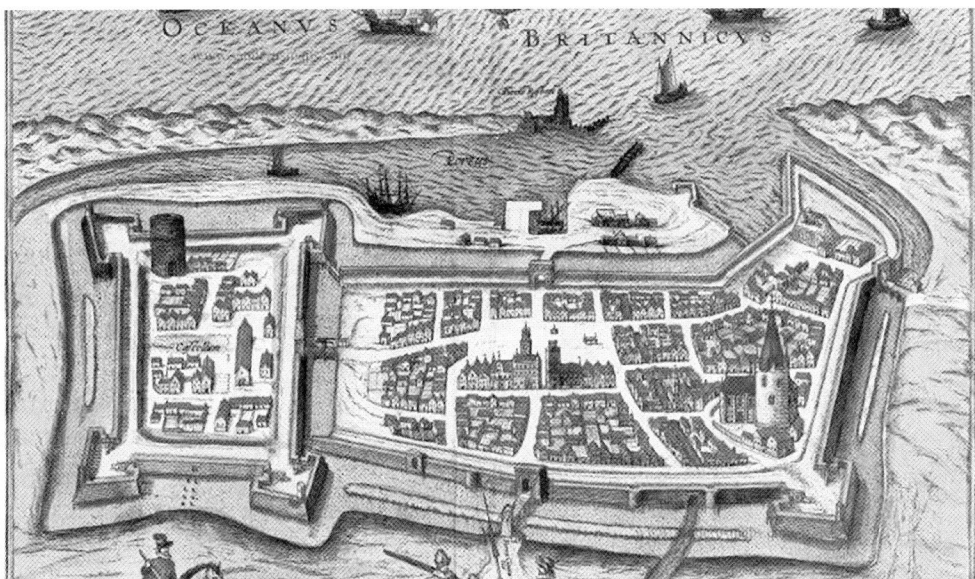

Key:

1. The Castle
2. The Laterngate
3. Staple Hall
4. Town Hall
5. Exchequer
6. St. Nichola's Church
7. Staple Inn
   (Formerly Prince's Inn)
8. St. Mary's Church
9. Rysbank Tower

ENGLISH CHANNEL

HARBOUR

MARKET PLACE

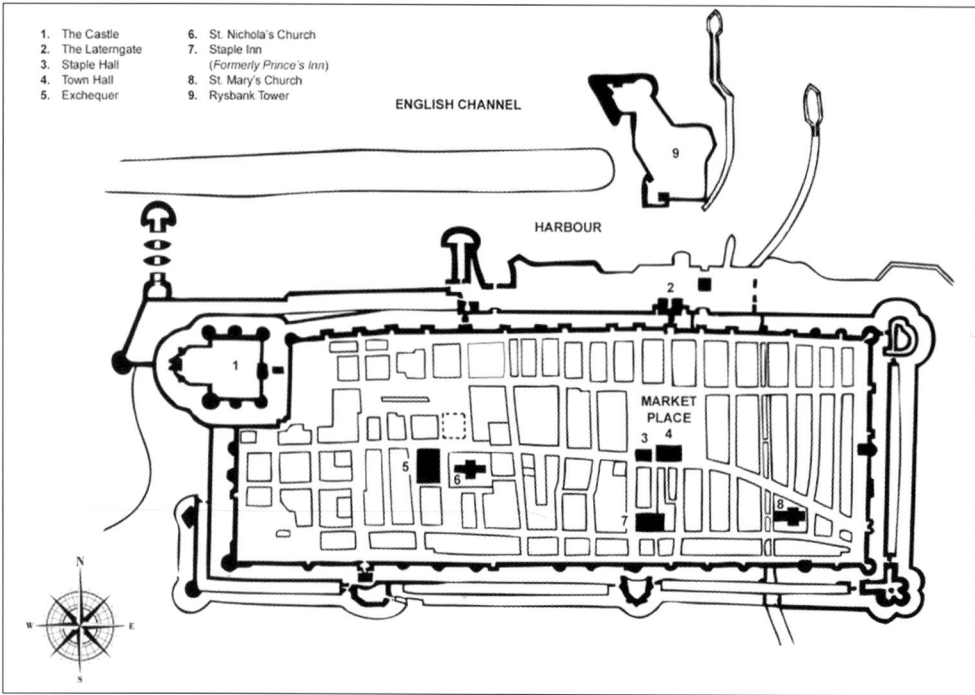

Above: A street plan from the sixteenth century, featured in the *Calais Chronicle*.

Left: A depiction of Calais harbour by Stefano Della Bella in the 1640s.

A sixteenth-century drawing of Calais from the water, showing the hospital of the Franciscan sisters outside the gates, on the left.

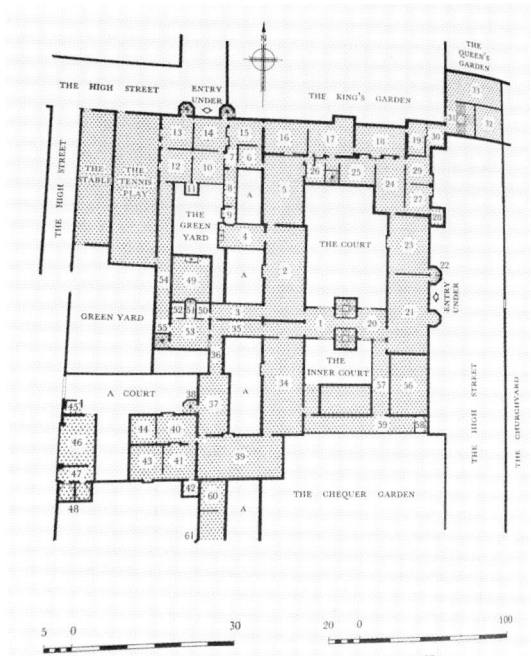

Right: A floor plan of the Exchequer, where the royal party stayed in the autumn of 1532.

Below: William Hogarth's 1748 painting of the Calais Gate, possibly the Lantern Gate, as supplies of roast beef are being unloaded from the harbour to a tavern.

Above: The Chateau at Pont-Remy, where Anne Basset was sent to stay with the Rouault family in November 1533.

Below left: The gate to the Staple Inn in Calais, all that remains of the house the Lisles moved to in February 1536.

Below right: Early twentieth-century photograph of the gate to the Citadel of Calais.

Above: Early twentieth-century photograph of the Place d'Armes in Calais.

Below left: John Bourchier, Lord Berner, Lieutenant of Calais until 1533, into whose house the Lisles moved.

Below right: Oudart du Bies, Marshal of France, and a correspondent of Arthur.

Above left: Thomas More, Chancellor and devout Catholic, executed in 1535 along with John Fisher, for refusing to swear the Oath of Succession.

Above right: Thomas Cromwell, correspondent of both Honor and Arthur, responsible for the monastic visitations and implementing reform.

Left: Statue of a Virgin and Child, *c*.1270, from Abbeville Cathedral, which Honor may have seen on her pilgrimage and visits.

Above left: Pilgrim's badge depicting the shrine of Thomas Becket in Canterbury Cathedral.

Above right: Reliquary of Thomas Becket, *c.*1180–90, Limoges, France, typical of the items seized by the English Crown during the Reformation.

Above left: Eleanor Manners, née Paston, Countess of Rutland, who took Katherine Basset into her household.

Above right: Mary Arundell, Honor's niece, who took Anne Basset into her household.

Left: Hearse cloth donated by the Lisles' agent, John Husee, to the Company of Vintners in 1539.

Below: Dover Castle, overlooking the port which was the usual point of embarkation for Calais. Arthur and Honor visited King Henry here soon after Anne Boleyn's fall in 1536.

Jane Seymour, to whom Honor sent quails during her pregnancy and who took Anne Basset into her household just a week before her death in childbirth, October 1537.

Anne of Cleves, whom Honor welcomed to Calais in December 1539, on her way to become Henry VIII's fourth queen.

Edmund Howard, Lord Comptroller of Calais and father of Catherine Howard, upon whom Honor's herbal remedies had unexpected effects.

Catherine Howard, fifth wife to Henry VIII, accused of adultery with Honor's correspondent, Thomas Culpeper.

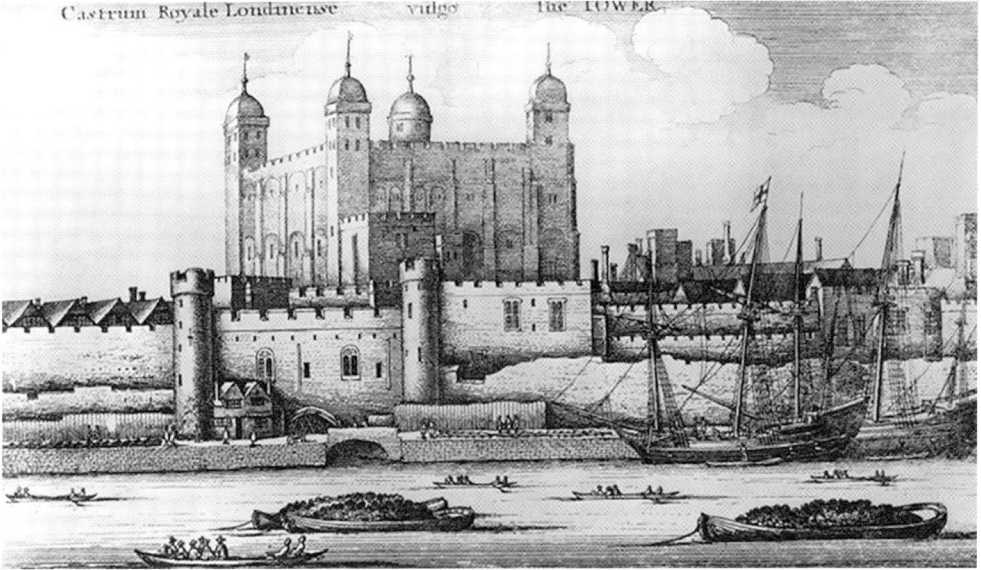

The Tower of London, to which Arthur was unexpectedly sent in 1540, and remained for the next two years.

The coastline at Tehidy, north Cornwall, to which Honor retired in 1542 and lived out her days.

Left: Engraving of Honor taken from the tomb she commissioned in 1533 for her first husband, John Basset.

Below: The Basset family tomb in the churchyard at St Illogan's, near Tehidy.

the autumn of 1535, which prevented her from writing, but planned to visit her own daughter after Christmas, when she was due to give birth 'eighty leagues hence'. She wrote to ask Honor whether Mary might accompany her, and if Honor wished to send cloth for a winter gown, or if Anne should procure it herself.[37] In the end, Honor sent some fabric which was made into a gown and coat.

Supplying the table could also be a challenge in Calais. Honor was appreciative of edible gifts sent by her friends, and reciprocated in kind. To John Kite, Bishop of Carlisle, she sent wine and a barrel of herring in January 1534,[38] and in February, two barrels of herring went to Arthur's Plantagenet cousin, Henry Pole, Baron Montague, who reported that three galleys had arrived at Hampton bringing Spanish oil and wine.[39] Richard Norton received venison and wine in July[40] while Cromwell received the luxury gifts of sturgeon and baked crane.[41] Edward Ringley, who was planning to return to Calais for a visit, sent Honor a venison pasty from London in high summer, which can hardly have been particularly fresh upon arrival. Venison was a high-status, well-prized meat, which John Grenville sent the Lisles for their table at Christmas, following it to Calais himself a few days later, and perhaps helping them feast upon the remains of it.[42]

Unfortunately there were occasions when the transportation of food items across the Channel did not go as planned, and the dispatch of live creatures for the table required planning, to keep the meat fresh. When Honor had sent Anne eighteen dotterels, the birds travelled across the Channel live in cages, being slaughtered at Dover. Unfortunately, on another occasion, when she dispatched twelve dozen quails in similar fashion, nine died on the journey, although they were still delivered and probably consumed as intended.[43] When 'last year's salmon' was sent to the Lisles by the Prior of Christchurch, it was already baked and stored in barrels, but had to endure a further wait as the merchant was experiencing troubles. The Prior also sent them a live ox which survived the journey, and the Lisles sent him two storks, one of which was drowned on the journey.[44] Servants could also create difficulties, such as when John Atkinson wrote that their ship would have dispatched sooner, except 'your man Candelar is so drunken every night that he causes great trouble, and has hurt one of your chief carpenters'.[45]

Honor's skill with medicinal herbs was well known among her circle of friends. Lord Edmund Howard, Comptroller of Calais, frequently suffered from ill health including gallstones. Honor made up a recipe for him of her own devising, which he diligently took, delighted that it caused his stone to break, bringing him relief. It had, however, another unexpected side effect: 'it hath made me piss my bed this night, for the which my wife hath sore beaten me, and saying it is children's parts to bepiss their bed'.[46] Honor had made him 'such a pisser that I dare not this day go abroad', and asked her to give his apologies to the Lord Treasurer who was expecting him for dinner.[47]

Gifts could help build new relationships when Honor was not there to do so in person. Henry's closest friend and former brother-in-law, Charles Brandon, Duke of Suffolk, had remarried his young ward, Katherine Willoughby, following the death of his wife Mary Tudor. Honor would have seen Mary at court during the four years preceding her departure to Calais, perhaps with particular interest as a former queen of France, but Mary's increasing ill health kept her away from the centre of her brother's world. She died shortly after Anne's coronation and six weeks later, Suffolk took to wife the 14-year-old former fiancée of his own son. There is a chance Honor may have seen Katherine before, but it is more likely that she had remained in the countryside, so any acquaintance would have been brief. In order to build the connection, Honor sent the young bride the gifts of a dog and some 'good wine'. In return, Katherine wrote thanking her for her kindness, and sending Suffolk's best wishes, hoping to be commended to Arthur, as 'one who would be glad to be acquainted with him'.[48] Wine features regularly in the Lisle letters as the most common form of gift given and received among Honor's connections. As well as being a most welcome gift, to cater to most budgets, it was easily portable in barrels and would not perish like livestock. On one occasion in March 1535, Husee delivered wine to Cromwell and his son Gregory, five other members of court, John Basset and Mr Skerne, and enquired about malvesy and muscatel for the Lisles.[49]

Another correspondent whose name would be significant in the years ahead was Thomas Culpeper. Two Culpeper brothers, both with the name Thomas, worked for Cromwell, but the younger (and more famous) one served as an agent for the Lisles in 1535, sourcing items for them. He was obsequious in sending his good wishes to Honor that June, sending her out a buck and asking if there were any novelties she desired that he might send for. In return, Honor helped Culpeper find a spaniel he wanted and later sent him a hawk, for which he wrote to thank her as 'a kindness I can never deserve'.[50] In October 1535, she sent him two bracelets of her colours, 'according to your desire. They are of no value, but that it was your gentle request to have them'.[51] A similarly ill-fated correspondent was

Henry Norris, Henry's closest friend and Groom of the Stool, who was commanded by the king to write to Arthur and enquire about yet another of the ever-popular spaniels.[52]

The Lisle retinue continued to grow, with new employees recruited from England being issued with papers for their safe passage to Calais. Soon after their issue in April 1534, the Lisles were joined by Richard Appowell, alias Powell, a mercer from Wells in Somerset; Robert Hodson, a butcher, and William Partriche, a pewterer, both from Rye in Sussex; Robert Joysse, a carver from Waldon in Essex; and Richard Grove, a London grocer.[53] The papers were signed by Arthur and sent to England to smooth the men's passage. Appowell, at least, was employed as a soldier at 8d a day, but had not yet taken up his commission in March 1535, so that Cromwell wrote to Arthur to question the delay.[54]

Good, trustworthy servants were hard to come by, and some of the existing ones had already caused trouble and expense. One in particular, William Petley, was the cause of a disgruntled letter Arthur received from William Grett of Faversham, complaining that Petley owed him for three hogsheads of wine, two of claret and one of white, a further tun and another 'piece' of wine, for which he had not paid. Grett asked Lisle to send him 50s recompense, for which he was prepared to forget the rest, otherwise he would need to apply to the king's council to settle the debt.[55]

John Husee was also trying to find Honor 'a waiting gentlewoman', and had in mind an 'Aragonese who dwelt with my lady Mary ... who speaks good English'. This woman, a Mrs Jermoyne, was greatly in demand and was 'the best cradlewoman in the land, well brought up and a good cook', although Husee was having no luck in securing her.[56] Eventually he announced that she was to marry a Gascon and serve no more, whereupon he offered a substitute by the name of Mrs Durdane, 35 years old, of good condition and known to Mrs Kingston.[57] By April 1535, he still had no luck, though, offering a Miss Barrat, aged 20, who 'works well and is book-learned', and had dwelled until recently with the Duchess of Norfolk.[58] The arrangement may have been tried, but did not work out, as in July, Husee was replying to Honor, 'I am sorry that your gentlewoman likes you no better ... I will do [my] best to procure you such a one as you desire, which will be hard to come by'.[59]

Most of those who dealt with the Lisles held them in high esteem, as their affectionate greetings and thoughtful gifts attest. Along with many others, John Rokewood thanked Honor for remembering his children, and William Kingston asked for her help with a horse, thanked her for her special token and sent her an 'alms purse and somewhat therein to relieve the poor people at her pleasure'.[60] Francis Bryan wrote to Arthur and Honor together, showing his awareness of their closeness, 'because ye be both but one soul, though ye be two bodies, I write but one letter'.[61] Bryan was a good friend to the Lisles, willing to offer advice and warnings where necessary. When Arthur was having difficulties with Richard Whethill, he wrote to assure him 'he has such friends at court' that his adversary 'has little chance of success in his suit', but he went on to offer Arthur 'friendly counsel on two points'. Firstly, Bryan advised Arthur 'to consider he is the king's officer and to fear no man in doing right', and secondly, Bryan had been informed that Arthur was 'no good husband in keeping his house, which is a great undoing of many men'.[62] This comment is not a slur upon Lisle as a husband, as may appear to modern eyes, or any criticism of his relation with Honor, to whom Bryan proceeded to send his good wishes. The idea of husbandry related to thrift, economy and the careful, tight budgeting of a household, incurring little waste or excess. The implication was that the Lisle home could be a little more efficient, perhaps with their bills paid on time.

This was certainly the case when it came to settling accounts. The Lisles enjoyed their luxuries but did not always pay their debts, with the result that their merchants could be left out of pocket. John Husee tried his best to supply the Lisles with the kinds of spices and delicacies required of a household with royal connections, with very little thanks. In one particular dispatch, he sent a chest containing 101 pounds of expensive fine sugar set in twelve loaves, two pounds of cinnamon, two of ginger, a pound each of cloves, mace and sandalwood, ten pounds of pepper and half a pound of isinglass, which was used as a setting agency in jellies and other desserts. Husee had spent the day before searching all of London for the kinds of dishes Honor wanted, although he could not find more than a dozen.[63] Eventually, he was able to send a basket of eight dozen dishes on a ship called the *Julyan* of Erith, at 5d per pound, despite the pewterer being 'the naughtiest fellow that ever I knew'.[64] On another occasion, Husee was disappointed with the quality of sugar offered by Portuguese merchant, Sebastian Pinto: 'three chests that were wet with salt water' which had been baked and dried again. Pinto was asking 5d per pound for it, although Husee insisted it was not worth 3d. The merchant was also selling mace, which was 'wet and worthless' and the only good spices he had to offer were cloves, again at 5d per pound.[65] In December 1535 though, despite sending them sugar loaves, cinnamon, ginger, anise, liquorice, nutmeg, mace, cloves, almonds, raisins and figs, Husee had to warn the Lisles that their grocer remained unpaid and unhappy, by which he had 'lost a friend' from whom he might have purchased spices for £30 or £40.[66] The draper was also unpaid. Husee was the one to suffer, having paid out all his wages on the Lisles expenses so that he had nothing left to live upon and was suffering 'much ado'. He asked again at the end of the year:

> *The grocer and chandler call incessantly for money, and would*
> *not have dealt with me if I had not promised to see them paid*
> *out of hand, as your Ladyship wrote that the money should be*
> *sent without fail ere this. Further, I see no help for it, but after*
> *all the charges I have been at, I must lose my wages.*[67]

The Lisles were being chased for more significant debts, too. Sir Brian Tuke, Henry's secretary, wrote quite frankly to Arthur, although whether his inability to pay bills was down to lack of funds or poor organisation is unclear. To this, Arthur replied that he or Honor would come to court at Lent in order to petition the king about their debts.[68] Tuke replied:

> *Apart from this I should have been compelled to write to your*
> *Lordship of your own matter. During the seven years and more*
> *that I have been treasurer of the King's chamber, I have not*
> *received a penny of your debts to the King. I hope you take me*
> *for your friend, but being the King's debt if I do not receive it*
> *or tell the King, what shall I do? Or how would you esteem a*
> *servant that served you so? The debt is great.*[69]

Tuke and Bryan's comments may have awakened in Honor's memory the former criticism that Cromwell had made about Arthur listening to her too much. She clearly knew more, too, about the matter to which Bryan alluded, writing to Thomas Legh, one of Cromwell's men, about the 'great unquietness she has had by reason of evil tongued persons'. Legh informed her that the party concerned had been spoken to, as Honor wished, and that 'henceforth credence will not be given to some persons as it has been heretofore'. He hoped that 'by the grace of God she will be able to withstand all her adversaries' and sent her three gold and three silver cramp rings to replace some he had borrowed from her when passing through that May on embassy to Hamburg.[70] Legh would later send her a piece of camrick and seek out the damask caffra she desired, patterned with 'florse' or flowers.[71]

However, Legh was soon to end up on an opposing side to Honor in terms of religion. In the summer of 1535 he would join Cromwell's team of Ecclesiastical Visitors, gathering information about the monasteries ahead of their dissolution. Legh's new role did not appear to affect his relationship with Honor, as she continued to instruct him about the purchase of material and other desirable items. Cromwell, too, wrote to reassure Honor, contradicting the report that he was displeased with her. He knew no cause for the rumour, he wrote, and if she continued 'to act as he hears that she does, and as he doubts not she will do' she would always find him 'as ready to do her pleasure as any friend she has'.[72]

In October 1535, a letter written by Cromwell's agent, William Popley, who was also married to a West Country Basset, reveals that he was named in the complaint against Honor, although he denies the accusations, which were related to her close involvement in Arthur's business:

> *Has received her letter complaining of a report made to his master that she intermeddles much in lord Lisle's business concerning the King's causes. Knows of no such report, but his Master on some slender occasion of some insolent person touched the matter a little in his letter to lord Lisle. Assures her that neither he nor Hussey could do anything to try out the knowledge thereof. His Master favours lord Lisle as it becomes him to do, and is well pleased with everything that he does according to his honour. He is somewhat plain where he loves, and lord Lisle no doubt considers this. She will perceive this from Mr. Waterbaylly, who is a friend of lord Lisle and her. She must take no discomfort from his master's letters. He means no ill towards her.*[73]

Family too, were affected by rumours and misinformation. Anthony Wayte, Arthur's relative who had previously sent him advice and cures, now feared that Honor distrusted him. It seems that a lack of communication was responsible. Wayte wrote in April 1535 after having received no correspondence from the Lisles, and asking for reassurance so that his master, Thomas West, 'may have no cause to think unkindness of your husband, or be discontented with me'. Honor's last letter, he claimed, had suggested 'unkindness and mistrust' on his part, which 'considering your kindness, it would be most unnatural in me to feel'.[74] Honor had responded to Anthony by 5 May, when he replied that he was glad to hear of her good health and that wrongs had been redressed.[75] He visited Calais that summer, where he received 'great cheer' and 'manifold kindness'.[76] Later, his cousin, William Wayte, sourced and dispatched twelve ounces of saffron and two barrels of good white salt to the Lisles, adding that he 'wishes they were full of angels' (coins) instead.[77]

For all his devotion and care in the service of the Lisles, not even John Husee was immune to negative whispers. In March 1535, he felt compelled to write to Arthur after realising 'how ill Mr Tate has reported' of him, 'which I must with patience bear'. After some run-in concerning candlesticks in lieu of rent, in which Husee had been asked to leave Tate's property, he stated that 'their so saying shall conceive small honesty and much less worship'. Husee insisted he was at the Lisles' disposal: 'I remain here on your business and if you wish me to set it aside I shall come in haste to Calais' and that he would 'not forsake Lisle till Lisle forsakes him'.[78] Even if Husee's services were ten thousand times better, he wrote, being well meant, 'they were nothing to compare with the goodness' he had found in the Lisles.[79] 'I trust', he continued to affirm, through the following month, 'that whatsoever if reported, Calais shall not be of me forsaken while your Lordship is there deputy'.[80] As Arthur and Honor were beginning to realise, even those with best intentions might be misrepresented across the Channel.

Ten

Heresies and Reform
Summer 1535

It was impossible to ignore the changes Henry VIII was making as 1535 progressed. Perhaps Arthur saw the irony when he was asked by the new Archbishop of Canterbury, Thomas Cranmer, to investigate the case of one errant individual named Thomas King, who was living in Calais at the time. King was reputed to have left his wife, Eleanor Saygrave, in order to cohabit with another woman, denying all knowledge of his former vows. Cranmer requested Arthur's assistance in seeing them both punished, being himself unaware, or more likely unprepared, to comment on the similarity with another king's marital situation.[1]

Others within Arthur's jurisdiction found themselves in trouble for being more vocal. Charles Arundell sent a deposition to Calais against one Guilliam Cowschier, a skinner of St Omer, for saying that 'our sovereign lord king Henry was a wretch, a caitiff and no Christian man, having two wives and a concubine', agreeing with a friend who commented that it was a pity 'of the King's life to forsake the noble blood of the Emperor and to take a poor knight's daughter'. Cowschier was safely outside the English boundary at St Omer, but he had recently visited Calais to attend a wedding and noted all its secrets and weaknesses, 'where it might be most easily entered' and stating 'it were little mastery to win the town in a quarter of a year'.[2] This was treasonous and exposed the town's weaknesses. It was especially important to stamp out any disruption or potential security breaches, as once again, Henry was considering visiting Calais. As Thomas Warley wrote to Honor, 'the common saying in Court is that the king will be in Calais about Whitsuntide'.[3]

However, Henry had more important business on his mind. After breaking with Rome and establishing himself as the Supreme Head of the English Church, he intended to dispense with what he saw as the wealthy but anachronistic bastions of popery, some of which had grown indulgent and irrelevant. In the spring he launched a programme of monastic visitations, recruiting servants to travel across the length and breadth of the country to visit and record details of every religious institution, such as Thomas Legh. Detailed accounts were produced of their assets and abuses, which were presented to Henry by the end of May, in a document named *Valor Ecclesiasticus*, giving him the necessary ammunition to begin a nationwide programme of closures. It was also the role of the Visitors to ensure that all inhabitants swore the Act of Supremacy, which had been passed by parliament the previous November, and so was treason to refuse. As everyone knew, treason was punishable by death, and Henry was not to be tested on the matter. This new act created a crisis of spiritual conscience for many religious figures who were reluctant to set aside their lifelong adherence to the Pope, and were forced to choose between him and their king, potentially imperilling their mortal souls.

Anthony Wayte wrote to Honor in April, describing how his Lord, Thomas West, Baron de la Warr, was newly appointed a visitor, or 'chief commissioner for the valuation of the spiritual lands'. West had recently visited Chichester, with an entourage of a hundred gentlemen, with great enthusiasm to 'stomach the honor' (*sic*) of the job, although his 'great age (made him) scarce able to bear it'. West was, in fact, only around 60 at this point, and would live on to the age of 79, dying in 1554. There were a number of religious establishments in the area, which would have been known to the Lisles as a little way along the coast from their Hampshire home, with Blackfriars and Greyfriars in Chichester itself. West's party had dined on fish in the Bishop's Palace at Chichester with around 700 guests, spread through the large hall, the parlour and great chamber, where West was based 'for warmth', with other commissioners.[4] News of the visitations spread in advance and the commissioners were greeted often with suspicion, hostility and threats in some cases,[5] with good reason; both establishments in Chichester would be dissolved in October 1538.

Considered as part of England, any religious houses within the Calais Pale were also subject to this new scrutiny and closure. In his 1908 book, *Calais Under English Rule*, G.A.C Sandeman wrote 'probably these various institutions were suppressed at the time of the reformation, but singularly little is known as to how that movement was accomplished in Calais'.[6] This simply isn't true, as the State Letters and Papers record Arthur's involvement in the dissolution of key religious establishments in the town. The process is integral to Honor's story.

In March, Arthur was tasked to investigate the Franciscan sisters of the hospital situated 'without the gates' at Calais, in 'honour of the Virgin Mary, St Francis and St Elizabeth of Hungary for sisters of the third order of St Francis'.[7] An illustration included in the *Chronicles of Calais*[8] shows the town from the water, from outside the North, or Lantern Gate. On the left-hand side, a small church-like building with tower, cloisters and outhouses is visible, overlooking the harbour, where the Franciscan sisters lived.

When Arthur went to assess the sisters in late March 1535, perhaps it was one task that out of all his official duties might have suggested Honor's presence too. Although he had jurisdiction over the women, his religious disposition and sensitivity may have led him to bring his wife into the small all-female environment of nine, run by matron Jane Meyns. No doubt Honor already had at least a connection of patronage with them, given her correspondence with other similar figures further afield. It is possible that she had previously visited them, bringing gifts and praying with them. Initially, it looked as if the community might withstand the dissolution. As Arthur wrote to explain to Cromwell, the majority of the 'sisters of the house of religion' were 'mostly strangers', meaning they were likely to have been French or Flemish, or of other nationalities, and therefore were not obliged to 'be obedient to the King's Act'. Regardless, he sent in Sir Hugh Conway to make an inventory of their possessions and forbade them to depart until the king's pleasure was known, but the Calais Council was in agreement that 'they were better away', due to their foreign status.[9] However, just three days after writing this letter, the sisters chose to submit, and all nine of them acknowledged the Royal Supremacy, with matron Meyns signing for them.[10]

Within Calais itself, the community of White Friars, located on the block next to the Lisles, would remain untouched for the moment. Its prior, John Dove, would play a significant role in the future of the Lisles, before White Friars itself was dissolved in 1539, with its estates, gardens and wool making industry granted to Arthur.

A little to south of Calais stood the Benedictine Abbey of St Leonard, outside the ramparts at Guisnes. An earlier inventory shows the extent of the nun's scope and wealth, drawing tithes, rents, wheat, forestry, poultry and more from the surrounding area, overseeing local schools, a leper house, meadows, mills and ships.[11] Within the town walls stood an eleventh-century Benedictine convent, also under the jurisdiction of St Leonards. With Guisnes under English control, it is possible that Arthur visited these places too, unless Lord Sandys was sufficiently recovered from his illness and returned to Calais to do so. No doubt word spread among the monastic community about what these visits meant, and what the future might hold, just as it did in England. Perhaps they also began the process of secreting holy relics and their best treasures, out of sight of visiting eyes. When Archbishop Thomas Cranmer's chaplains arrived in Calais, to assist Arthur, perhaps they were doubtful that the Catholic Lisles would be sufficiently diligent in the pursuit of Henry's ruthless agenda. Such a task cannot have been easy for Arthur, but Henry required it, and Cranmer's chaplains were watching his every move. Ahead of the impending dissolution, some nuns and monks retired with a small pension, but others may have sought permanent residence in religious houses beyond the Pale, in France, where they were safe from English reform.

The scope of investigation widened, as Arthur worked with the royal commissioners to search out 'the extent and yearly value of all the spiritual benefices and promotions on this side of the sea'. He had run into difficulties with the Abbey of Sandingfield, 'the master of which refuses to declare the ordinary rents or lands of the house'. Also present was his friend, Philippe de Chabot, Seigneur de Brion, Admiral of France, who favoured the abbot highly, so Arthur thought it good to meddle no further with him 'until the king's pleasure be known'.[12] Halting his investigation because of his friend's allegiance may have been diplomatic, but the time for diplomacy had passed. The decision would cause Arthur trouble.

At some point during the visit of Cranmer's men, suspicions were aroused about the Lisles' religious sensibilities. At the end of April, Cranmer wrote to thank Arthur and Honor for their 'gentle entreating of his chaplains late at Calais', and to address accusations made 'by some of Cranmer's house, of [Arthur] being a papist, although he had given so little reason to be considered' so.[13] Cranmer proceeded to give a brief lecture about the nature of Henry's objections:

> *It is not so much the person of the bishop of Rome, usurping the title of Pope, but the whole papacy and see of Rome, setting up the Pope as a God of this World that is to be detested. And since the Word of God was against the Pope and his vices, the Pope. in turn, set himself against the Word of God, extorting it out of the true sense, and suppressing it. The chief thing to be detested in that see is that it hath brought the professors of Christ into such ignorance of Christ. Moreover, the Pope has impoverished all Christendom for the maintenance of his own estate.*[14]

Finally, the Archbishop offered reassurance, as 'though some have suspected Lisle of favouring this usurped power, Cranmer, perceiving both lord and lady Lisle inclined to promote the Word of God, will stand to their defence either before the King and Council or elsewhere'.[15] However, lingering doubts about the Lisles' commitment to reform refused to die.

In the summer of 1535, papal tensions in England were complicated by a decision made by Pope Paul III. An unsigned, anonymous letter in the State Letters and Papers collection was written, reputedly, 'in the hand of Lisle's spy'. It contained the information that 'a messenger of the Pope crossed to England on Tuesday night with a cardinal's hat for the Bishop of Rochester, and a bull to excommunicate the King if he refuses to release Rochester or let him wear the hat'. It warned Arthur that any agreements he made with his friend the Admiral, 'will be broken by the Pope, who will excommunicate the King of France if he does not quit your alliance, and the Pope and King will then destroy you'. As if this was too dangerous a message to bear, the spy then begged to be dismissed from Arthur's service.[16] This put Arthur in a highly inflammatory position, highlighting his own Catholicism and good border relations with his French neighbours – indeed, the very reasons why he had been originally selected for the role – but the spy's insinuation that Arthur had been seeking some sort of secret agreement with Brion, an admiral of France, came dangerously close to treason.[17] For the time being, though, it appeared that the spy's message had not been leaked.

The situation in England was escalating fast, especially in relation to treason and heresy. Agents and friends of the Lisles kept them updated about persecutions of those who refused to swear the Oath of Supremacy. At the time that Cranmer's agents were in Calais, Husee described to Arthur how ten monks from the Carthusian monastery of London's Charterhouse had been taken to Newgate gaol, while the city sheriffs remained in their establishment, preparing for dissolution.[18] He followed this with another letter describing how on 4 May, 'three monks of the Charterhouse, one of the brethren of Sion, and a priest, were drawn, hanged, headed and quartered'.[19] This was the start of two years' worth of Carthusian martyrdoms, where dozens died in prison before reaching the traitor's death, until the house was closed for good in 1537.

Anthony Wayte wrote from the Inner Temple, another of the seats of legal training in the city, where heretics were being questioned. His role there is unclear, whether he was a student, or was present as part of his Lord's retinue as a visitor, but he described how twenty-three people from the Netherlands, twenty men and three women, some residents, some new immigrants, were being questioned over their 'no less than damnable opinions'. These included 'that Christ hath not the nature of God and man; that Christ born of the Virgin Mary took no part of the substance of her body; that the bread consecrated by the priest is not the incarnate body of Christ; that baptism given in the state of innocence to children does not profit; that if a man sins deadly after being baptised, he shall never be forgiven'.[20] They were being interrogated by John Stokesley, the Bishop of London, sitting in a court at St Paul's, finding the foreigners so 'stiff', or inflexible, in their beliefs that there seemed 'small hope of their conversion' ahead of judgement being passed the next day. If they proved obstinate, said Anthony, it was still doubtful whether Henry would condemn them, or send them home 'to their country to suffer according to their laws and deserts'.[21] He concluded with a comedic touch that had its roots in truth, that it was 'rumoured that a person should be committed to the Tower for saying that this month will be rainy and full of wet, next month, death, and the third month, wars. He will be kept there till experience shows the truth of his prophecy'.[22]

Later, Anthony would write to describe more changes. A mixture of archaic practices and reform sat side by side in the city. At St Paul's, five bishops and abbots wore mitres in a 'great and solemn procession, carrying the sacrament under a canopy to pray for the recovery of Francis I from a bout of sickness'.[23] On the other hand, preachers were advocating clerical marriage, which had always been strictly forbidden and changes to how people received the sacrament, along with questions about the existence of purgatory.[24] The Ten Articles, published in July 1536, still permitted prayers and masses to be said for the dead, but asserted that the existence of purgatory, its name, and the experience of it, was 'uncertain by scripture'. Superstitious practices were to be avoided, and although it was still permissible to own religious images, worshippers were no longer allowed to kneel before them or make offerings to them. Images were only to serve as reminders of virtue and good works, but were not in themselves to be actively worshipped. Common practices such as sprinkling holy water, carrying candles, ashes, clerical vestments and the sale of indulgences were derided as having no intrinsic power to heal or offer salvation, despite past centuries imbuing them with the power to do so as substitutes for God's forgiveness.

This was one of the most significant changes for 'ordinary' Catholics, who through generations had devoted prayers and gifts in the hopes of assisting the souls of their loved ones out of limbo and into the Kingdom of Heaven. They were accustomed to lighting candles in memory of the dead, worshiping in churches lined by the chantry chapels of the wealthy, and having their church calendar punctuated by memorial days. All of this established a strong connection between the living and the dead, and the very real sense of survivors assisting souls who had passed, giving them an additional sense of purpose and faith. Honor would have drawn comfort from remembering her family in this active way, as is seen in the tomb she commissioned for her first husband and the remembrance of his anniversary. The practice also encouraged ties between the Church and its congregation, who would invest their time and prayers wisely, in the hopes of receiving similar devotions themselves, and securing their eternal bliss. Suddenly, ideas that were not just comforting, but considered essential, were being questioned. The impact of this upon the older generations of devout Catholics who had lived this way for decades, is difficult to underestimate.

When Arthur's spy had written about the Pope's messenger bringing a cardinal's cap for the Bishop of Rochester, at some point in May, no one could have estimated the result of this action. John Fisher, formerly Bishop of Rochester, and Sir Thomas More, formerly Henry's chancellor, were still imprisoned in the Tower of London as a consequence of their refusal to sign the Act of Supremacy. When Pope Paul offered a cardinal's hat to Fisher, it was in the hopes that this would save him from punishment, but the idea backfired, bringing about the opposite effect and sealing his fate. Henry refused to let the symbolic hat enter England and arranged Fisher's trial for 17 June, then sped through his execution a week later, to avoid an outcry among the English people who were likening him to John the Baptist. With St John's feast approaching on June 24, Fisher was executed two days before the feast, and his head was placed on a spike above London Bridge. When an inventory was made of Fisher's worldly goods, the majority of his current correspondence, totalling forty-six letters, were found in his gallery window, but among the fewer letters in his personal chamber were several from Arthur.[25] It was a further link to Papacy that the Lisles did not need.

Fisher's death was followed by that of Thomas More. Previously so close to the king that he was something of a father figure, as well as an efficient Lord Chancellor, More was a devout Catholic for whom the reforms of Protestant Europe were heresy and the Pope remained the supreme authority. Having been previously implicated in the treason of Elizabeth Barton, and refused to swear the Oath, More went on trial on 1 July, relying upon his silence to appear in agreement with what he was asked to accept. This proved insufficient, and after the jury had swiftly found him guilty, he explained how no 'temporal' or earthly man could be Head of the Church, as it was contrary to Church laws, while the Statue of Supremacy opposed the Magna Carta. He was executed on 6 July. No doubt Arthur would have known More well. He was at court through the period of More's rise to power, whose closeness with the king meant they would often have been in proximity. Honor is likely to have known him during her time in service to Anne Boleyn, possibly Fisher too. Apart from the personal loss of two long-term peers, the significance of their deaths must have been as shocking for the Lisles as it was for much of England, if not more so.

Reform prompted more reform. Sir William Fitzwilliam, Treasurer of the King's Household was sent out to Calais in May 1535 with a commission to improve things. He was a man long known to Arthur, as the Earl of Southampton, Captain of Guisnes and Admiral of England, who had served in Henry's court since his accession. Now he was charged with investigating Arthur's management and the efficiency of Calais. This may have come about as a result of observations made by Cranmer's Visitors the previous month, building on previous doubts held by Cromwell and Bryan about the Lisles' efficiency. Mixed messages came from Edward Fox, Bishop of Hereford, who wrote to Arthur that the king had 'declared in presence of the Council … his very great regard for' you, but still intended to 'reform all disorders in Calais and the pale', for which purpose he was sending out Fitzwilliam.[26] In any case, it was another blow to Arthur's authority and would have no doubt caused concern in his household. Nor was Honor able to exercise her usual gifts of hospitality as Fitzwilliam was concerned to keep his distance, writing to ask Lady Garneys whether he might lodge with her, giving the feeble excuse that 'the wholesome walk he may have in her garden will be conducive to his health'.[27] Once he had arrived though, the hard work began.

On 17 June, Arthur gave instructions for a general search throughout the twelve wards of Calais, recording population figures and supplies of wheat, salt, oats, beef, wood, coals and other necessaries. This yielded the information that there was a total of 4031 residents in the area of the town and Pale, living under the jurisdiction of an alderman, who at that time were: Sir Richard Whethill, William Prysley, Thomas Prowde, John Massingberd, Christopher Conway, William Snowden, Griffith Appenriff, Thomas Tate, Thomas Hollonde, William Johnson, Robert Baynham and Thomas Skryven.[28] Arthur was also requested by Sir Thomas Audley, who had replaced More as Lord Chancellor, to 'send a just declaration of the value of all his lands, goods, plate and jewels, with the view of being assessed for the same', as well as his rent for the past year.[29]

Arthur produced a series of articles addressed to Fitzwilliam and the other commissioners outlining his plans for the improvement of Calais. These included the poverty of the Calais brewers, the role of the soldiers in the king's retinue, the presence of strangers in the town who were not to be trusted in emergencies, the replacement of thatched rooves with tile or slate, the sale of grain outside the town, the disrepair of houses and the question of whether marriage should be permitted between English residents and strangers.[30] Fitzwilliam seemed satisfied, writing to thank Arthur for the 'good cheer' he had received while visiting, and promised that he would soon learn the king's pleasure.[31]

Briefly, all seemed well. Then, a report reached Arthur that Cromwell was displeased with him as the result of rumours of war spreading through Calais, prompted by the son of his old adversary Richard Whethill bringing his father's 'stuff' to this town. This makes sense if the 'stuff' was spears, pikes or armour, or other military gear. The situation was further complicated because Robert Whethill had married Jane Grenville, so perhaps had used his connection to the Lisles, or stored items on their property. Arthur added that he was 'not himself the author of the report', and whilst Whethill junior was about this business, Arthur had been 'with his wife at a place he has three miles from Calais', and had left the keys with the marshal, who had contacted him about Whethill's carts. Rumours of war had spread through the town as a result, which Arthur had done his best to pacify. Cromwell might also have been angry about the forfeit of 'the wools', which was a matter in which Arthur had been forced to act swiftly, seeking advice from Henry Norris because Cromwell had been ill at that point.[32] Arthur added that he trusted Cromwell above all others and appears to have been so concerned about a misunderstanding, that he added notes in his own hand to the letter's margin that he had been unable to halt the spread of the rumour.[33]

Arthur was deeply affected by the misunderstanding, elaborating in a further letter:

> *to be plain with you as my special good master and friend, the residue of your said letters were couched after such sort, and went so nigh unto mine heart, that I could minister unto me such cause of sorrow that never thing grieved me so much in my life hitherto. For I have lived in this world at God's pleasure unto this day, and never went about the bush with any man. And now to have it laid to my charge, and specially by*

you, that I should use myself after that sort towards my most dread sovereign Lord and King, of whom dependeth all my life and living, it is the greatest heaviness that ever fortuned unto me. And surely I had rather be under the ground than that either the King or you should worthily conceive any such opinion of me. Wherefore, Sir, I most heartily desire and pray you to interpret my writings and sayings as proceeding from him that meaneth as faithfully and as sincerely to deal with the King's highness as becometh his true liege man, and in all such things as his Highness shall commit unto my charge, to execute the same with as much truth and diligence as my poor wit can extend unto.[34]

The summer of 1535 was tense and full of drama. With the monastic visitations, the enforcement of the Act of Supremacy in England, and the deaths of previously revered men such as Fisher, More and the Carthusian monks, pressure was felt in Calais to conform and reform. For Arthur and Honor, this meant an additional level of scrutiny into the state of Calais and its religious houses, the latter being at odds with their privately held Catholic beliefs. At such a time, when it was vital to be seen to be supportive of Henry's changes, cross-channel communication again failed to dispel criticism and rumours, forcing Arthur once more to insist upon his loyalty. It must have been a stressful few months in the Lisle household.

Eleven

The Lisles at Home
Early 1536

In February 1536,[1] the Lisles finally moved out of Lord Berners' old home into the Staple Inn. They had been pursuing it since the previous spring, when Husee first explored the possibility of their occupancy, being delayed by Cromwell for various reasons. This central, significant building, more like a mini palace, contained its own apartments, parlours, chapel, armoury, guardrooms, counting house and cellar, as well as a bakehouse, ewery, buttery, pantry, chaundry, spicery and brewhouse, and now had been handed over to the Crown by the Staplers in part payment of their debts. Honor remembered its potential from the autumn of 1532, where she had accompanied Anne Boleyn to dance before Francis I and seen it hung with gold and silver cloth, dazzling in the light of hundreds of candles.

The detailed inventory made of the Lisles' possessions in the Staple gives a fascinating snapshot of the inside of their home, confirming the material details of Honor's letters. When entering the house, a visitor would be received in the great parlour, where the walls displayed rich tapestries and the floors were spread with Turkish carpets and embroidered cushion and a cupboard showcased their plate. Beyond that lay the great chamber, with more tapestries, where they might sit upon chairs and stools of crimson velvet, or drink from one of the thirty glasses kept in the closet, or be offered a remedy from one of six gallipots, or earthenware medical pots. Here, local dignitaries and visiting ambassadors would have been entertained. Inside Arthur's chamber were four new Turkish carpets, a great bedstead with bedding of embroidered cloth of gold and crimson satin, and a red and blue sarcenet quilt.[2]

The inventory allows us to look around Honor's private rooms, as if she had just left them. In her dining chamber, carpets covered the board, cupboard and windows for privacy and warmth, while a painted cloth depicted Holofernes, the invading Assyrian general beheaded by Judith, was on display. Honor dined at a long table, seated on a chair covered with crimson velvet, while her guests occupied stools or benches made comfortable by twenty-eight cushions. Hangings of green say were on hand when she wanted a change. Honor's bedroom contained more luxury, confirming the details about her style that pervade her letters. Her bed was dressed in tawny velvet and blue satin, with a cushion of Bruges satin, a chair from Flanders with a gold cushion, five red carpets with blue crewel work, feather-stuffed mattresses, blankets, pillows, more Turkish carpets and nine pieces of tapestry. There was also evidence of clothes-making and interior decorating, with lengths of cloth of tissue, tinsel, crimson satin, crimson velvet, red embroidered cloth and pieces of needlework. Her daughters' bedroom held red say hangings, bedding and basins. It appears that red was a particular favourite colour.[3]

The inventory allows us to open up the Lisles' wardrobes and peer inside. This really allows us an unprecedented glimpse of how Arthur and Honor appeared in their new home setting and as they appeared about the town. Their clothing is symbolic in many more ways that the quality of their fabric or the type of fur they wore, or their gold and jewels, as indicative of status. For the historian, it represents the absence of their physical bodies, intimate and personal, conjuring up their presence as no other forms of record can. Arthur's possessions speak of his position, contemporary fashions and his own preferences, but we know from the letters that he was partly dressed by Honor too, and that she sourced many of these items from England. His gowns are up-to-date but sombre, in the popular tawny caffa damask, with facing of black rabbit fur, or in black satin guarded with black velvet, embroidered and adorned with grey rabbit. Also hanging in his wardrobe was his formal parliamentary robe, juxtaposed with the more personal white night gown, more fur gowns, and a magnificent cloth of Arras gold and silk which retold the story of St Luke.[4]

It is an absolute treat to look inside Honor's wardrobe. The items within reflect not just a woman of her status and times, but one who took particular interest in how she adorned her body, with the exacting standards that kept her agents in England searching for the correct quality of silver cloth, or who relished the setting of a new jewel. Her gowns were made of black satin lined with buckram, tawny velvet, black velvet lined with white taffeta turned up with powered ermines, black velvet furred with miniver, or ermine, or lamb. Her kirtles were of gold, tinsel, black velvet, tawny satin or velvet and purple velvet; she owned nightgowns of similar coloured damask, a scarlet petticoat, a taffeta cloak and a buckram cloak case, a pillion cloth guarded with velvet and black velvet foot cloth. Also housed in her wardrobe was the saddle made by Robert Action of Southwark, 'with pommel, copper and gilt', and other garments embroidered with stars and angels. In a chest were stored rolls of silk, frontlets of gold and crimson velvet, sleeve, partlets, bonnets and placards for gowns, as well as a great Bible.[5]

Among Honor's jewels were three girdles of goldsmith's work and pearls, that she would have worn about her waist. These may have come from London, perhaps from the royal goldsmith Cornelius Hays whilst the Lisles were at court, or sourced by agent Richard Blount in Bruges, or were perhaps the work of the local Calais craftsmen from whom King Henry had made purchases in 1532: Alart Plumer, Latronet, Symon Quanden, Jenyns and John de Grane.[6] One of them may have created Honor's gold chain made from 198 links, or her black enamelled one of 282 links. Kept inside a black desk, she had many strings of beads of amethyst and gold, pearl and gold, white and black enamel and some golden ones called French beans. There were also gold aglets, the metal caps that bind the end of laces, cords or ribbons, gold clasps on velvet, gold buttons, pearls for sleeves, gold spoons, a gold thimble, a gold hawthorn with twenty diamonds, a gold rose with four diamonds and three pearls and four bunches of the cramp rings that feature so often in Honor's letters. Her rings were set with sapphires, emeralds and rubies.[7]

More wealth was found among the Lisles' plate, which was usually displayed on cupboards in dining rooms, with symbolic designs. One of the salt cellars displayed the Bourchier arms of Lord Berners, suggesting that the plate of his that the Lisles had petitioned to take over in 1533 was mixed up here among their own possessions. Among the usual bowls, cups, pots and dishes, were cups with covers featuring an armed man, a lion, a diamond, crowns, roses and mulberries. Some had clear dynastic significance, such as the enamelled 'white rose in a red', the portcullis associated with the Beauforts and the pomegranate, symbol of Catherine of Aragon. Basins and ewers bearing the device of the falcon and fetterlock had formerly belonged to, or were gifted to the Lisles by, Anne Boleyn. There was also a silver seal that had come from the dissolved friary, a shaving basin, beer cups and candlesticks. In one of the wardrobes was a stained cloth bearing the portrait of the Emperor and Empress as well as twelve masking gowns with hoods and caps of buckram which were probably left over from the visit of Henry and Anne in the autumn of 1532. The chapel contained evidence of the Lisles' continuing Catholic faith. There were priests' vestments of crimson and blue velvet with gold crosses, a tablet embroidered with a crucifix, another featuring Our Lady and an altar piece embroidered with the knots of the Bourchier family. There was a chalice, a bell, a bottle to cast holy water, a holy water stock and sprinkle, a pyx for consecrated bread and a pax which was kissed during mass.[8] The vivid picture emerges from these material items of a wealthy, stately Catholic family with royal connections.

The Lisles also owned a farm in the countryside, to which they could retreat from Calais. Situated three miles from the town, it might have been due south in the farming area of Coulogne, near an ancient chateau, or east towards the flat lands of Fort Vert and Marck, where present day farms stand, or west in the direction of Fréthun and Coquelles, around the location of the Eurotunnel terminal. Alternatively, it may have been at Landreteun, on account of Honor's friendship with Jenne de Quierete, lady of Landertyn, who wrote to Honor in 1536 from 'your house of Landreteun',[9] and later offered fruit from her garden, although on a present day map, the only approximate place, Landrethun-le-Nord, is closer to ten miles south than the three Arthur claims. However, it is not impossible that Arthur meant three miles outside the Pale of Calais, rather than three miles outside the town itself, confirming the quiet French village of Landrethun-le-Nord as the likely spot.

What the Lisles considered a farm was, in fact, a substantial property containing a hall, chambers, parlour, buttery, bakery, kitchen and loft, with an additional milkhouse, cheesehouse and stables.[10] Like the Staple, the walls were hung with painted hangings and red and green say, furnished with cushions, curtains, carpets and footstools, while the two bedrooms were supplied with feather beds, bolsters and blankets.[11] By 1540, it sustained a bull and sixteen cows, three mares, two horses, three male colts, twenty-three ewes, a lamb, two boars and four sows.[12] There were also beehives, a spinning wheel and a candle mould, as well as the equipment needed for the manufacture of dairy produce, so the place was pretty self-sufficient and must have retained a basic staff during the Lisles' absences.

Honor continued to hear news from her Basset home of Umberleigh. Sir John Bonde, her priest, wrote to inform her about the numbers of salmon in her ponds and the amount of timber required, and informed her about the difficult relationship between her stepdaughter Jane and her sisters, who could not please her. Nor was Jane happy with recent items that Honor had ordered for her, including feather beds and sheets, as well as her having two cows, a horse and a greyhound, which was always with her or else lying on a bed day and night. Bonde also informed Honor that he would not forget the obit of her late husband, Sir John, in keeping with the traditional practise of remembering the dead on the anniversary of their passing.[13] Jane could have been in her forties at this point, or older than Honor, and was unmarried. Still living in her childhood home, she occupied a corner chamber and the buttery, often in conflict with Bonde, whom she accused of living a 'bawdy and unthrifty' life. Soon after, Jane herself wrote to Honor, thanking her for the flock and feather beds, bolsters, pillows, cushions and coverlets she had sent. Contrary to what Bonde wrote, she complained that the chapel was 'unserved' save for a weekly mass, and that her letters were opened before she had a chance to read them.[14] Two of Jane's sisters, Anne and Mary, were already married, but Thomasine still lived at Umberleigh, finding Jane so difficult that she ran away early one morning to stay with Mary.

Better news came from Honor's own Basset daughters. Anne had accompanied Jeanne de Saveuses, Madame de Riou, on a pilgrimage during which they saw the Holy Tear of Our Lord, which probably refers to the Benedictine Trinity Abbey in Vendôme, to the west of Orléans, around 250 miles south of their Pont-Remy home. The tear was encased in rocky crystal and supposedly brought from the Holy Land by the abbey's founder, Agnes of Burgundy. Pilgrims would press it to their eyes, as the tear was thought to cure blindness. Again, this shows how connected the Lisles were to old Catholic practices, at a time when shrines and relics in England were being destroyed. Anne had also been given a new necklace, which Jeanne wrote could be worn around her neck or waist, as she wished, adding that the girl was considered handsome and a 'good sort' by all.[15] Honor wrote that she could not thank Jeanne enough, and was sending a servant with money for the necklace, but had been unable to dispatch fish to the family as she had wished, as 'it is by default that the king's money is not come this time as it hath been accustomed'.[16]

In mid-March, Honor sent tokens to the daughter of Jeanne Rouault, Mary Basset's guardian, who was due to deliver a child, including a blanket and 'a girdle that hath been about the body of St Rose'.[17] In response, the daughter sent Honor 'a little silver cup and a head of St John to put in a cabinet'.[18] Such practices had been common during Honor's life, and she had possibly even used this girdle herself as part of the rituals of childbirth, but in England they were now considered superstitious. Among Henry's mandate for the monastic visitations of 1535 was that establishments should 'not show no relics nor fayned [feigned/fake] miracles for increase of lucre [money]' but should entreat visitors to donate to the poor instead of laying money before images or relics'.[19] The holy relics of England's religious houses had long been under attack as idols by thinkers like Erasmus, Tyndale and Latimer; now they were swiftly confiscated and destroyed, including, from Reading Abbey, 'oure lades gyrdell of Bruton, red silk, wiche is a solemne reliquie sent to women travelyng [travailing] wiche shall not miscarrie in partu' and 'Mare magdalens girdell, and that it wrappyde and covride with white, sent also with gret reverence to women traveling, wich girdell Matilda the empress ... gave unto them (*sic*)'.[20]

In August 1536, as the monastic closures were beginning, Honor's friend, Anthoinette de Saveuses, Jeanne's cousin, sent her an 'image of our Lady', cramp rings, a gold coin and coifs from her religious house at Dunkirk.[21] John Bekynsaw, James' guardian in Paris, sent her a diamond to fit her brooch of the Assumption of Our Lady, while Hugh Giles, a Calais archer, ordered her patterns of two brooches to be drawn, one with the image of Our Lady, the other with a personage sitting under a cloth of state.[22] Again, these small acts reaffirm Honor's continuing adherence to Catholic practices, even as they were being forbidden.

Jeanne Rouault had removed her family to Abbeville for safety, for 'fear of the evil times', which probably related to an outbreak of plague or the sweating sickness, but could also refer to impending war between France and the Netherlands.[23] Mary wrote to her mother from Abbeville, glad that she had already been informed of the move, and thanking her for sending her twenty-seven pearls and a crown. In return, Mary sent Honor a pair of knives for her cabinet, 'as she has none of the same make'. She was had found another teacher locally for the spinet, was to have a satin gown trimmed in time for Easter and had also found time to visit her sister Anne at Pont-Remy.[24] In fact, the sisters were now only five miles apart.

Mary also wrote to her sister Philippa, who was then aged around 20, and living in the Staple with Honor, Katherine Basset, Arthur and his daughter Frances Plantagenet. She missed her sisters, wishing she might spend an hour with them each day to teach them French, but she was so happy that if she could only see her mother often, she would be 'right well content ... never to return to England'. Mary sent Philippa a purse of green velvet, a little pot for Frances, a gospel to Katherine and a parrot to Arthur, 'because he maketh much of a bird'. She asked Philippa to present it to him, in the hopes that he would send her some 'pretty things' for Easter, adding that she hoped the Lord would 'give you a good husband, and that very soon'.[25] A week or so later, Mary wrote again to her mother, thanking her for a beautiful white girdle and saying that all she needed now were sleeves, as her others were 'all used up', and sending her a needle-case and 'a gospel to carry with her paternosters'.[26]

It appears that in the early part of 1536, during Lent, Honor and Arthur did go to England, in response to Sir Brian Tuke's questions about their debts. Apologising to Jeanne de Saveuses for not having written sooner, Honor explained that 'my Lord and I both were sent for to have gone into England, and other impeachment therein sithence hath been the cause thereof'.[27] This must have only been a brief visit, the result of which had been satisfactory, as no action was taken against the Lisles, although it was significant that Honor was summoned to accompany Arthur. It meant that her role in their partnership was acknowledged, even if it was also sometimes questioned, but that she had the opportunity to present herself to the king and affirm her loyalty. One of Arthur's letters to Francis Bryan at the end of January reveals that 'whereas my wife and I moved you to desire the King to forgive me my debt to him, of which the greater part is for suretyship, by which I never profited, nor did I ever borrow from his Grace, I bind myself to perform what my wife promised'.[28] This suggests that the main negotiator in the matter was Honor, and that Arthur was prepared to follow whatever course of action she suggested on the matter.

No doubt the Lisles took the opportunity to see old friends whilst in England, but may have found an uneasy mood at court. Catherine of Aragon had died in January, finally allowing Anne Boleyn to become the uncontested queen. However, Anne had recently uncovered Henry's flirtation with her maid of honour, Jane Seymour, which resulted in a physical altercation between the two women. Then, on the day of Catherine's funeral, Anne had miscarried a male child, of around three months gestation. Reputedly, Henry had muttered that God would give him no more sons by Anne. The Lisles may have even been at court at the time, finding the mood much altered since their departure, shortly after Anne's triumphant coronation. Henry's tone was ominous, but Anne's fate was not yet sealed.

It may have been during their visit to court that Arthur recruited new servants for the Lisle household. Grants were issued in February for the safe passage of Thomas Wilson and Baldwin Roper, both London mercers, Thomas Dockington, a salter from London, and Thomas Layer, a yeoman of Ovington, Essex, who were joining Arthur's retinue. The dates spanning 1–14 February 1536, suggest the period of time that the Lisles spent at court after their interview with the king.[29] It may be that they stayed at the Red Lion in Southwark during this period, as Honor's brother-in-law, Thomas St Aubyn, sent a dozen puffins there from her Cornish estate of Tehidy, either in anticipation of their arrival, or to be sent on to them.[30] The Red Lion was often used as a base by John Husee, which may also explain the reference.

Back in Calais, Honor continued to be at the centre of a network of communications. This was essentially economic in nature, but which also served to further strengthen ties with friends and associates. After much difficulty, Thomas Runcorn managed to source skins for her in Lyons, as 'good ones are very scarce' costing 10 crowns a pelt.[31] Henry Norris wrote asking for Arthur to send him a couple of red and white spaniels, sending into France for them if none were to be had in Calais.[32] A Gentleman of the Privy Chamber, and one of Henry VIII's closest friends, Norris was then in high favour, as the Lisles learned; the king had given him £200 a year, 'which he has gone to take possession of, and it will be a fortnight before he returns'.[33] Norris would soon come to regret his return to court.

Sir William Kingston thanked Arthur for sending him a horse, offering to look after the animal, so he would 'always be sure to have a horse in England'. He also gifted Honor a 'purse of wood, that it may long endure to keep money, for almost I can wear none purse for lack of money' and he was 'done with play', instead enjoying the game 'pennygleek'.[34] Thomas Warley sent Honor a velvet frontlet lined with black satin, some gold damask and promised a velvet bonnet to come, at the cost of 26s.[35] He followed this with the news that he had attended court to acquire Honor a kirtle, perhaps the same one in Anne's livery that she had previously sought, of cloth of gold, paned like the illustration he included.[36] Later, Husee confirmed that Anne was sending Honor a pair of sleeves as a gift to match the kirtle.[37]

In case the Lisles were inclined to forget, or ignore any of the recent religious changes, Cranmer sent them a preacher called Mr Hore, whom they had apparently appreciated last Lent, who was bringing to Calais a learned man called Nichols, 'begging you to assist the doctrine of the Gospel'.[38] Diplomatically, Arthur wrote to thank Cranmer for sending them, adding that they had 'done much good since their coming', and asking for them to be sent every Lent, 'for the erudition of the people in these parts'. He added that Honor sent her greetings, but not what she thought of Hore's sermons.[39] The dissolution of the monasteries was on Arthur's mind too, as he wrote seeking reassurance to William Popley, who told him there was 'no intention to put down the monastery of Glastonbury or any worshipful house, but it is thought all houses under 300 marks shall be suppressed'.[40] As it happened, Glastonbury would be dissolved in 1539, with the abbot hung, drawn and quartered on the nearby Tor.

Honor and Arthur continued to maintain friendly relationships with their French neighbours, besides the Rouault and de Bours family. Honor sent Ysabeau de Morbecque a cramp ring,[41] while another Ysabeau du Bies, offered her a little monkey,[42] and her father Oudart du Bies supplied them with deer from Boulogne.[43] Unfortunately, Oudart had to contact Arthur again shortly afterwards, when the servant of a Gascon merchant coming from Zeeland in the Netherlands had been robbed of 'eight angelots by some of your subjects at the bridge of Nuyllay', and asked for assistance in resolving the matter.[44] This may have been an isolated incident or an indicator of the unrest that was heading their way.

The Lisles' peace was being threatened by a wider European picture of conflict between Francis I and Emperor Charles V. After a long series of clashes over territory in Italy, war was threatening to erupt again following the death of Francesco II Sforza, Duke of Milan, who had no heirs. With both France and the Empire laying claim to the territory, Calais was potentially threatened, sitting just a few miles from the border of Charles' Netherlands, where troops were gathering. Arthur wrote to warn Cromwell that the Duke of Guelders was preparing his men for battle, minting new silver coins and ordering his men at arms to keep three horses 'to be ready in a short space', instead of the usual two.[45] Calais' neutral status made it attractive. Soon after, Arthur noticed that 'divers subjects, both of the French king and the Emperor', who bordered 'upon both the king's pale here, have desired leave to unload certain of their goods here', to be safe during future occurrence of war. It was rumoured in Flanders that the armies would 'spoil our marches, because the king (Henry) assists the French with 20,000 men'. Arthur wanted to do 'nothing to embolden our neighbours, whether friends or foes', but feared that troops might be suddenly blown over the frontier.[46] In response, the words of the king's secretary and Bishop of Winchester, Stephen Gardiner, feel a little glib with their meteorological metaphor:

> *There is no news; but whether there shall be war or peace is like doubtful weather. The weather is cloudy, and much preparation there is, and in Savoy hath fallen a few drops of rain, for 300 of the legionaries of France be dispatched by men of war of the duke of Savoy, which issued out of a castle at the town of Montmillian beside Chambery but there is no war yet with the Emperor, and the sun may shine yet and disperse these clouds.*[47]

Arthur informed Gardiner that war had been declared between Francis and Charles on Sunday 12 March at Gravelines and every man was commanded to his garrison.[48] The Captain of Gravelines had detained a man called Derick coming from Cologne, who was attempting to reach England with books by German reformer Martin Luther on his person, and Arthur wrote to him sternly in an attempt to secure his release.[49] The Captain replied that the Emperor had asked him to be vigilant for such heretical books and that not only was Arthur's reproach that he had ill-treated an English subject unfounded, but that Arthur had done nothing to preserve amity but had made malicious interventions.[50] This letter was incendiary to a man like Arthur, who wrote back that Derick was the king of England's servant and the Captain's reply was 'not honourable or neighbourly', but in direct contrast to the amity with the Emperor. He advised that Derick be set free at once, and the Captain refrain from 'irritating the king of England as he has often done'. In a final touch, Arthur could not resist asserting his status:

> *Few persons are acquainted with the captain's boasted nobility of birth, but every one knows Lisle's parentage. If the captain were come of noble lineage, his manner would be more courteous.*[51]

Honor's response to the threat of war, in writing to the Rouaults, was that 'it displease me greatly the war that is apparent, for your sake as much as it were for myself, trusting in God some good appointment shall be made that it shall cease'.[52] She feared it would threaten the Lisles' position and alienate them from friends and family, and summoned her son James from school in Paris back to Calais. From there James went to join his brother George at school with the priest Jehan des Gardins at the house of La Heuze[53] in St Omer, much closer and safer.

Mindful of war, Honor also wrote to her friend Jenne de Quierete at the Landreteun farm, asking whether she would feel safer if she moved into Calais, but while Jenne appreciated the kindness, she stated 'I have no occasion to retire to Calais or elsewhere, for the governors of the two princes do not prevent my being at home where I am, for they know well I have no ill intention, and am a widow, without power to do harm'.[54] Soon, the French would attempt to take Turin and Milan, whilst Charles marched his armies south into Provence to take Aix. This fresh eruption of the Italian wars would last until 1538, but England would have far more dramatic events to concern itself with.

Twelve

Thunder Round the Throne
1536

Suddenly, in the late spring of 1536, bad news arrived in Calais, timed to coincide with an outbreak of plague. Honor received a letter from John Davy, informing her that her Basset stepdaughter, Thomasine, had died. Having reached her forties, and remaining unmarried, Thomasine had recently run away from her home at Umberleigh, probably to escape her overbearing sister Jane, while some historians have framed it as an elopement.[1] Having found shelter with her other sister Mary, she was returning home at Easter when she fell ill and died, 'full well and virtuously', according to Davy, who promised Honor he would 'honestly keep' her month's mind. He also arranged for the arms of her parents to feature on the black say that draped her hearse.[2] Honor had had very little to do with Thomasine. The girl had been sent away to live with the Daubeney family as a child, and may have spent a brief period at Umberleigh while Honor was a young wife, but it is unlikely they had seen each other since her marriage to Arthur.

On Good Friday, 14 April, the Lisles' agent, Thomas Warley, wrote that Anne Boleyn's mother, the Countess of Wiltshire, thanked Honor for a pair of hose she had sent her and asked when she might be seeing her again. According to Warley, Elizabeth Boleyn was 'diseased with the cough, which grieves her sore', but that he had told her that Honor was 'very desirous to see the queen and her ladies and gentlewomen'. A letter from Honor had been delivered to the king, but according to Sir Richard Page, Henry had not yet opened it, but he was waiting in anticipation of the reply.[3] The letter may have related to the proposed Calais visit, about which Warley had been informed that 'the King will be at Dover in three weeks at the farthest', with Anne and their entourage.[4] Arthur was pleased to hear of their imminent arrival and promised to send a hogshead of 'hegge wine, such as I am wont to have for your Grace's drinking'.[5] Soon after, George Boleyn confirmed the impending visit, 'within this fortnight', writing to Arthur to prepare for his own arrival in the town and make such arrangements as was necessary.[6] However, two weeks later, both Anne and George would be in the Tower on charges of treason. This timing demonstrates just how unexpectedly, and how rapidly, Henry turned against Anne and her circle.

On 22 April, Arthur was writing to ask for Richard Page's assistance in resolving his ongoing conflict with Robert Whethill, and to ask Henry Norris to ask the king if Arthur might have the priory of St Mary Magdalene in Barnstaple, Devon, as he thought it 'would not be long out of the king's hands'.[7] Barnstaple was only ten miles east of Bideford, and eight miles north of Umberleigh, so this may well have been a request on Honor's behalf, and it is likely that she had connections with the nuns. The priory was later granted to the Howards.

Five days later all still appeared well to outside observers. John Husee reported that Page had left court, until the start of his next period of waiting upon the king, but that he had obtained permission, through Henry Norris, for Arthur to attend court in person. 'The King granted it willingly and said he would be glad to see you.' He added that Henry was to begin his journey to Dover on 4 May, and that Arthur could speak with him in person regarding his interest in Barnstaple Priory.[8] Husee advised Arthur to be ready to depart from Calais on 5 May, so that he might travel back with the king.[9] Behind the scenes, though, the net was already closing in. Henry had instructed Cromwell to investigate Anne's behaviour and find evidence of adultery and treason. Courts of Oyer and Terminer had been established on 24 April to investigate crimes that occurred in Kent and Middlesex, the main locations where Anne would be charged. A day later, Henry was still referring to her publicly as his 'most dear and entirely beloved wife'. It may be, though, that Anne had an inkling of the trouble brewing, as on 26 April, she asked her chaplain, Matthew Parker, to look after her daughter Elizabeth, should anything happen to her.

Still, the Lisles planned for a royal visit to Calais. On April 28, Husee wrote to Honor that 'the Queen expects my Lady to meet her at Dover, as Mrs. Margery Horsman informed me, and on Tuesday next the King and Queen will lie at Rochester. On Monday I intend to leave for Dover or Sandwich, to await the coming of your Lordship and my Lady'.[10] Honor and Arthur must have been frantically busy, making arrangements to entertain their royal guests, sourcing supplies, arranging lodgings, cleaning and tidying up the town and ensuring themselves and their households were suitably attired. The following day, Anne had words with both Mark Smeaton, her lutist, whom she accused of being in love with her and reminded him of his lowly status, and with Henry Norris, whom she said was 'looking for dead men's shoes', and would wish to wed her if anything happened to the king. This was enough to seal their fates. On 30 April, the trip to Calais was quietly cancelled, Henry and Anne quarrelled, and Smeaton was arrested, questioned and reputedly tortured by Cromwell.

The first indication that something was wrong reached Calais on 1 May, when Honor's nephew, John Grenville, informed them that 'the king's journey to Dover is prolonged'.[11] Grenville was unaware that Henry and Anne had attended the May Day Joust where George Boleyn was leading the challengers, after which the king rose abruptly in his seat and rode away with Henry Norris. The next day, 2 May, Thomas Warley clearly had not yet heard anything, writing to Honor that Henry was supposed to have been at Rochester 'but he has changed his mind, which was not known until Sunday at 11 o'clock'.[12] As Warley wrote, George and Norris were being arrested and sent to the Tower, followed shortly after by Francis Weston, Nicholas Brereton, Richard Page and the poet Thomas Wyatt. Out of this group, the Lisles had been closest to Anne and George, and had been corresponding with Norris and Page through the month of April, asking them to advance their various causes.

Arthur's first response was one of panic. On May 8, he wrote to Henry, fearing he had somehow overstepped the mark and that his loyalty and ability might also be called into question:

> *Pleaseth your highness to be advertised that not long since I wrote unto your Grace, desiring the same to be good and gracious lord unto me, for as much as no man in this town was ordinarily charged with keeping of household ... as well as in banqueting and feasting of strange ambassadors and other foreign potestes and great personages... I have done although the same might be further than my powers extend... Praying God to send your Grace long and most joyful life, with suppedation of your enemies...*[13]

To Cromwell, Arthur was even more explicit:

> *I thought it most requisite to open my mind unto you ... and seeing there are many things now in his gracious disposition and hands, by reason of the most mischievous, heinous and most abominable treasons against his most gracious and royal*

> *crown and person committed, I wholly trust that his Grace,*
> *being good lord unto me, will vouchsafe to employ some*
> *part of those same upon me ... by your good mediation and*
> *furtherance.*[14]

At this point, Anne's fate was already sealed. On 9 or 10 May, a specialist swordsman from Calais was summoned to London in order to carry out her execution. This allowed him enough time to cross the Channel in anticipation of her trial and guilty verdict. There is no conceivable way that Arthur and Honor cannot have known this man. Richard Turpyn, author of the *Calais Chronicles*, who lived in the town until his death in 1545,[15] adds that Anne met her death 'by the hands of the hangman of Calais, by the sword of Calais', but gives no further details. The usual method of execution in Calais was by gallows, which were erected in the central location of the market place as a visible deterrent, and would have been operated by this same individual. The gallows are mentioned in the *Chronicles* several times, notably for drawing a swarm of bees on the morning of 12 June 1538, and for the hanging of heretical priests William Richardson and William Peterson on April 10, 1540.[16] Calais was of a size that it would not have needed more than one executioner, and the mystery man would have likely required Arthur's permission to depart.

Arthur's stepson, John Dudley, described very minimally for Honor, on 10 May, how he was 'sure there is no need to write the news, for all the world knows them by this time. Today Mr. Norres, Mr. Weston, William a Brearton, Markes, and lord Rocheforde were indicted, and on Friday they will be arraigned at Westminster. The Queen herself will be condemned by Parliament'.[17] On the day that Norris, Weston, Brereton and Smeaton went on trial, 12 May, Sir John Russell's letter to Arthur reminded him of his former connection: 'Today Mr. Norres and *such other as you know* are cast, and the Queen shall go to her judgment on Monday next'.[18] Husee added more detail, explaining that they had been condemned to be 'drawn, hanged and quartered ... tomorrow or Monday', but that Page and Wyatt were thought to be out of danger, although Page was 'banished the King's court forever'. Husee was unsure of the 'divers considerations, which are not yet known', upon which Anne and George were to be charged.[19] The next day, he reported rumours circulating about the prisoners' fates:

> *Here are so many tales I cannot tell what to write. This day,*
> *some say, young Weston shall scape, and some that none shall*

die but the Queen and her brother; others, that Wyat and Mr. Payge are as like to suffer as the others. The saying now is that those who shall suffer shall die when the Queen and her brother go to execution; but I think they shall all suffer. If any escape, it will be young Weston, for whom importunate suit is made.[20]

Honor must have been initially confused, or doubtful, about the accusations against Anne, as she asked Husee directly about the nature of them, the queen's confession, and who the witnesses had been. Husee replied that he had been told little about the confession, 'but what was said was wondrously discreetly spoken', and named her accusers as Lady Worcester and Nan Cobham[21] (likely to have been Anne Bray, Baroness Cobham). Husee wrote openly about Anne's guilt, in an attempt to direct Honor's feelings in support of the king. His implication that 'any good woman' must find the queen's crimes 'abominable and detestable' was a warning that Honor would have been a fool to ignore:

Madam, I think verily, if all the books and chronicles were totally revolved, and to the uttermost persecuted and tried, which against women hath been penned, contrived, and written since Adam and Eve, those same were, I think, verily nothing in comparison of that which hath been done and committed by Anne the Queen; which, though I presume be not all things as it is now rumoured, yet that which hath been by her confessed, and other offenders with her by her own alluring, procurement, and instigation, is so abominable and detestable that I am ashamed that any good woman should give ear thereunto. I pray God give her grace to repent while she now liveth. I think not the contrary but she and all they shall suffer.[22]

Under such direction, it would not be surprising if Honor, like many of her peers, made the pragmatic decision to believe the accusations against Anne and her co-accused. Whatever her previous friendship had been, based upon serving Anne at court and in Calais, and the exchange of goods, her ultimate loyalty was to Henry. If she had any doubts whatsoever about Anne's character and actions, she was wise not to express them, but to accept the situation, given her inability to change it and her distance across the Channel. However, Honor was only human. The suddenness and severity of Anne's fate must have taken her by surprise, especially since she had been preparing to host the queen in Calais. Perhaps Honor was shocked by the accusations, disappointed and angry at Anne's perceived deceptions, following Husee's tone, or maybe she pitied Anne for the situation she found herself in. Regardless, life had to go on. If Arthur had not already advised her so, Honor probably already understood that the best way to deal with traitors was to distance herself from them, no matter how close they had previously been. She would have known that her own survival depended upon it.

Honor did write to one survivor of the events of that summer, Sir Richard Page, with whom she already had a long-standing connection. The banished Page wrote back gratefully in July, two months after the executions, thanking her for her kind remembrance and explaining that he was 'long ago at liberty'. Despite his ordeal, he stuck to the line that 'the King is his good and gracious lord', but that he had not yet 'greatly assayed to be a daily courtier again', bravely saying he was 'more meet for the country than the court'. He was keen for Honor to visit, adding that 'no lady or gentlewoman in England shall be more welcome to his poor cabin' and asking if she would visit him if she 'comes into these parts'.[23] Honor's friendship with Page, along with those friends she had lost, was a reminder of how quickly and easily the mighty could fall, even those closest to the king.

Calais Constable, Anthony Pickering's letter to Honor of 19 May mixes up the details of domestic life with the tragedy of national scandal. He wrote that he had delivered a quantity of gold dye for her kersey fabric, but that it cost more than anticipated and Honor owed him a further 2s 6d. Without drawing breath, he proceeded straight to the news that George Boleyn, Norris, Weston, Brereton and Smeaton 'were put to death on Tower Hill' two days earlier, and that Anne had been executed that morning 'in the presence of a thousand people'.[24]

Understandably, despite his best efforts, John Husee was unable to get an audience with Henry at this time. He reported how Henry had not been abroad (going out) these past fourteen days, except into his garden, and by his boat at night 'at which times it may become no man to prevent him'. What Husee did not know, is that Henry was travelling down river to visit Jane Seymour, for whom Cranmer had issued a dispensation for Henry to marry in the hours following Anne's death. Husee reported how the five men died 'very charitably' by the axe, and that Anne 'suffered with sword this day within the Tower, upon a new scaffold, and died boldly'. He hoped that now the 'matter of executions are past (he may) soon speak with (the king) and deliver the Lisles' letters, adding later that a new coronation was expected at Midsummer,[25] and subsequently quoting Michaelmas.[26] Indeed, Henry wasted no time, marrying Jane Seymour in the queen's closet at York Place on 30 May, just eleven days after Anne's death.

Finally, in July, Arthur and Honor met Henry and the new Queen Jane. Husee wrote to them with only four days' warning, as the royal party were setting out for Rochester, then heading to Sittingbourne, Canterbury and from thence on to Dover, where they would stay for two days. Husee advised that the Lisles had better cross the Channel quickly and be waiting at Dover the day before Henry's arrival, and warned they would probably have simple lodgings, given that the court needed to be housed.[27] Bowing before the new queen, Honor may have been struck by the contrast between Jane and her predecessor, with her pale looks and placid, peaceful manner. She had probably met Jane before, as the daughter of Sir John Seymour of Wulfhall may have been at court as early as 1527, serving Catherine of Aragon, although she was definitely present in 1532, while Honor was with Anne. Whatever she thought of the new queen, and her rise to power, Honor curtseyed and showed Jane the due deference her new position demanded. Jane was pleased to see Honor, though, as Husee was able to write mid-August: 'the queen has spoken of you divers times since your departing from Dover'.[28] After their meeting with Henry, Arthur came away satisfied, having received the promise of £100 of the recently dissolved monastic lands. That September, the Lisles were jointly granted the suppressed Augustinian priory of Frithelstock, Torrington, six miles south of Bideford, which was one of the first to have surrendered, in August 1536. Along with the accompanying church, tower, manor house, rectory and nearby manor of Broadwoodwidger, the estate was worth £92 4s 8d.[29]

The day after the Lisles met Henry, news arrived of the death of the king's illegitimate son, Henry Fitzroy, Duke of Richmond and Somerset, at the age of 16. Henry was devastated, having possibly pinned hopes of succession upon the young man as his only living son. Honor and Arthur were probably still in Dover, preparing to depart, and may have joined in the prayers for the soul of a young man they had entertained at Calais.

In the wake of the Boleyn fall, the Lisles were typical of their times and class in seeking to turn the situation into an opportunity. Arthur wrote very soon after the men's executions enquiring about the redistribution of their titles, lands and assets, soon enough for Sir John Russell's reply to be dated 23 May, six days after George's death. Arthur's letter had included the request 'to have something of what came to his hands by these gentlemen's deaths', so Russell had spoken to the king about it, but others already had their eyes on the prizes, so 'he said that all things worthy of you had been given away before your letter came'.[30] The death of Norris had also lost Arthur a considerable agent and patron, and he now appealed to Sir John Russell and Sir Thomas Heneage, hoping to find a replacement, with Husee informing the new candidates of the 'losses you have sustained by Mr Norris' death'.[31]

Letters John Husee wrote to Honor on the day of Anne's execution may have prompted her next move. He described how 'most of the late Queen's servants are set at liberty to seek service elsewhere', and 'your ladyship hath two nieces with the Queen, daughters to Mr. Arundell':[32] Mary, a daughter of Honor's closest sister, and possible twin, Katherine Arundell of Lanherne, and Mary's half-sister Jane. Honor saw this moment as the opportunity to place one of her daughters at court, offering both Anne and Mary Basset as ladies for Jane Seymour's household, considering recalling both girls from the De Bours and Rouault families. Aged around 18 and 16, they were attractive, well-presented and popular, with their letters demonstrating the usual interest in clothes, dogs and the ability to speak French. On June 6, Husee responded 'as touching the preferment of your ladyship's daughter unto the queen, I will at the delivering of my Lord's letter unto Mr Heneage, move the same'. Husee had high hopes that an answer would be 'easily obtained, but what answer I have, and how I do speed your ladyship shall be shortly advertised'.[33]

Husee spoke about Anne Basset to another important court figure who was another of the king's aunts. Margaret Pole, Lady Salisbury, was Arthur's cousin, a remnant of the Plantagenet age, who was twenty years Honor's elder. Her son, Reginald, had fled aboard, refusing the Oath of Supremacy and even attempting to incite European rulers to rise against Henry. His mother had been exiled from court as a result, but was briefly welcomed back in the wake of Anne's fall. Now Margaret promised to speak on Anne's behalf, but feared that it would take time, as Anne was too young, although Husee promised to try and show Mr Heneage that 'Katherine is of sufficient age'. In addition, it appeared that there was no current vacancy, as 'the queen had all her maidens 'pointed already ... if the queen hath her while determined number appointed, I suppose this suit will the later take place'.[34] The assumption was that Honor and Arthur would come to England in time for the new queen's coronation, but Husee noted that Honor had not sent a token to Jane, so offered her a gold ring himself, on her behalf.[35] No coronation occurred and Jane's household was full. For the time being, Anne Basset would have to wait. Although the advantages they hoped to seize upon Anne's fall had not materialised, the Lisles had at least survived the catastrophic events that took some of their friends and associates. But while they benefited from its spoils, did they heed its warning?

Thirteen

Pregnancies
1537

In the autumn of 1536, Honor suspected that she was pregnant. She had been married to Arthur for seven years and was then 43, with her youngest child being 10 years old. Arthur was considerably older, and although they may have wished for children, it is likely that by this point, Honor had already given up hoping. Forty-three was old for a successful pregnancy in Tudor times, when many of her aristocratic peers had given birth in their late teens and had become grandmothers by the time they reached Honor's age.

Given the timing of her anticipated lying-in, Honor must have conceived, or thought she had conceived, in or around October 1536. It was a difficult time, with Arthur constantly dealing with the consequences of war, keeping up to date with accurate news, dealing with prisoners and negotiating for the release of captured Englishmen, infringements in the Pale and with the aftermath of a ship carrying his timber being stolen by the French. Worrying news also came from England, where rebellions in the north, known as the Pilgrimage of Grace, had erupted in protest against Henry's break with Rome and the dissolution of the monasteries. Congregations had watched as the Visitors confiscated their crosses, chalices, plate, bells, jewels and other items of religious ceremony, many of which had been the gifts and bequests of local families. Over 20,000 people rose in rebellion after the closure of Louth Park Abbey in Lincolnshire, burning the registers compiled by the commissioner and beating the Lincoln chancellor to death. To many devout Catholics, whose lives had been shaped by the practices of the old faith, and the comforting presence of the monasteries, the uprising signalled hope. On one hand, Honor may have felt sympathy for their cause, but on the other, she was aware that they were challenging the king's authority, which was an act of treason.

In November, Honor wrote to Anne Rouault, Madame de Bours, requesting that she send some oysters, which may have been an early pregnancy craving, or could have been recommended as beneficial.[1] Honor was also trying to source quinces from St Omer, another potential result of her condition, but as these were out of season, none of good quality were available.[2] However, Honor was keeping her news secret, perhaps following the usual custom of waiting until she had safely passed through her first trimester. Anne would learn of her pregnancy during a visit by James Basset, prompting her to congratulate Honor, 'from what he says, you are *enceinte*, and I pray that you may have joy of it,'[3] adding later that she would like to assist Honor when she was brought to bed, with Mary Basset wishing she could be there to warm the infant's clothes.[4] John Husee had heard the news by letter, commenting that 'I am glad your ladyship is so well sped. Jesu send you a son!'[5] Later, this expanded to 'I pray God send her ladyship a good and fortunate hour, and therewith a son ... that name surviving and spring anew, which would make many joyful heart ... who send your lordship long life with much honor',[6] sentiments which he repeated in almost every letter over the coming six months. When Honor's due date approached, he upped this to twins: 'two jolly boys'.[7]

As the end of the year approached, Honor was feathering her nest, ordering tawny damask for 7s 6d the yard from England,[8] and violet cloth and cloth of gold frieze from St Omer.[9] She anticipated needing supplies and support for when the baby arrived in the summer, and with supply ships threatened by the war, was ordering well in advance. With other potential waiting women having failed to impress, Husee now offered her 'a gentlewoman, which is a maiden and unmarried, that lately dwelled with my lady Waldon, and is of 30 years, a good needlewoman, and also she can embroider very well, and will be content to wash and brush and do anything else that your Ladyship will put her to'. In return, the servant required 40s and a livery.[10]

In December, Husee announced that the 'northern men have obeyed the King's proclamation and submitted to mercy', before adding 'no news here please me so well as that your Ladyship has so well sped in advancing the name of the noble Plantagenet. If I thought it should not be painful I would never cease praying unto God that your Ladyship might have two goodly sons, as I have full hope that God will show his handiwork'.[11] When Husee delivered the Lisles' New Year gifts to the king, and informed him of Honor's pregnancy, he told Henry that they attributed it 'to your satisfaction in seeing the King at Dover', upon which Henry was 'very glad and wished my lady a son'.[12]

Honor's news spread swiftly among her London suppliers, with the mercer William Lok sending her a special pregnancy 'stomacher of cloth of gold', and adding that he prayed that if it was God's pleasure 'it may cover a young Lord Plantagenet, as I do understand by divers is well forward, of the which I am very glad'.[13] Richard Lee, a surveyor of Calais, congratulated the Lisles from London after Honor had sent him some marmalade: 'it hath pleased God to visit her with a child, he most heartily thanketh her good ladyship for her marmelado. I pray God make your Lordship a glad father and my Lady a glad mother'.[14] John Hutton, the Lisles' agent in Flanders added a similar message, that he would 'pray to God to make her a glad mother and send my lord a young son'.[15]

Sir John Wallop, Lieutenant of Calais Castle, wrote with some intimate advice, having been informed by Arthur of Honor's condition. Wallop rejoiced 'firstly for both your sakes', and secondly because 'it gives hope both to my wife and me, considering not to be so long married as you two, and either of us being younger, man for man and woman for woman'. Wallop was 46 at this point, and married to his second wife, Elizabeth, having fathered no children as yet. He hoped that if he 'retire once quietly to the castle, such good fortune may ensue unto us, and so much the rather if your abode and my lady's continue at Calais'. Wallop seemed to have some knowledge of childbirth though, as he sent Honor two bottles of water 'which I brought from Avignon, meet for that purpose, especially when she comes near churching time'. Apparently this special water could bring on labour, making her 'the more readier by five or six days if she will use the virtue of the same', as it was 'restraintive and draweth together like a purse'. The water could also raise women's breasts that had become long, making them 'higher and rounder', to which Wallop tactfully added, hoping he had not impugned Honor's appearance, 'peradventure shall be good for some of your neighbours. As for my lady, needeth not'.[16]

Jenne de Quierete at the Landreteun farm, wrote offering Honor 'the use of anything in her house' [the Lisles' farm] upon hearing of her pregnancy. She added that she could 'well imagine the pleasure it must give to her lord and her to obtain what they have so much desired, as Lady Lisle expressed' when with her, and sent along some fruit from the garden.[17] Lady Rutland had been unaware of Honor's pregnancy, being absorbed with her own, and probably retiring into her lying-in chamber at some point in late November. She sent her best wishes via John Husee six days after she had been through her churching ceremony in mid-January.[18] Guillaume le Gras had acquired a girdle for Honor, which was commonly used during childbirth, and an image, which is likely to have depicted one of the saints, especially one associated with childbirth.[19] Geoffrey Wolfet, Clerk of the King's Closet, requested that if Honor bore a son, they should consider the king as godfather.[20] When Lady Beaumont's daughter was christened in February, Husee wrote to Honor to inform her that the baby's sponsors, or godparents, were Queen Jane, Princess Mary and the Lord Privy Seal, perhaps intending to suggest that Honor chose similarly.

In February, the Countess of Rutland sent Honor some parcels of 'necessaries' and Husee advised her that Mr Scott, her tailor, said that the fashion in nightgowns was 'such as your ladyship already has, made of damask, velvet or satin', but she was to have two ermine bonnets and her waistcoats were to be made of white satin, edged and turned up at the band with ermines'.[21] He was investigating whether Honor might use some of the hangings and carpets from the queen's wardrobe, as lying-in chambers were usually fully lined, covering walls, floor and windows, to maintain a constant temperature and keep out the light, which was costly. This was even the case when Honor's due date was expected to fall in July.[22] Lady Sussex sent a rich bed pane of ermines bordered with cloth of gold, two or three fine lawn sheets and a traverse.[23] Lady Rutland was able to procure one bed for Honor's use from the royal wardrobe, but nothing more, while Husee kept pressing for six pieces of tapestry and six carpets. He was unable to send Honor spices, as the spicer had died and 'his wife is a limb of the devil with whom I will not deal', but he did enclose a welcome gift from Queen Jane, being a pair of beads set with gold.[24] Husee also hoped it might be possible to borrow a font from Canterbury for the child's christening. The Prior of Christchurch, Canterbury, though, was unable to supply carpets, as they were 'burned when the king's visitor lay here'.[25] However, at least Husee had obtained a holy water stock with sprinkle,[26] (for uses contrary to the Ten Articles) and the cradle was ready.[27]

Unanimously, the well-wishers hoped that Honor was carrying a boy. It is not necessary to look further than the experiences of Catherine of Aragon and Anne Boleyn to demonstrate how important sons were to the aristocracy, and Arthur had, as yet, only fathered three girls. A potential son would carry forward the Plantagenet name, to 'survive and spring anew'[28] as those concerned were aware, as well as being the only child of the marriage. John Hutton was explicit in wishing Honor would 'recommend me to your little boy in your belly, the which I pray God to send into your arms to your comfort and your lord's'.[29] He had heard that Honor was experiencing nerves and fears as her pregnancy progressed, hoping to reassure her: 'the knowledge of your noble heart and most gentle request emboldens me to write. I have nothing to write but to devise what may cause your Ladyship to be merry and to forget all fantasies by days. As for the nights, my good lord will keep you waking, as I do my wife, whom I sometime make as weary as though she had watched upon'.[30] It is clear from the comments of the Lisle's numerous well-wishers that this was a much-longed for and desired pregnancy.

Early in 1537, Honor's niece, Mary Arundell, married Robert Radcliffe, Earl of Sussex. Radcliffe's father had been beheaded in Calais after supporting Perkin Warbeck, but his son had risen to become Chamberlain of the Exchequer. Initially, it had been hoped that Katherine Basset could join the household of her cousin, the new Countess, but Mary 'had three women already, which is one more than she is allowed'.[31] Next, Honor considered to place her with the young Countess of Suffolk, Katherine Willoughby, who was then 17, with a 2-year-old son, but age gave Honor pause, though, wondering if she might be too young[32] to offer the kind of role model and guidance that she required for Katherine. Instead, Honor turned to her friend, Eleanor Manners, née Paston, Countess of Rutland, also part of Jane's new household, who was willing to oblige. Katherine was still in France in February, when Husee wrote that if she came over to England as planned, 'she must have double gowns and kirtles of silk, and good attirements for her head and neck'.[33]

In May, it was announced that Jane Seymour was pregnant. She had been married to Henry for almost a year, with the child due in October. Husee described how she was 'great' with child and would be 'open-laced with stomacher' by Corpus Christi day at the farthest.[34] Honor sent Jane a gift of 'fat quails ... which her Grace loveth very well, and longeth not a little for them', with a second consignment of two or three dozen to be killed at Dover for freshness, which Husee conveyed to Hampton Court. The Countesses of Rutland and Sussex were waiting upon Jane when she ate them, and seized the moment to influence the well-fed queen to suggest the acceptance of one of the Basset girls into her household. The Lisles were also asked to look out for 'peascods or cherries' as there would be none ripe in England until midsummer, and would merit the senders 'great thanks'.[35]

As the result of her friends' efforts, it was arranged that both Basset girls, Anne and Katherine, should be sent over to court, but their good fortune came with a warning:

> that her Grace will first see them and know their manners,
> fashions and conditions, and take which of them shall like her

> *Grace best. They must be sent over about six weeks hence,*
> *and your ladyship need not spend much on them till you know*
> *which her Grace will have. They will only require two honest*
> *changes, [of clothes] the one of satin the other of damask.*
> *At their coming the one will be put in my lady of Rutland's*
> *chamber, the other in my lady of Sussex's, and when it is*
> *known which the Queen will have, the other will be put with*
> *the duchess of Suffolk, and then be apparelled according to*
> *their degrees.*
>
> *And for as much as they shall now go upon making and*
> *marring, it shall please your ladyship to exhort them to be*
> *sober, sad, wise and discreet and lowly above all things, and to*
> *be obedient, and governed and ruled by my Lady Rutland and*
> *my Lady Sussex ... and your ladyship's friends here ... and to*
> *serve God well and be sober of tongue.*[36]

Jane's court was very different from that of Anne Boleyn, being conservative, strict and formal, which underpinned Husee's advice. He explained that he did not wish to sound too patronising, only helpful, adding:

> *I trust your ladyship will not take this my meaning that I should*
> *presume to learn your ladyship what is to be done ... but I do*
> *it only of pure and sincere zeal that I bear to them for your*
> *ladyship's sake ... for your ladyship knoweth the court is full of*
> *pride, envy, indignation and mocking, scorning and derision,*
> *therefore I would be sorry but they should use themselves*
> *according to their birth ... and all their friends will be glad of*
> *them ... doing otherwise, it will be your ladyship's discomfort*
> *and discontentaion, and their undoing.*[37]

Honor took to her chamber in June. This was a ritual that usually occurred around a month before the expected day of delivery, in a room that had been well-prepared and equipped for several weeks' worth of lying-in. Hung with tapestries and carpets, with a well-stoked fire, and supplies of cushions, blankets and linen, it would be her retreat until she had recovered from the ordeal, attended exclusively by women. Sir Richard Hart wrote to Arthur at the end of the month that he was glad 'to hear that her Ladyship has taken her chamber'. He had been pleased to receive news from her by letter and echoed many views that 'her good delivery will be joyful to all her friends … will be glad to hear of a young lord Lysley'(*sic*).[38] John Husee also wrote that everyone at court was anxious to hear of her safe delivery.

Honor was expecting to give birth in July. As the days passed, she kept in touch with news of her daughters and the progress of Queen Jane's pregnancy. However, the weeks passed and no child arrived, even though predicting the correct date was an inexact science. While Honor clung to hope, so did the many friends waiting to hear her good news. On 7 August, Husee sent a cushion, having heard report that she was in pain.[39] Two weeks later, he was expressing his sorrow at Honor's 'ways of lamentation and sorrows [and causeless] as my full trust in God is, for your ladyship is not the first woman of honour that hath overshot or mistaken your time'.[40] He added, correctly, that many noblewomen, 'Empress, Queen, Princess nor Duchess', had been through a similar ordeal, echoing Catherine of Aragon's experience of a false pregnancy, or pseudocyesis, in 1509. Yet while he tried to reassure her and told her not to mistrust herself, he cautioned that if 'it might chance otherwise (which God forbid) yet should not your ladyship take it so earnestly' and he would rather 'die than your ladyship should despair in yourself'.[41] Even as late as 5 September, Richard Wingfield wished to Honor that God would make her a joyful mother,[42] but Honor's hopes must have been fading.

Towards the middle of September, Honor received a letter from her niece, Margaret Grenville, which offered her comfort in this dark time and expressed the views that many held towards her:

> *Good madam, take you no thought for no thing worldly of this transitory world, for I trust ye have love of God. It is a good token, for ye have the love of the people as much as any woman that ever I heard of. Be joyful in our Lord, and no doubt He will send you comfort. It is a token of the love of God when he sends trouble, and especially to them that be good. There is no need to counsel you to take patience. I am sorry that you should have any grief, for I know you of old, for you would no trouble to any living creature. We heard you and my lord would come into these parts. I and many others would be right glad if it might so be.*[43]

During these weeks of hope and pain, Honor was visited by a Parisian doctor named Le Coop, who gave her extensive dietary advice. He diagnosed her as being of 'a cold complexion as it appeareth by your colour and your flesh, which is very delicate' and for this reason, 'gathering together many and divers cold slimy humours within your body'.[44] This caused Honor to experience a shortness of breath, or a 'disease in the right side', which required purging. Otherwise, the illness could gather in her back and give her gallstones, or in the guts and lead to colic; sometimes it ended up in the womb, 'where if they fortune to stick fast and congeal together, there engendereth with also the blood that is retained a swelling even like as the woman had conceived ... which deceiveth and abuseth many folks'. In the doctor's opinion, this was the cause of Honor's disease and he offered her a small purgation to rid herself of the additional matter, 'ye shall on certain days use of a little drink which Mr Philbert shall give you' to keep her body 'pure and clean'.

The rest of Dr Le Coop's advice was dietary. According to the Galenic theory of the four humours, to contrast Honor's natural disposition to coldness, she was to eat hot and dry foods, nothing raw, and especially not 'cold meats, as powdered beef that is cold, or cold veal or venison flesh ... except of pheasants, nor of mutton', which he believed had caused the humours to build in her belly in the first place. She could eat broth or stewed capon, hens, chickens, pigeons or woodcock but must avoid raw or partially cooked fruit and herbs, only eating them mixed with sources of heat, such as hyssop, parsley and chervil. Borage and sage would be beneficial to her, as were pastry, tarts, pie and cakes, with 'a little marmalade for to comfort your stomach or else a pear well roasted betwixt two ashes with sugar and wine sweetened with sugar to rid herself of evil influences'.[45] If she kept to this diet, the doctor promised that 'ye shall find yourself well and that your disease will go from you'.

Help of a more superstitious kind came from Anthoinette de Saveuses, who sent Honor 'une ensangie' (an enchantment) with which she had 'touched the head of St John the Baptist and Amiens', and was intended to relieve her suffering. Anthoinette added that she used to have a fine piece 'of the point of a unicorn's head', which she had been given by a great lady and had been 'very careful [with] on account of its properties', but she had lent it to a sick person and never received it back.[46] However, she did have a mere sliver of horn to send, and begged Honor to set it in gold or silver for her use. These pieces of what were, actually, narwhal tusks, were prized in Tudor times as guards against poison and disease. Among the spoils collected from the English monasteries in 1540 was a 'great piece of unicorn's horn, as is supposed' from Glastonbury, along with the images of saints.[47]

Honor must have been devastated at the realisation that she had never been pregnant. Her house was filled with the gifts and items that friends had sent to assist her lying-in, and she faced the task of explaining her predicament to her many well-wishers, from France, England and Calais. Those items that had been lent to her would also need to be returned, although Husee wrote that those of the king's wardrobe were 'prepared to forbear the carpets a reasonable time'.[48] Jacques Groutier invited her to spend time at the priory or abbey of Notre Dame at Dieppe, promising to fetch her himself and send her back to Calais with 'an honourable company'.[49] At the age of 44, Honor had to face the likelihood that she would not bear another child, and there would be no more inheritors of the Plantagenet name.

Honor probably emerged from her confinement in September, and turned her attention to her two daughters, Anne and Katherine, who were about to depart for court. Jeanne Rouault was sad to see Anne go, having treated her like her own daughter; 'you do me honour by leaving her with me', as she was 'ladylike' and 'improving every day in her bearing'. Mary Basset, left behind, also regretted her absence, and perhaps the opportunity she had missed out on.[50]

Honor took on board the advice she had been given by John Husee and others and ensured her girls were attired suitably to impress. She sent to Guillaume le Gras for French ladies' hats, crepes, crespins and taffetas, 'for now the ladies here follow the French fashion'[51] and gave her daughters the best advice she could. On 1 September, Husee asked that the girls depart as soon as possible, as Queen Jane was asking for them and was due to take to her chamber soon. By the second week of September, Anne and Katherine had arrived in London and had been received by the queen, who rapidly made the decision that she preferred Anne. Despite this, the girls were both 'merry and in good health'. Anne was sworn into her household, and was to lie in the chamber of Lady Sussex, who gave her a kirtle of crimson damask with matching sleeves, although she also needed to have 'such apparel' as was written in 'Mrs Pole's book of reckoning', within two months.[52]

It seemed that Honor's French purchases had been misjudged, being perhaps too evocative of Anne Boleyn's style. Initially, she was permitted to 'wear out her French apparel, so that your ladyship shall thereby be no loser', but afterwards, she must conform. Although nothing became Anne so well as the French bonnet, in Husee's opinion, she must have a new bonnet of velvet and a matching frontlet. It may have been due to her difference in style that Henry had reputedly noticed Anne and commented on how pretty she was, but these evoked dangerous shades of déjà vu.[53] Two weeks later,

Husee informed Honor that Jane insisted 'Anne shall wear no more her French apparel', and that she required a black satin gown, a gown of velvet and pearl trim bonnet before Jane's churching, and that her smocks were too coarse and needed replacing.[54] Katherine was to stay with the Countess of Rutland, and was promised a gown of taffeta, but had expressed the desire to be with her cousin Mary Arundell which 'might be brought to pass',[55] although she already had an extra lady in her household. Having been kept away from court during Anne's reign, Princess Mary had been welcomed back by her sympathetic new stepmother, who was building bridges between the princess and her father.

A week after Anne was sworn in, Jane entered her confinement at Hampton Court. Anne would have played a minor role here, assisting with keeping the room warm and the queen's needs supplied, whiling away the hours with prayers, reading, music and sensible talk. On 12 October, after a long and gruelling labour of almost three days, Jane bore the son that Henry had been waiting twenty-seven years for. Anne attended the infant's christening in the palace chapel three days later, wearing a gown of black velvet turned up with yellow satin, with a new satin one planned for the queen's churching, which would usually be three to four weeks afterwards.[56] However, the rejoicing at court only lasted a short while before Jane's condition began to deteriorate, and she died on 24 October. Anne was one of the mourners at her funeral on 12 November at St George's Chapel, Windsor, having received lengths of black cloth for mourning clothes.

In February 1537, the wedding had taken place of Arthur's daughter, Frances, and Honor's eldest son, John. It was held in the private chapel of the Staple, with a licence procured by John Husee from the Archbishop of Canterbury, so that they could be wed after a single calling of the banns, instead of the usual three.[57] This implies a sense of urgency. Couples were usually not allowed to marry during the period of Lent, which would have begun on February 28 that year, given that Easter fell on 11 April. The young pair may have wished to marry before that period of abstinence, or else there was another reason for the speed. On 7 April, John Husee wrote to congratulate the Lisles who would 'soon be a merry grandfather and grandame'.[58] With pregnancies not usually announced until the end of the first trimester, out of the necessity of being certain, Frances may well have wished to be married before her condition became visible.

The couple were well supplied for their wedding, with silks, scarlet kersey, garnishings, a tawny gown with fur, bonnets, gold chains, new hose, clasps, diamonds and a cap with a white feather for John, all from England, although Husee advised they would have been much cheaper bought in Flanders.[59] Again, it was all done in a hurry, as Husee commented 'we could not have made more speed for our lives, and I hope it will come in season'.[60] John Dudley sent three does to Dover to be shipped out to Calais, Husee sent spices, and venison was dispatched from Hampshire to furnish the wedding breakfast table.[61] Mary Basset was recalled from the Rouaults for the wedding and while Madame de Bours regretted her absence, she agreed it was 'right she should be'.[62] Mary herself wrote, asking that Anne de Bours be allowed to accompany her home, 'as she will be sorry to leave her'.[63] After this visit, it was decided that Mary would return to Calais on a more permanent basis, perhaps due to the consequences of war that were still encroaching into the Calais Pale and beyond.[64]

While Honor would have been pleased to celebrate the wedding, and at news of Frances' pregnancy, it cannot have been easy after the year she had just had. From England, news also came that her niece Lady Sussex, Mary Arundell, had delivered a baby and was being churched.[65] It would appear though, that James and Frances' first surviving child, a daughter named Honor, was not born until May 1539, so it is possible that Frances lost this first pregnancy and conceived again in the summer following her wedding.

Fourteen

Shrines and Sacraments
1538

While immense change swept through the English monasteries, with shrines and images destroyed before the very eyes of pilgrims, Honor clung to her old ways. In recent years, her letters had been full of correspondence with local priests, nuns and abbesses, as part of her extended network, and the rituals of pilgrimage, prayer and mutual gifts, some of which were holy items. Worse still, some were considered superstitious under the new reforms, like the piece of 'enchantment', the unicorn horn, the birthing girdle or the images or tablets of saints or Our Lady, that were used as objects of devotion, and the focus of prayers.

In early 1538, Honor accepted the gift of a falcon from Jacques de la Motte, the Abbot of Ardres[1] and was invited by Anthoine Brusset to visit St Beze at Gravelines, 'now that the weather is so fine for pilgrimages'.[2] She sent her frequent correspondent, Anthoinette de Sauveuses, two breviaries, or books of daily service, perhaps knowing that her friend had struggled in saying her heures for the past two years. Along with the book, she sent a rich covering, although Anthoinette was unsure whether she would 'dare use it to cover at night the cup of the Holy Sacrament when it shall be on the altar'.[3] That July, Honor took Mary to stay with Anthoinette at the Abbey of Bourbourch, before she went on to visit Adrienne de Mortaigne at Gravelines. The Lisles also kept abreast of the news of monastic closures, especially those close to home – Hampton, Southwick and Portsmouth – hearing that the famous Blood of Hailes Priory had been seized, and the 'most parts of the saints whereunto pilgrimages and offerings were wont to be made are taken away'.[4]

Then, an incident occurred in Calais that prompted the town to come under scrutiny from Cromwell. In line with the instructions being carried out across the Channel, attempts were made in Calais to take down images and icons in the town's churches and chapels, perhaps by Arthur, or the council, or members of the clergy. Attention focused upon the little shrine of Our Lady set into the town wall, at which Henry himself had made an offering when he visited with Anne Boleyn in October 1532. The intention had been to remove the image of Our Lady, on account of the 'abuses and superstitions' attached to it, but this was not accomplished, supposedly due to the reaction, or fear of 'tumult' among the residents. Arthur may have been present on this occasion, or else it might have been his decision to halt the action, even though this constituted a refusal to obey orders.[5] Ultimately, as Lieutenant, it was his responsibility to ensure that the king's law was carried out, but he had to balance this with preventing rioting in his town.

In May 1538, Cromwell wrote to Arthur, displeased at this 'contempt of authority' which he urged must be rectified.[6] It seemed though, that the image of Our Lady in the Wall was merely the tip of the iceberg. Word had reached England that Calais was 'in misorder by certain sacramentaries there' (followers of the sacraments) which surprised Cromwell, as Arthur had been informed of his 'desire for the repression of errors and the establishment of unity in the King's subjects' but had not declared the presence of any 'lewd persons'.[7] Cromwell laboured his point, clearly angry, adding how strategically important Calais was in 'avoiding all danger arising from diversity of opinions in matters so high and weighty'.[8] Arthur's heart would have sunk to read that this information had been passed on to Henry, who commanded Cromwell to investigate, sending the letter 'without favour or affectation'.[9]

Arthur wrote back at once, having 'examined the truth' with Thomas Scriven (the current mayor, 1537–8), Sir Robert Wingfield and the upper marshal and chief porter of Calais. Regarding Cromwell's accusation that Our Lady in the Wall was not removed, 'in a manner to imply contempt of authority', Arthur insisted he had received 'no order to the contrary' and such a thing should not be done 'without express orders' and that there had been 'no tumult'.[10] Acknowledging the depth of feeling on the matter, he proceeded to ask how future tumult might be avoided. Issues arising from the image of Our Lady in the Wall may have been a miscommunication, but it revealed that there was a degree of resistance among the locals.

There certainly was a degree of religious apathy in Calais. In 1532, it had been reported that out of twenty-six clergymen resident in the town and wider Pale, thirteen were absent, an additional four were royal appointments, so not present either, and one was attached to the Chamberlain, leaving a total of eight remaining clergy, less than a third of the Calais provision. Five years on, in 1537, out of the 1700 residents of Calais, only ten or twelve were attending services at the main church of Our Lady and Mass was largely ignored.[11] Some historians have put this down to the influence of the Lisles, such as G.A.C Sandeman, who cast an indiscriminating blanket of blame upon the 'papist tendencies of Lisle and his wife'.[12]

It was noted, at the time, that Arthur and Honor might not share the same approach when it came to the old Catholic practices. Some of the relics from Calais churches had already been surrendered, and shipped back to England, including a saint's bone which proved to have come from the tail of a sheep. John Husee presented these to Cromwell, who 'rejoiced not a little' and was glad that Arthur had 'come to so good a point'. Husee replied that the Lieutenant was 'always indifferent' to such items, whereupon Cromwell asked whether Honor was too. Husee replied tactfully that 'there was no doubt but she would be won and little and a little',(*sic*) but the dangerous implication was that Honor's 'bad' influence and superstitious practices had not gone unnoticed.[13] Husee warned Arthur that he should soon be summoned to court.

It was at this point that a controversial figure arrived in Calais, whose actions would contribute to the Lisles' later downfall. Adam Damplip, alias George Bucker, was a young English preacher, formerly chaplain to the Bishop of Rochester, who had recently visited Rome and Germany. He appeared in Calais with a coin of endowment from Reginald Pole, Arthur's cousin, who had been made a cardinal late in 1536 and remained in exile. Due to the family connection, Damplip was welcomed by the Lisles, hosted in their home, and Honor had provided him with some clothing.[14]

John Foxe's 1563 *Book of Martyrs*, championing the Protestants who suffered for their faith, unsurprisingly makes far more of the Lisles' connection with Damplip as part of his attempt to blacken Honor's name. After he had preached three or four times, Foxe claims that Damplip was 'so well liked for both his learning, his utterance and the truth of his doctrine' that not only the soldiers and commoners gave him 'marvellous great praise' and thanks, but that Arthur had 'offered unto him a chamber in his own house, to dine and sup every meal' with them, as well as a servant or two to wait upon him. Apparently, Arthur promised to meet his expenses, including whatever books he wanted, in order to encourage him to stay among them and preach. Foxe states that Damplip refused this offer and sought instead quiet lodgings where he would not be 'disturbed and molested', rejecting Arthur's second suggestion that he lodge with William Stevens, along with the rich food the Lisles sent him from their home, explaining that a 'thinne diet was most convenient for students'.[15] If Foxe is to be believed, the Lisles were throwing money and wealth Damplip's way but he virtuously refused.

Damplip was granted permission to preach in the White Friars Church, beside Lord Berners' old house. He was asked, perhaps by Arthur, to speak about the dismantling of another Calais shrine, known as the Resurrection. Here, it was claimed, three holy wafers had been buried in the ground and congealed into one, turning into the flesh of the newborn baby Jesus. When the shrine was demolished, and found to be filled only with stone and iron, much of which fell apart in the process, Damplip was asked to explain this to the people and crumbled the remainder of it before the eyes of the congregation. Damplip then caused confusion when he spoke against the doctrine of transubstantiation, the literal translation of the bread and wine into the body and blood of Christ. At the time, it was believed that Henry still supported this practice, so John Dove, the White Friars Prior, made objection out of fear of being guilty of treason. Arthur and his council issued Damplip with a warning:

> *Order made by the Council of Calais, 19 June 30 Hen. VIII., present, Viscount Lisle, Sir Richard Grenville, marshal, Sir Thomas. Palmer, porter, Robert. Fouler, vice-treasurer, William Sympson, under marshal, and John Rokewood, baillie of Marc. Setting forth that whereas certain chapters have been read at the White Friars by Adam Damlip, [sic] priest, who has set forth matters touching the Sacrament of the altar which have aroused controversy, to the prejudice of the King's retinue and the town, the lord Deputy sent for the Commissary of the Archbishop of Canterbury, who had licensed Damlip to preach, and warned him that tomorrow, Corpus Christi Day, if Damplip shall preach otherwise than may stand with the King's pleasure, I will charge you, Mr. Commissary, with the same, because it is you that have licensed him to read and preach: and therefore I discharge me and charge you, Mr. Commissary, with the same.*[16]

Cromwell requested that Arthur send him a list of the articles that Damplip had preached, and was suitably unimpressed by it, and the length of time it had taken for Calais to react. There was no point being polite and discreet about it, Cromwell insisted, as heresy was like a sickness which must be halted in its progress before it could spread too far:

> *I have received your letter dated in this month with a schedule of articles preached by one Adam Damplipe, [sic] as it is alleged, by permission of the Commissary, which Damplipe you judge to have been an author of the erroneous opinions which have lately appeared at Calais. I have perused those articles and find them very pestilent. I wonder they were not objected to him before, when he was accused of the matter of transubstantiation; but if he taught them he taught most detestable heresy, and if the Commissary consented to it he is unmeet for his office and deserves great punishment.*
>
> *In answer to the points of your said letters, what I wrote before about appeasing such slanders discreetly and charitably I now repeat, being the counsel that I would follow myself, not seeing but offenders may as well be punished without too great a tumult ... to be plain with you, dangerous diseases, if seen in time by a good physician, may be remedied; but if the physician wink till the infection be more deeply settled, all his cunning may not be able to restore the sick man; and we be no less in fault who labour not to avoid evil from our neighbours... The evil, as you truly write, will labour to pervert the good, and he that neither fears God nor esteems the King's injunctions is no meet herb to grow in his Majesty's most Catholic and virtuous garden. If therefore you know any more of that sort, I doubt not you will immediately inform the king.*[17]

Cromwell had raised his concerns with Arthur about the presence in Calais of 'an infection of certain persons called Sacramentaries', who denied the 'Holy Sacrament of Christ's blessed body and blood'. This aspect of the mass was a stumbling block for the early days of the English Reformation and gave rise to much misunderstanding. Despite his dissolution of the monasteries and confiscation of holy relics, Henry still clung to the old Catholic belief of transubstantiation, which held that the bread and wine was literally transformed into the body and blood of Christ, merely retaining the shapes of the humble offering. In Germany, where the Reformation was significantly more advanced since Martin Luther had pinned his ninety-five theses to the door of a church in Wittenburg, a less literal interpretation of the mass was favoured. Luther supported the idea of consubstantiation, where the bread and wine were metaphors for Christ's body and blood. Sacramentarians supported the Lutheran view of consubstantiation, against Henry's doctrine, and Cromwell called for them to be examined and punished if they refused to reform, 'to the example of others, and see such errors totally extinguished'.[18] With so many immense changes occurring in such a short space of time, there was a hesitancy in Calais, and other places, an uncertainty about what was expected, and which of the changes were to be lasting.

Religious dissent was spreading among the soldiers and commoners of Calais, 'who spoke against the Sacrament of the altar, saying it was not in a knave priest to make God, that the mass was not made by God, but by the invention of man, and that a mouse would as soon eat the body of God as another cake'.[19] In May 1538, several papists had been identified in the Pale, including Thomas Cockes, curate of Marc, who 'raised such slanders ... that do apply themselves to the word of God', and claimed a local woman said she was 'as good as Mary who had made her husband cuckold.'[20] Others in Calais claimed that the mass was being used to sing for the souls of dogs, hogs and ducks, and as a consequence, the town was getting such a bad reputation that French butchers were refusing to supply it.[21] Such sentiments reflected similar dissent to that which was being voiced in England at the time. When the monastic Visitor, Richard Layton, colleague of Honor's friend Thomas Legh, had visited Canterbury, his lodgings in the Prior's House had mysteriously caught fire. Items such as statues and altar slabs had been taken out of the cathedral and integrated into domestic settings in homes in the city, with one individual saying he could 'piss holy water' better than that kept in the font.[22]

Afraid of putting a foot wrong, Arthur pleaded ignorance, replying that he was 'not learned in such matters, nor no man of this town'. He had, therefore, asked both the men concerned to give him 'their opinions in writing under their hands and seals', which he sent straight to Cromwell for his judgement. He added that he had examined 'an unthrifty fellow who doth much slander the mass', but reserved his punishment until knowing Cromwell's pleasure.[23] The Council of Calais then wrote asking for clarification around the practices of the sacrament and whether they should accept any deviations from what the King's book set out. Arthur tried to draw on his personal connection with Cromwell, asking 'not as a councillor but as a special friend'.[24] This reply reveals his willingness to serve the king and follow his rules, but also a lack of decisiveness and action, passing the responsibility for justice and reform in Calais back into Cromwell's hands. It was precisely this kind of indecision that allowed suspicion to be cast upon the Lisles later on.

Arthur was still concerned about Adam Damplip's activities in Calais. Damplip had recently preached a sermon 'of the Sacrament of the altar in a way much at variance with the King's book, which has caused great offence and made many people not care for the mass, and wish they had never heard mass in all their lives'.[25] Arthur appealed to Cromwell, who 'can discuss the scripture better than I can' and sent him Damplip's words, 'that you may know whether they should be maintained or corrected'. Clearly, Arthur felt uncomfortable in interpreting these finer points, and the position of Calais as being unrestricted to visitors from France and Flanders, opened it to the influence of both traditional Catholics and reformists: 'I assure you both in France and Flanders they repute us but as heretics, and that we are out of the league with the Emperor and the French king, and they trust to have war with us'.[26] Torn between the reformers and the 'popish dregs', Arthur insisted that he would obey Henry 'to the last drop of my blood' and that 'nothing since I was born ever went so near my heart as this', but he had not received an answer to his three letters to Cromwell on the matter.[27] His anxiety here is palpable.

Soon after this, Adam Damplip left Calais, travelling to England in the custody of an Edward Corbet, who delivered him for examination to Archbishop Cranmer at Lambeth Palace. Corbet's letter to Arthur reveals more about the tension in Calais as the result of religious reforms. He had informed Cromwell how Arthur had managed the difficult crowd of soldiers who came to hear Damplip preach, along with many strangers, one of whom offered him 'over-thwart language' for which he was committed, and that Arthur had ordered a constable and his company to be present.[28] One such individual, perhaps the man Corbet mentions, was named as a Calais smith, Thomas Delingcourt, who was to be brought to England to 'answer for his lewd behaviour'.[29]

John Foxe attributes Damplip's departure and subsequent interrogation entirely to Honor, who he is determined to make the scapegoat for the preacher's fall. Arthur, who according to Foxe, was 'of a most gentle nature, and of a right noble blood', was 'fiercely set on, and incessantly enticed, by the wicked Lady Honor his wife, who was an utter enemy to God's honour and, in idolatory, hypocrisy and pride, incomparably evil'. She reputedly 'being daily and hourly' influenced by fellow Calais Catholics Sir Thomas

Palmer and John Rokewood, 'two enemies to God's word', to complain against Damplip, writing 'very heinous letters' to the Privy Council 'against divers of the town of Calais, affirming that they were horribly infected with heresies and pernicious opinions',[30] even after Damplip had left the town. Foxe's agenda is transparent. Nothing emerges from any close reading of Honor's letters to suggest that she was a woman prepared to complain so bitterly to the Privy Council in a way that would have undermined her husband on such an important matter. Nor do Foxe's sources appear to be first hand.

Cromwell was not satisfied with interrogating Damplip alone. The net closed around Calais, taking as its first victim John Dove, Prior of the White Friars, where Damplip had recently preached. Even though Dove had intervened and complained about the content of his speech, he was now questioned regarding his history and beliefs, providing an interesting insight into the biography of a man Honor and Arthur must have known well. It seems Dove decided to go to England himself 'to recant things by him mis-spoken', and set the record straight.[31] The interview included details about his promotions and route to Calais, whether Arthur had appointed him and how many members of the council he considered to be his friends, who shared his views. He was asked who had encouraged him to hear Damplip preach, and who had asked him to depose against Damplip in England. Cromwell also wanted to know what connections he had with certain English bishops, what was the content of letters he exchanged with them and what was meant by certain words in those correspondences.[32]

The examination broke Dove, who wrote to Arthur during his absence, hoping that Honor would fulfil a promise she made to apply for ownership of the White Friars. 'I hope it may be done shortly', he added, 'as I am weary of the heavy burden'. He was prepared to surrender all claim to the house, asking Arthur to produce paperwork 'under our convent seal to render to you all the title we have', as 'the people shall not wonder at me in surrendering it to your Lordship'.[33] The Lisles did accept the surrender of Dove's friary, objects from which were found among their inventory in 1540.

In September 1538, Honor and Arthur made a visit to England in the wake of this, probably to help clarify matters and clear their name. While Arthur remained with Cromwell, Honor returned in order to care for Mary Basset, who was unwell. She had been suffering from a fever for five weeks, 'it still attacks her every day and we do not know what remedy to apply'. Honor wrote to Madame de Bours after having promised to send her news of seeing the king: 'I can hardly tell you how well he received us. All our affairs have succeeded as well as we could desire'. When they left court, Henry made them 'beautiful presents' promising Arthur 'he shall not want anything he can do for him'.[34]

Arthur's letters to Honor during his absence reveal that despite recent miscommunications about religious reform, his efforts at court to clarify their intentions had been successful. From Canterbury, he wrote that Henry was 'never better lord to him', and Cromwell had promised him 'money, clothes, a collar and shirt'[35] and, he believed, £400 a year, although this turned out to be 400 marks, which was considerably smaller.[36] John Husee wrote that Arthur had slept every night in Cromwell's lodging 'and was never out of his company but when he went to the King'. Cromwell officially granted him the Calais White Friars and all its lands, for the duration of his life.[37]

Arthur's stay in Canterbury coincided with a seismic milestone of the English Reformation: the destruction of Thomas Becket's tomb at the start of September 1538. Since the former archbishop's murder in 1170, pilgrims had crawled upon their knees to visit the glittering shrine of a man who had defied a king and reputedly worked many miracles since. The shrine drew visitors from all round the world, immortalised by Geoffrey Chaucer, giving rise to something of an industry in Canterbury. Visiting it was a theatrical experience, as it was raised on steps behind an altar, with a stone arcaded plinth, a gilded casket containing bones and a canopy, which could be raised and lowered by pulleys. The casket was studded with all manner of jewels and the great Régale of France, which Louis VII had left there in 1179. Writing twenty-five years before Arthur's visit, the Humanist, Desiderius Erasmus, described how 'every part glistened, shone and sparkled with rare and very large jewels, some of them larger than a goose's egg'.[38] When the canopy was raised before the prostrate pilgrims, silver bells rang and a priest came out to touch the jewels with a white wand. Amid this piece of staging, many felt spiritually cleansed and physically healed, as the stained glass windows paralleling their journey through the cathedral attest.[39]

John Husee wrote to Honor on 8 September, that Cromwell's agent, Richard Pollard, was busy day and night 'in prayer with offering' to St Thomas' shrine and head, meaning the piece of Becket's skull, or corona, that was usually on display in the chapel of that name, as well as 'other dead relics'. But Husee got this wrong – in fact, Pollard was assessing the shrine, before Cromwell swept in to dismantle it and remove more than 400 relics, images and jewels, including Becket's staff.[40] It is even possible that the destruction had already begun, with some historians placing the final phase of the shrine's dismantling on the very day Husee wrote his letter.[41] The significance of this destruction, in the heart of the city where Christianity was founded in England, and which had been a centre of worldwide pilgrimage for centuries, is impossible to underestimate. Whether the bones of the saint were rescued ahead of the event remains a mystery. Arthur was in Canterbury during this time, staying with Cromwell, close to Henry. Was there discussion of the process? Did he witness the removal of gems, bones, pieces of the gold casket? If he saw or overheard even the slightest hint that this was taking place under his nose, he can have been left in little doubt about the seriousness of Henry's reforms.

Cromwell was also working on a series of religious injunctions which were published in the second week of October. The main focus of this change was to remove Latin as an exclusive language that created a barrier between God and the ordinary worshipper. The rules included that at least one Bible in English must be set out in every church before next Easter, where parishioners might read it. Everyone was to be encouraged to read it, interpret it for themselves and have their questions answered. Upon every Sunday or holy day, the priests must recite the Pater Noster, or Creed, to the congregation in English, so that they might learn it by heart, and teach their children and servants the same. At Lent, priests should examine those who confessed to them, to check they knew the articles of faith in English. Icons, pilgrimages and offerings were next to come under attack. Sermons should forbid those acts of 'idolatry and superstition' such as 'wandering to pilgrimages, offering of money, candles, or tapers to images or relics, or kissing or licking the same, saying over a number of beads, or in such-like superstition', which did not promise of rewards, but was 'contrary to the great threats and maledictions of God'. The use of all false cures, images of waxes, devotional images and acts of pilgrimage were to cease at once.[42] John Husee wasted no time in sending these to Arthur on October 16, who was now back in Calais, with the instruction to display the injunction 'in every place in your house, hall, chamber, gate and other offices, that you being head may be a light to the inferiors'.[43] Surely, if Honor was still clinging to her superstitious ways, this was the time to give them up.

Fifteen

Mine Own Sweetheart
November 1538

In November 1538, Honor went to England 'to defend the right'[1] of her eldest son, John Basset, whose inheritance was being threatened by Lord Bridgewater. This Beaumont inheritance should have come to him from his father's grandmother, Joan Beaumont, and included Honor's former home of Umberleigh. In the meantime, these had been granted to Lord Daubeney, later Bridgewater, to whom one of the Basset girls had been intended to marry. No such marriage went ahead but Bridgewater retained the inheritance, an act of 'extortion to defraud'[2] the family. John was due to come of age in 1539, and take possession of his lands and properties, but this involved paying certain fines and recoveries to the king, so Honor travelled in person to request Cromwell's assistance. She was absent from Calais from about a month, during which the most affectionate and informative of her letters were composed.

Honor crossed the Channel on 7 November, landing at Dover around ten o'clock at night. The passage was slow but fair, and although she was sick once, she was merry enough, adding, however, that she would have been merrier if she were sailing towards her husband. The landing had been difficult, with 'evil chance' running the ship against the pier, but Honor had already disembarked by that point, and gave Captain Lamb two crowns to get it mended. She began her letter to Arthur that night, but there was no provision to send it, so she had supper and listened to tales being told before bedtime. She was anxious that her letter had been left by the courier, John Nele, who departed early at 3 a.m., probably to catch the tide, and tried to reassure Arthur that it was not intended as an unkindness that he had not heard from her sooner. She was waiting for the arrival of John Husee, as they intended to ride to Sittingbourne that night, but the weather was 'boisterous'.[3]

Honor and Husee met at Canterbury, where they began their journey up to London. It was proving costly, as Honor had already spent 40 crowns and was now informed that she was unable to stay at the home of Sir Christopher More,[4] because Mr Long of the privy chamber was lying ill there. Instead, Honor stayed at the home of 'one Archer near Sir Brian Tuke's in Lothbury',[5] a London street in Broad Street Ward which is just north of Bank Street tube station today. A contemporary map[6] shows it running from Ironmonger Lane in the west to Broad Street in the east, starting outside the entrance to the Guildhall, passing many large dwellings with gardens and terminating by the Draper's Hall, just before the Austin Friars. Honor had not yet been gone for long, but the expense and the change in plan already made her 'very anxious to return'.[7]

Honor arrived in London on Saturday, 9 November, and met with Cromwell on the following Monday. After he had been a 'very good lord' to her and John, 'both for my suit and your annuity',[8] Honor travelled out of the city to see Henry who was currently at Hampton Court. Set amid the beautiful Surrey countryside, on the banks of the Thames, Cardinal Wolsey's old palace was a miniature town in itself, with beautiful surrounding grounds. The easiest way to approach was by boat, so Honor took a barge, probably from the Queenhithe steps, downriver to join the court, a journey that may have taken an hour or two, depending upon the tide. Upon arriving, Honor was met at the privy stairs by Thomas Heneage, and conveyed her to her chamber 'where was a rich bed furnished, and nothing lacking for me nor my folks'.[9] She was soon reunited with her daughters Anne and Katherine; her friends including the new Lady Suffolk, Katherine Willoughby; her niece Mary Arundell, Countess of Sussex; Eleanor, Countess of Rutland and others.

As a mark of respect, Honor was 'highly feasted' at court – the banquet was 'the best I was ever at, and was partly made for me, I had not expected it'. One account noted that 'they lay all night in Court and had banquets in their chambers, and the King's servants to wait upon them, and did not take leave till four o'clock after dinner next day'.[10] Afterwards, Henry showed her around the 'conveniences' of the palace and promised that no one should be allowed to meddle in the business of John's inheritance. Honor took the opportunity to thank Henry for his goodness, and reported that he was 'very gracious' towards Arthur.[11] After she returned to London, Honor sent Henry some boars heads as a thank you gift, which he was pleased to receive.

She wrote to Arthur with affection:

> *I hope soon to despatch my business, for I would fain be with*
> *you. You promised me after my departing you would dine at 10*

*every day and keep little company because you would mourn
for mine absence; but I warrant you I know what rule you
keep and company well enough since my departing, and what
thought you take for me, whereof you shall hear at my coming
home. By her that is more yours than her own, which had much
rather die with you there than live here.*[12]

Indeed, Arthur was missing Honor greatly. He addressed her as 'mine own
sweetheart' and said he lay awake thinking of her at night so that he could
not sleep – he never 'longed so much for anyone, since I knew a woman'.
On a more practical note, he wrote that his agent would bring her money
and asked for her to send him a velvet night cap and a cloth cap; she could
hall all his plate if she wished for it.[13]

After visiting Henry, Honor met with Cromwell regarding Arthur's
annuity and the White Friars. She came away hopeful, reassured by his
promises of assistance, although she would 'know more of his mind in
a day or two'. Honor hoped to see the infant Prince Edward before her
departure, and anticipated that her business would soon be finished.[14] She
sent Arthur half a doe, but kept the other half because she was due to dine
the following evening with Cromwell's son, Gregory, and Richard Pollard,
the dismantler of Becket's shrine whom Arthur had met in Canterbury. It is
difficult to imagine how this meeting went if Honor was aware of Pollard's
recent actions. Was she cautious at dinner? Did they discuss the religious
reforms? How did Honor feel when faced with the agent of destruction who
was attacking her faith? No doubt she concealed any private feelings and
played her gentle, diplomatic role well.

On the same day that Honor dined with Richard Pollard, Henry was
investigating heretics at York Place, or Whitehall, as it had now become.
John Husee described for Arthur how scaffolding, bars and seats were
erected on both sides, with a high place at the end for the king. Henry
appeared around noon, and was seated amid 'the most part of the lords
temporal and spiritual, bishops, doctors, judges, serjeants at law, the mayor
and aldermen of London',[15] on order to hear the testimony of a John
Nicholson, alias Lambert, who had been an English chaplain in Antwerp,
who had denied certain articles of the sacrament:

*The King's Majesty reasoned with him in person, sundry times
confounding him, so that he alone would have been sufficient
to confute a thousand such. It was not a little rejoicing unto*

all his commons and to all others that saw and heard how his
Grace handled the matter; for it shall be a precedent whilst
the world stands; and no one will be so bold hereafter to
attempt the like cause. Alter the King had confounded him by
Scripture, so that Lambert had nothing to say for himself, the
bishops and doctors exhorted him to abandon his opinions, as
his Grace did also: but he refused, and will have his deserts.
The matter lasted from noon till 5, when he was conveyed to
the Marshalsea.[16]

A proclamation was also made on the same day against the import, selling or publishing of heretical books, and various other practices. There was to be no disputing of the sacrament except by those learned in divinity, but holy bread, holy water, kneeling and creeping to the Cross on Good Friday and Easter day, the setting up of lights before Corpus Christi, bearing of candles on Candlemas day, purification of women, and offering of baptismal chrisoms must be observed till the king please to change them. Priests known to have wives or to intend marriage were to be deprived of their positions, and those marrying after this proclamation to be imprisoned at the king's pleasure. Finally, the new rules stated that Thomas Becket, 'sometime Archbishop of Canterbury, shall no longer he named a saint, as he was really a rebel who fled the realm to France and to the bishop of Rome to procure the abrogation of wholesome laws, and was slain upon a rescue made with resistance to those who counselled him to leave his stubbornness. His pictures throughout the realm are to be plucked down and his festival shall no longer be kept, and the services in his name shall be razed out of all books'.[17]

Sometimes it must have felt to the Lisles that they were clinging to a world that was rapidly dissolving. On one hand, Henry was welcoming and feasting Honor at court, whilst on the other, he was attacking the faith that had been her guiding light for a lifetime. The internal struggle that she must have experienced would surely have been echoed by many others of Henry's subjects, torn between loyalty to their king and their beliefs. Honor and Arthur sought short-term comfort in their relationship and the domestic comforts of their life together. Arthur wrote to his wife about some white cloth he had sent, and asked her to look at the three geldings that he wished to buy. He sent her some baked partridges and a French wild boar pasty, a baked crane and kersey to make a petticoat from.[18] In his next letter, he was glad to hear of her kind reception by the king, and admitted he had partly broken his promise to dine every day at ten, as he had been so well feasted by Calais friends that he could not miss Honor during the day. At night, however, 'I swear God I sleep not one hour together for lack of you'. Arthur also informed her that a powder she had made up had saved the life of one Hyffield, who had been unable to pass water for four days and 'prayeth heartily for you'. He would send her some French wine, but hoped she would soon return, as he 'would not be without [your] company so long for £100.'[19]

Honor also corresponded with other family and friends. Her daughter-in-law, Frances, John Basset's wife, wrote that she and Philippa had received Honor's letters and she was dispatching the items Honor had requested, including the key to her coffer. Frances had improved a little from her illness of the autumn: 'my breast is somewhat amended, though I have had sore pain in it', while Philippa was now experiencing an ague, or fever. Frances hoped Honor would find a border for a long cushion in a matching shade of green and needed some blue material for the 'inner part'. She asked to be recommended to her husband John, 'my bedfellow Mr Basset. I long much to hear from him'.[20]

Sir Richard Wingfield's second wife, Jane, a friend of Honor's in Calais, also wrote to inform her that Arthur and all the council had dined with them, although they had 'desired greatly to have had your Ladyship … but in your absence you were drunk to by my Lord and all your good lovers'. She added that Arthur said he 'thought the time long of your absence and would for no good that you should lack him so long again'.[21] The Lisles' former quarrel with the Wingfields, over reclaiming his house built in the marshes, appears to have abated. Arthur would have dined at their 'great mansion house' by the Boulogne gate in the town, but they also owned a number of houses and tenements bought from Baron Sandys standing on the north-west side of the market place.[22]

Another Calais correspondent, local vintner (wine seller) John Worth, informed Honor that Arthur was 'in good health and merry, the merrier for receiving a letter from you this day'. However, he confirmed that Frances and Philippa were still both suffering from the fever, despite Frances' brave words, but thought Frances' health would improve if her husband were to visit her. He included a long list of people sending Honor their best wishes and eagerly anticipating her return, from the Wingfields and Whethills, other ladies and families, and even 'all your poor neighbours', serving as reminder of how popular she was in the Calais community.[23]

While Honor was in England, another tragedy was playing out among the Plantagenet survivors. This cut right to the heart of Arthur's family and its resistance to religious reform. The trouble had been brewing for several years, with the breach between Henry and his cousin, Reginald Pole, a papist currently in exile, whom the Pope had made a cardinal in 1537. Pole was also charged by Paul III to organise funding for the northern rebels of the 1536–7 Pilgrimage of Grace, which had ended in the brutal suppression and execution of its leaders. Earlier in 1538, the Pole's cousin, Henry Courtenay, Marquess of Exeter had been involved with uprisings of traditional Catholics in Devon and Cornwall, which had supposedly intended to overthrow the king and replace him with Courtenay. Arrests were made of Courtenay's correspondents, which included Reginald Pole's brother Geoffrey, who implicated the cardinal under duress, but also his elder brother Henry and their mother Margaret. As survivors of the old regime, the Pole family were the closest claimants to the English throne. This took place in November 1538, while Honor was in England.

Margaret Pole, Countess of Salisbury, was Arthur's first cousin, the only surviving child of Edward IV's treasonous brother, George. Once responsible for raising Princess Mary, she had briefly returned to court in 1536, after Anne Boleyn's fall, although she later withdrew. While Honor was in London, Margaret and her eldest son Henry were arrested and taken to the Tower. Rumours circulated that all were 'like to suffer death', on account of their connection with Reginald, and 'would have made foul work in England'.[24] Margaret was then 63, a grandmother who had suffered the executions of her father and brother, and the absence and strife caused by her son Reginald; she was likely to have been guilty of little else than being a devoted mother. She would have all her titles, lands and properties confiscated by an Act of Attainder, reserved for traitors, the following May, when Cromwell produced a tunic, supposedly found among her effects, bearing the five wounds of Christ. This was taken to be evidence of her support of a Catholic plot.

Honor and Arthur must have been concerned about the tenuous downfall of an elderly lady of Plantagenet blood, thrust into the Tower, devoid of all comforts. With hindsight, it is easy to spot precedents for their own downfall, but with Henry and Cromwell professing kindness and support, despite their former adherence to old practices, the Lisles may have been lulled into the belief that they could weather the storm.

As Honor's time in England began to draw to a close, her letters hint indirectly at the uncertainty of unfolding events. In contrast to the way she had been welcomed and feasted, now Cromwell and the king were more distant. 'I have come here at an ill time', she wrote, and 'the time for my present business is so unsuitable that if I appointed a time this seven years I could not have chanced in such another'.[25] Honor would certainly have been aware of the tension and heard rumours circulating about the Poles as evidence was gathered for their trials. Cromwell was exceptionally busy as a result, so that Honor had to wait four days to see him, only to be told he was unable to meet with her just yet. She dared not leave court until she had done so, fearing she might evoke his displeasure for having done so.[26] A week later, she was still waiting to see Cromwell when she wrote to Arthur 'mine own sweet heart, even with my whole heart root, I have me most heartily recommended unto you. I have received your letters, but so pressing is the King's business that for eight days I have not been able to speak with my lord Privy Seal'. She 'would have been with the King before but for the said lord's displeasure, which I would not gladly have'.[27] Again, this indicates Honor's vulnerability and the dependence of the Lisles upon the good favour of Henry's chief minister. She clearly felt that favour could easily be withdrawn as the result of a slight breach of protocol. Just in case, she added to the bottom of her latest letter to Arthur: 'please burn my letters'.[28] Henry Courtenay, Marquess of Exeter, Henry Pole, Lord Montagu and Sir Edward Neville, brother of Henry's wife, were executed on 9 December in the Tower. For the time being, Margaret remained incarcerated, to lament her losses. Historians have subsequently concluded that much of the evidence relating to the supposed Exeter conspiracy was fabricated or circumstantial, and that the greatest crime committed by the innocent Poles was to be in correspondence with Reginald, who was the king's real target. But like the Boleyn scandal of two years earlier, Henry had decided he needed scapegoats and Cromwell had provided him with the 'evidence' he needed.

In her final days at court, Honor saw Prince Edward, then just past his first birthday, 'who is the goodliest babe that ever I set mine eye upon' and prayed that God would 'make him an old man, for I should never be weary of looking on him'. She had also seen Princesses Mary and Elizabeth, both declared illegitimate and stripped of their titles. She had even dined with the Earl of Bridgewater, and hoped he would be reasonable regarding John's inheritance after Henry had 'shaken [him] up' if not, the king would do her no wrong. Cromwell even suggested they would receive £1000 from him.[29] Arthur sent her thirteen partridges and asked her not to forget the gown she was having made up for him, along with six dozen black ribbon points and two pairs of hose. He suggested she look for some venison and send it out for them to enjoy at Christmas.[30] He 'longed to hear' from her, and for her return home, 'for whom I long as much as a child for his nurse'.[31]

Frances wrote again at the end of November to reassure her mother-in-law that Philippa was much better and that the pain in her own breast was 'amended'. She had also received a letter from her husband John, and passed on gifts from Calais residents of a gold ring with a diamond from Mr Boys, a sapphire ring from Lady Garnish and a turquoise ring from Mrs London. Upon her return, Honor was to be met outside the gate of Calais by a Mr Gray 'with his cap in his hand, while Philippa sent her mother a token of Our Lady of Boulogne, like a pilgrimage badge, a slightly dangerous gift given the religious climate.[32] Arthur replied that he would have sent Lamb's boat to fetch her 'if he knew of her return to Dover'.[33] The pair now longed to be reunited, and for Honor to escape the tension at court. She wrote 'as to your writing that you never longed so sore for me, your desire in that behalf can be no vehementer than mine. I can neither eat, sleep nor drink, my heart is so heavy, and it will never be light till I am with you'.[34] In reply, Arthur repeated that when 'I think so much on you I cannot sleep I'the night when I think on you in two hours after' and echoed the sentiment that 'there was never child thought so long for his nurse, as I do for you'.[35]

Honor was home in time for Christmas, brought safely back across the Channel in Lamb's ship. Anthoinette de Saveuses knew she had returned because on December 20, one of Honor's servants delivered to her monastery a piece of gold, by which she 'perceived by these tokens that you had returned from your voyage, and I thank God you have accomplished your object'.[36] Anne Weston, widow of Francis who had been executed in the Boleyn downfall, wrote that she was glad Honor had 'escaped the great jeopardies of the sea and is safe come home again, after so merry a journey'.[37] Honor may have considered her trip far less than merry, but no doubt the Lisles were happy to be reunited and enjoyed the season together as a family, safe in their Calais enclave.

Sixteen

The Gathering Storm
1539

1539 began quietly enough for the Lisles. Honor continued her patterns of friendship, patronage and gift-giving with her connections in England, the Pale of Calais and France. She sent flowers and the 'best baked partridges that ever he has eaten' to Brian Tuke and his daughters, along with a puncheon of French wine from Arthur's cellar, and in return, Tuke promised to send her venison once it was in season.[1] Diligent as ever, John Husee was arranging for a suit of vestments of bawdkin which were going to cost at least £40,[2] had already purchased Honor some ling and stockfish at 45s, and advised her that her quilts were not to be stuffed with say because it would breed moths. Honor's velvet was dyed but had not yet dried because of the wet weather[3] and a spaniel Honor had sent for Lady Suffolk had not yet been delivered, but he would give it to her himself the next day.[4] Soon after, he sent the Lisles raisins, almonds, rice, thirty eels,[5] eighteen puffins in a barrel[6] and was chasing up a waistcoat for Frances and some carp pasties.[7]

Honor continued to exchange news and gifts with her closest female friends. Jeanne Rouault and her sister-in-law, Madame de Bours, remained important to her long after her daughters Anne and Mary had left their households. 'You do me so many kindnesses', wrote Anne Rouault after receiving a barrel of herring and two salmon, that 'I know not how to deserve them' and begged to hear from her often.[8] With Anthoinette de Saveuses, Honor exchanged linen and clothing items, such as bonnets and coifs, which the nuns made for sale at Bourbourch.[9] Honor remained in touch with her daughters in England, Anne and Katherine, who remained with the Countesses of Arundell and Rutland respectively, awaiting such time as Henry VIII might remarry, whereupon they could attempt to gain entry into a new queen's household. Henry's reputation as a husband and reformer had damaged his chances of marriage with many of the main European dynasties, and that year he turned to the Protestant Duchy of Cleves, sending out ambassadors to enquire about the availability of princesses there.

In May, Anne Basset was among a group of women who travelled down to Portsmouth to view the ninety war ships in the harbour, including the new great ship, the *Harry Grace à Dieu*. Anne, who was now 18, appeared to be in favour with Henry, who had previously commented on her beauty and given her the gift of a saddle. Anne was one of ten female signatories to a letter written to Henry from Portsmouth, describing the ships as 'so goodly to behold that in our lives we have not seen (excepting your royal person and the lord prince your son) a more pleasant sight'. They thanked him for the entertainments he had 'bestowed' upon them and lamented his absence. Henry later asked Anne to write to Honor requesting that she send him more of the 'codiniac of the clearest making' (quince paste) and of the 'conserve of damsons' as soon as possible, as he 'doth so well like'[10] the ones she had sent before. On another occasion, Honor sent Henry some 'goodeneke' which he tasted and enjoyed, prompting Anne to remark that 'your Ladyship was glad that ye could make anything that his Grace did like; and his Grace made me answer that he did thank you with all his heart'.[11]

After her exchange of bonnets with Honor, Anthoinette de Saveuses wished to send Anne Basset the gift of some gloves. However, she expressed concerns about getting Anne into trouble in England, because 'the religieuses there are wholly extirpated' and 'I should be very sorry that she should fall into any disfavour if it should be known that a religieuse had sent her a pair of gloves', especially as the gloves were embroidered with the name of St Anne. In the end, she decided it was safer to send the gloves to Honor instead, advising that they should be cleaned in cold water with white Spanish lye, so that Honor may forward them to Anne, or not, at her discretion.[12] Anthoinette was aware that something was making Honor 'ill at ease' at the end of April, although she does not specify what; perhaps it was all these religious concerns. In her next letter, she sent her the daily prayers of the convent.[13]

On March 18, Deputy of Calais, Richard Wingfield, died in the town. By the terms of his will, he bequeathed Arthur and all members of the council a gilt spoon for remembrance. Arthur would have attended his funeral in the north-east side of St Nicholas' Church, in accordance with his final wishes. Wingfield had long held reservations about the religious reforms being made, and had actively resisted Lutheranism, but in the last month of his life, he had written directly to Henry, seemingly having had a change of heart. The king had been provided, he said, 'to restore again the principle of Christianity abolished by the sorceries of those who usurped the authority of God and of princes'. Previous attempts at reform had failed due to 'lack of pure mind' but applauded Henry upon the success of his 'holy enterprise'. Perhaps Wingfield was aware that his death was approaching – he only wrote his will three days before his death – and was making his repentance. I 'would not for all the good of the world' have 'died in [my] former ignorance', and this matter seemed of 'right great importance', the most important he had ever written.[14]

That spring, Edward Seymour, Lord Hertford, brother to the late Jane, had paid a visit to Calais in order to inspect the fortifications there and at Guisnes. With their former dispute over John Dudley's inheritance behind them, gestures of friendship were made, and Honor appears to have suggested the possibility of the Seymours taking Katherine Basset into their household.[15] Edward was influential at court, as Prince Edward's uncle, so it would have been a politic move. However, after speaking to her daughter, Honor changed her mind, informing Seymour that Katherine still wished to remain with Lady Rutland, so she was 'very loath' to remove her from there.[16] Katherine was also set to attend the wedding of Gertrude Manners to the son of the Earl of Shrewsbury, to which purpose, Husee delivered her 'twelve yards of white damask, two and a half yards of carnation velvet, one roll of buckram, and half a yard of velvet for a partlet'.[17] In May, the heavily pregnant Countess of Rutland explained to Honor that her husband wished her to go into the country to deliver her child and requested that Katherine might accompany her: 'She is as honest a gentlewoman as can be, and everybody seeing and knowing her, liketh her very well'.[18] Husee wrote to Honor that Katherine was 'determined to go'.[19] Honor herself was busy with the lying-in of her daughter-in-law Frances, who was delivered of a daughter that May, in Calais, who was named Honor. James Basset, who was still thriving in Winchester, wrote less than tactfully that he had heard 'his sister Frances has given birth to a child' but he 'always wished it would be a boy'.[20]

The threat of war continued to exert pressure upon Calais, although much of the fighting between Francis and the Emperor had taken place to the south, with Charles' efforts to conquer cities in Provence thwarted by the French alliance with Turkish naval captain and pirate, Barbarossa. The state of war did affect Calais though, and Arthur particularly, with Husee writing to warn him that if there was any likelihood of England having to join on France's side, 'there is no hope for the £400' that Henry had promised him the previous autumn.[21] Proving that Calais was in control of the situation, Arthur and the council wrote to Henry to confirm they had published his proclamations concerning the presence of officers and soldiers in the town, and outlining the provision of food available, which was secure in the town, but that their supplies from the marches were potentially in danger. They intended to carry out a thorough investigation into what was 'lacking in the fortifications and munitions', adding that there was no available timber for necessary repairs.[22] They assessed that Calais held 1000 soldiers while a further 700 were at Guisnes, all of whom needed equipment and supplies.[23] Anthoine Brusset wrote to Arthur from the Pale to set rumours straight that he had been fortifying the town of Ardres: 'he who told you so deceived you, for there is no truth in it... I do not love the French so much as to desire to gratify them in any way'. He also requested that a surgeon and physician, Master William, be allowed to 'gain his living in your town of Calais' because he had been unjustly banished from his French home after disagreements with officials, probably due to increasing hostilities.[24] A John Borough rode along the sea coast from Calais to Flanders and reported back to Arthur that he could see no provisions for war made there by the Emperor, only a single boat containing 180 men who claimed to be pilgrims, but that many ships were in disrepair save for 16–18 that had come for Portugal for the use of Charles, which remained untouched and had permission to return home whenever they wished.[25] Cromwell advised Arthur to wait and watch: 'my secret advice is that having a vigilant eye and await to the sure defence and fortification of the town ... you do nothing to the emboldening of the King's enemies or putting in fear his subjects more than necessary'.[26] A peace between France and the Empire would be signed in June, bringing this phase of their conflict to an end.

While war was abating, the uncertainty and urgency over religious reform remained. Despite having deferred his decisions to Cromwell, and following his advice, Arthur could not shake the doubts that seemed to have been settling around him since he had mistakenly put his trust in Adam Damplip. John Husee wrote to warn him that 'certain vile and lewd persons have bruited slanderous and most heinous words upon your lordship', but assured him that the 'lords of the Council took the matter as it was', and that Arthur should not 'take it so earnestly'.[27]

In June, the Six Articles were enshrined in law, enabling strict punishments to be enforced for those who disregarded them. As Husee confirmed, 'the sum of it is that, those who deny that the very body of God is there in flesh and blood, will suffer as traitors and heretics'.[28] Those

Sacramentarians who refused to believe in transubstantiation could now be burned at the stake without being given the opportunity to recant, and married priests were given until 12 June to separate from their wives, although the vows of religious women were being honoured. The Lisles were making efforts to enforce the new changes, chasing up dissenters and ordering French translation of the Bible, while requesting that any Husee could find in English might be sent out to them.[29] He dispatched one to them in June.

One of Cranmer's commissaries in Calais, Ralph Hare, was now accused of being a Sacramentarian, as well as keeping a concubine who had borne him children, and of bringing his cut corn and grass into church, threshing it before the sacraments, 'whereby all the said parish found them sore aggrieved therewith'.[30] Arthur sent Hare to Cromwell, along with several other suspects, including a barber named John Brook: 'the barber has declared openly that since he came into this country he never received the Sacrament with his good will'. Arthur was clearly tiring of the miscommunications and blame being assigned him, adding, 'I write nothing of malice but the thing proved be depositions'. He had always done his best to ensure the safety of Calais, although 'I know well your lordship has been informed of the contrary by others ... if I should be used as I have been, I had rather lie in perpetual prison, and so I will write to the king, if I can get no remedy from your lordship'.[31] According to Foxe, Hare was accused of speaking against the use of holy bread and water, and turned the blame back upon Arthur, because he 'could not be otherwise, coming out of a town so infected with pernicious errors and sects'.[32] No wonder Arthur was frustrated; he was trying to appease both sides, while each thought the worst of him.

More accusations were levelled against Calais inhabitants, who were taken into custody and sent over to Cromwell and examined in the Star Chamber. This may have come from Arthur, or from other members of the council, concerned about the consequences of not adhering to the Six Articles. William Smith, curate of the parish of Our Lady in Calais, was charged with 'the same heinous errors and pernicious opinions' as Hare and Brook, but in addition, he had 'spoken and preached against our blessed lady, against praying to saints, against doing good works and had eaten flesh with Thomas Brook together at Lent, in Brook's house'.[33] Ominously, John Butler, a commissary of Calais, was then charged with supporting and encouraging Adam Damplip, but he so 'humbly besought their Lordships ... to be good unto him', that he was dismissed, losing his job but not his life.[34] Butler had formerly complained about Arthur but appears to have many more complaints ranged against him, including theft, murder and keeping a mistress, so Arthur would not have felt his loss too keenly. Hare, Brook, Smith and another man from Marck were to recant and 'bear a faggot' through the streets and into the market place as penance, instructed to recant openly 'all his false doctrines, knowledging (*sic*) his offence' and to listen to a sermon.[35]

To Sir Anthony Browne, Arthur explained his dilemma of needing to enforce the new rules while not in full knowledge of them, all whilst facing resistance in the town. Even members of the council were opposing him in carrying out his duties:

> *We have had here such erroneous opinions against the Sacrament, with such light and evil communication concerning the mass, as I think has not been used or heard in any place, besides other evil opinions concerning Scripture, and banding of certain persons for maintaining them. I have been continually vexed therewith these two years, and would not live so another two years if the King would give me four times as much, for I cannot govern according to my bounden duty unless redress be had. Even now the Lord Chamberlain, Mr. Wallop, myself, Mr. Treasurer, the Knight Porter, and Mr. Rookewood, go about to redress the said opinions, but certain other of the Council are against us. The vintners and constables of the town, by the persuasion of certain subtle persons of the said opinions and evil sort, have written against us, so that I think such division has not been seen in this town. It has never been heard that any company or band of the retinue should write to the King's council in England without the knowledge of the Deputy and Council here.[36]*

According to John Foxe, who was writing with hindsight and a Protestant agenda, Henry was gradually becoming more and more angry at the dissention in Calais. 'The grudging minds of the adversaries were not yet satisfied', he wrote, 'but still suggested new complaints to the king's ears against the town of Calais, making the king believe that, through new opinions, the town was so divided, that it was in great danger to be overcome of the adversary'.[37] It seemed to Henry's new commissioner, Mr Currin, that the town was gripped by confusion and heresy, which had there not been a tendency towards leniency, could have resulted in a witch hunt, leading to a blood-bath: 'such a burning charity was in him and the rest of the commissioners, that had not God pitied the innocency of men's causes, there had a hundred been burned or hanged shortly after'.[38] Cromwell wrote to reassure Arthur that he 'never took Lisle to be a malicious man, but always thought him "of a good and gentle natural disposition", therefore there was no need to excuse himself'.[39] However, the blood-bath had only been delayed.

By the middle of the year, Arthur must have had great concerns about his future in Calais. A letter from Thomas Boys expressed surprise that Arthur had been troubling the king's council with his problems in the town and must 'certify the evil behaviour of certain persons' which he had been appointed to do. It appears Arthur was being accused of lacking leadership. Boys was preparing a book detailing 'the persons by whom these riots have been provoked' as Henry had been very angry to hear that some had eaten flesh in Lent and disobeyed the king's injunctions. He went on to warn Arthur that he 'has many enemies here, who say he loves not those that favour the Word of God. [He] heard one say to Thomas Broke that Lisle was a Pharisee', another replied he was a 'false knave and a heretic that so said', and that it was 'because you rebuked seditious and erroneous persons that they could not abide you'.[40] It must have felt as if Arthur alone was being blamed for being unable to rein in a volatile and potentially riotous situation. He travelled briefly to court that September in order to plead his case, where Henry 'welcomed and entertained him lovingly'.[41]

Then, the Lisles were suddenly needed again. The light of Tudor politics and international relations briefly illuminated Calais again, as it became once more a necessary location in Henry's marital plans. Katherine Basset wrote to Honor that 'we hear say that the king's grace shall be married', which might get her a position in the new queen's household.[42] After Hans Holbein had been dispatched that summer to Cleves, to paint what turned out to be one of the most controversial of all royal portraits, a contract of marriage had been drawn up between Henry VIII and Anne, sister of the Duke of Cleves. The Protestant bride was to travel across land, through Flanders and into the Pale of Calais, from where she would depart for England.

Hearing this news, Honor sent Anne a gift, which she received at Dusseldorf on 10 November, by the hands of Dr Henry Olisleger, Vice-Chancellor of Cleves, who had recently been in Calais. Anne was 'much pleased with it and still more with your affection'.[43] Arthur was asked by

Cromwell to visit the Exchequer, where Anne was to stay, 'and have it properly repaired', including examining 'the streets round it with a view to paving them. The whole town is to be put in cleanly order'.[44]

Anne set out from Cleves in mid-November with 263 attendants and 228 horses, proceeding at the slow pace of five miles a day.[45] Henry sent over a reception committee to welcome her, which arrived in Calais on 2 December, long before Anne, and they settled in to wait for her in their requisitioned lodgings. According to the ordinances prepared for her reception, Arthur and other dignitaries 'in their best array shall meet and receive her grace at her entry into the English Pale', making due reverence and salutations. From there, with 'honest and friendly semblance and entertainment', they were to conduct the party back into the town, 'whereby they may perceive themselves most heartily welcome'.[46] The Lisles drew on their local connections, with Anthoine Brusset securing Anne the best lodgings he could at Gravelines in exchange for them rewarding him with 100 quarts of malt.[47] Oudart du Bies sent a boars head and side[48] for their table, plus a 'mule harnessed for your service when the Queen of England comes to Calais'.[49] Chronicler, Edward Hall, describes how, on 9 December, at the turnpike on the English side of Gravelines, Anne was met by Arthur and all his spears and horsemen, attired in warlike gear, who led her back to where the Earl of Southampton was waiting, a mile out of town. Southampton, not Arthur, was Henry's official delegate, dressed in purple velvet and cloth of gold, accompanied by thirty men of the court, all hung with gold chains.

Anne entered Calais at the Lantern Gate, where Honor and other women of the town were waiting to meet her.[50] She paused to look at the 'ships lay in the haven garnished with their banners, pencelles and flags, pleasant to behold'; particularly two called the *Lion* and the *Sweepstake*, which were hung with banners of gold. The Calais guns sounded upon her arrival and the mayor came forward to present her with 100 gold marks.[51] The local dignitaries had turned out to meet Anne, in scenes reminiscent of the arrival of Anne Boleyn only seven years earlier. The merchants of the Staple lined up before their hall, dressed in their finery, to present her with another 100 gold marks. From there, she rode through the streets to the Exchequer, where she was to be lodged, and where Honor would be her chief hostess.

Due to the weather conditions, Anne would remain in Calais for fifteen days, where she was entertained by everything from 'goodly jousts' and 'costly banquets' to learning new games of cards. As the town's leading hostess, Honor was at the heart of these events, as her friend, Anthoinette de Saveuses, acknowledged later, by saying Honor had taken 'great pains' over the future queen's visit. Honor found her a pleasant woman, 'so good and gentle to serve and please'[52] and was happy to recommend her to her daughter, Anne Basset, awaiting her arrival at court. Henry was pleased to hear of Honor's 'good will and toward mind therein as thankfully as though your ladyship had waited on her Grace hither'.[53] It was not until after Christmas that the weather allowed Anne to depart, after which she landed at Deal, proceeded to Dover and from thence to London. On her way, she was intercepted by Henry at Rochester Castle, who decided that he did not like her, although he was already committed to the marriage. Desperately, he asked Cromwell to find him some means of escape, but there was none, and Henry married Anne of Cleves on 6 January 1540.

Seventeen

World About to Fall
March and April 1540

In the spring of 1540, concerns over religious turmoil in Calais came to a head. Tension had been brewing for the last three years, despite Arthur's best efforts to control a situation which was spiralling beyond the boundaries of his expectations. It is also clear that there was an element of distrust of Arthur, whether justified or not, and that he had been criticised in court circles for his inability to maintain order. Honor had also come under suspicion for her influence over him, and as John Foxe later summed up, her continued use of 'superstitious' practices.

It is difficult to understand just why Calais had become such a hotbed of heresy in the later 1530s, when many other places in England were also experiencing dissent. Or at least, that is how it had come to be viewed by Henry. Some historians[1] have seen the town as a testing ground used by Cromwell to further his religious agenda, where he pursued rules and punished dissenters more harshly than elsewhere. Perhaps it is Calais' location and size that make it seem that way. As England's gateway to Europe, any dissent in the town could legitimately have been considered as weakening England's defences. The country was only as secure as its foothold in Calais, which should act as a dam against the onslaught of heretical voices from abroad. As the events of 1540 would show, it was certainly considered to be a location from where a successful invasion might be launched. Also, because the town was small, self-contained and remote, a village mentality may have intensified instances of dissent, similar to how witch trials developed, where neighbours informed against each other and whispering campaigns threw around accusations. The steady stream of problems associated with Calais since the Damplip incident appear to have had a cumulative effect.

It began on March 9, when a commission was established to investigate the problem. Arthur was included in this, along with Honor's nephew by marriage, the Earl of Sussex, Lord St John, Sir John Gage, Dr Corein, Attorney-General John Baker and Richard Layton, one of Cromwell's Visitors for the Valor Ecclesiasticus who was now Clerk of the King's Closet.[2] Their task was to 'inquire into the origin of the disorder and divisions in the town of Calais and to take such steps for the reestablishment of order as they shall think expedient'.[3] They were to round up the offenders, examine them and punish them at their discretion, through banishment, discharging them of their offices, or committing to the king any who 'have deserved death'.[4] They must take action to prevent future abuses, take musters, examine the present fortifications and report back on the general state of the town. It is also possible to read this in a positive light, given the recent dangers of encroaching war, and the need to keep the town safe.

Arthur had been asking for assistance and clarification for years, and now that he was included in this commission, even with its focus on religion, this may have felt like a positive step for the Lisles. This possibility is supported by the letter Baron Sandys wrote to Arthur about how 'graciously the King has provided for the security of Calais and the abolishment of erroneous opinions and punishments of Sacramentaries'. Sandys reminded Arthur that he had already been vocal in his complaints of heretics in the town, for 'their own ill doings and the maintenance of Adam Damplip, an odious person who has infected many with his preachings'.[5]

The Calais Commissioners' report gives insight into the town under Arthur and Honor's occupancy in 1540. The information on wages reveals who the prominent residents were, their roles and expenses, whose faces and reputations were known to Honor on a day-to-day basis. Many of these individuals were people she had employed, or interacted with in her role as Arthur's wife, leading hostess and general patron and good lady. Arthur's expenses amounted to £680 13s 10d annually, from which he was paid 20 marks as a yearly award plus 2s daily, with an eighteenth part for his food and drink, plus wages for his spears, archers and soldiers. High Marshall, Sir Richard Grenville's, total of £338 19s 1d included the same salary as Arthur, with wages for twenty-seven soldiers. Sir Edward Ringley, still the Comptroller, had £181 4s 2d, out of which he received 18s a day, plus wages for soldiers and clerks. Sir Thomas Palmer was the porter, receiving 12d a day, William Simpson the Under Marshall got 18d a day, while Sir John Wallop, Lieutenant of the Castle, had a £20 reward, 2s a day and maintained 49 soldiers. Honor had exchanged letters with a number of their wives.[6]

The Calais High Treasurer was Baron Sandys, who in his absence was assisted by Sir Richard Weston, father of the Francis Weston who had lost his life in the Boleyns' fall. He was responsible for paying the wages of the men at arms and archers on horseback, and the archers and men at arms on foot, who must have recently turned out to greet Anne of Cleves. Also on their payroll were the tradesmen and craftsmen who had recently spruced up the town for Anne's visit: numerous masons and carpenters, plumbers, smiths and tilers, a purveyor of stuff, as well as the pensions of the Carmelite Friars, the expenses of individuals travelling to England and the cost of watches and banquets in herring time and Christmas, totalling £1,064 18s 3d.[7]

The report names the Calais officers Honor would have seen around the town, carrying out their business: Henry Palmer the bailiff of Guisnes; Thomas Fowler, the receiver of Marck and Oye; Robert Poole, collector of the rents; John Barthelet, searcher at Calais; John Hussay, searcher at Marck; Edward Peyton, overseer of customs at the Lantern Gate; Vincent Finch, beadle and serjeant of Marck and Oye; Sir Christopher Morris, overseer of the ordinance; and George Brown, master of the ordinance. Then there was William London, who received 4d a day for the keeping of the Staple Inn, whom Honor must have known well; Richard Lee, surveyor of the king's works; Henry Palmer, keeper of the forest of Guisnes; pursuivants William Flower of Guisnes and Gilbert Dethicke of Hammes; and the numerous constables and vintners of the town, and the porters. She is likely to have known Christiane Sackvyle, whose house was rented out at a cost of £17 6s 8d for the storage of ordinance, and the 'poor and feeble' George Gruffyth who had a pension of £50 for having served Henry VII. Surely Honor would also have been familiar with Thomas Tichet, a poor man who carried the post for 100s annually. Had the men of the day watch, John Lukes, Humfrey Persons, Thomas Holmer and Edward Hopton, witnessed the recent unrest and hurried to inform Arthur? Had he called upon the sergeants, Davie Selley, Thomas Lewis, Thomas Baker, John Clare, William Lake and Richard Cole, to try and contain it?[8]

New rules setting out Calais' security paint a picture of the town Honor knew. The four key gates – Lantern Gate, Milk Gate, Boulogne Gate and Water Gate – were to be opened at specific times, but in very precise ways, such as if the other three were open, the Lantern Gate was only to open to two wickets. On holy days and festivals it was to open thrice before noon, the first being at five in the morning, after the watch bell was struck, whilst it would close at nine at night. During the herring season, (Michaelmas to St Andrew's, or 29 September – 30 November) only the Lantern Gate was permitted to open, the others only with special orders from Arthur. The instructions continue to outline the details of who must collect the keys and how the gates should be opened and closed in relation to each other. At the end of each day, those who rented out lodgings were required to declare to the clerk how many strangers were lodging at their house that night, and where they had come from. Any strangers found in the town after dark, even at other lodgings, were taken to the prison.[9]

Each night the town was patrolled by a number of watches, drawn from the guilds, but if 'any fray be done by any of the watch, the party offending shall lose his life'. It was responsibility that the town took seriously, with the severest of consequences:

> *If any of the said search watch [find any of the stand watch] sleeping three times in the night and so take him by the nose the offender on the next market day shall be hanged in a basket over the wall, 10 or 12 feet from the water, with a loaf of bread, a pot of drink, and a knife to cut the rope when he will. The dyke keepers must be present with their boat to take him up when he falls. He shall be kept in the mayor's prison till next market day, and then banished the town for a year and a day. The watchman shall not suffer man, woman, or child to pass without the watch word, except those who have lodgings in the towers, and they must come up at the nearest stair. No one having the watchword must depart until the relief in the morning, nor give the word to any person on pain of death.*[10]

It was estimated that around 600 ships used the port of Calais in a year, both foreign and English, with an additional 80 being involved in the wool trade. Often, the same merchant ships returned ten or twelve times in a year, carrying wood, English beer and malt. Twenty-four ships 'belonged' to the town, with their owners listed, including a French man, some 'stranger born' and a 'Flemming dwelling without the gates'. The weight of the ships ranged between 15 and 60 tons, and there were 10 fishing boats, which plied the herring trade. At least 340 herring ships of strangers visited the port annually.[11]

Honor's world was small and familiar. The behaviour and movements of individuals came under regular scrutiny. Within the walls of Calais, precise and exacting rules governed every aspect of town life, especially in relation to safety. When turmoil broke out over religion, the contemporary ideas of good governance and the common weal, meant that the town's necessary harmony and peace were threatened. The sixteenth-century fear of 'misgovernance' ran from the home all the way up to the throne. Wives who ruled husbands were subject to criticism and ridicule, as Honor had experienced; servants who disobeyed masters, and subjects who broke the king's laws, could expect to be dealt with harshly.

While the religious turmoil in Calais was the backdrop to Arthur's fall, it was prompted by disobedience within his own household. This couldn't have been worse for the Lisles, and played into the narratives that Arthur was inefficient and Honor influenced him with her Catholicism. Two years earlier, in mid-April 1538, Arthur had taken on a new personal chaplain by the name of Gregory Botolf, or Gregory Sweet-lips, as he was known in Calais. He came from a Suffolk family, based in Sudbury, with three brothers remaining in 1540: Sir William was parson of Sudbury Church, possibly St Gregory's which displayed the head of Archbishop Simon Sudbury, killed by the rebels of the Peasants' Revolt; Robert Botolf still lived in the town; and John had moved to Leystoke, having been in trouble for debts to a London merchant.

When Botolf asked Arthur for permission to visit England in January 1540, Arthur had no idea that he was planning otherwise. When the Lisles' household was dissolved that June, it contained fifty-six employees, so Arthur's trust in Botolf may not have been so much naivety as a consequence of numbers. And Botolf had hitherto given him little cause to be concerned. Behind the scenes, though, the chaplain had been influencing two other of the Lisles' servants, Edward Corbet and Clement Philpot, the latter of whom was being considered at the time as a potential husband for Philippa Basset. Both were Arthur's gentleman-servitors, with Philpot having been recommended into Lisle's service by Sir Antony Windsor. Other men of the town were brought into Botolf's scheming: Edmund Bryndeholme, parish priest of Our Lady in Calais' and Corbet's servants John Browne and John Woller. Botolf's intention was to take Calais on behalf of Cardinal Reginald Pole and use it to launch an invasion of England. There is no evidence that Pole was aware of this plan, but he had been corresponding with Botolf and some of the other conspirators, and his familial relationship to Arthur had been previously exploited by Adam Damplip. Equipped with Arthur's permission to leave, Botolf, Philpot and Woller prepared to depart on 5 February, leaving the town before the Lantern Gate was ceremoniously locked in the evening, advertising their intention of waiting outside the walls in order to set sail for England on the 2 a.m. tide. They spent the waiting hours gambling in a tavern outside the gates, but when the time came to board the ship, Botolf was nowhere to be found. Philpot and Woller duly sailed, but Botolf had absconded to Rome.

Woller returned to Calais on 14 March, Botolf three days later, but Philpot not until 24 March. The morning after his arrival, Botolf went to greet the Lisles, whereupon Corbet asked him what he had been doing in France. Botolf's excuse was that he had been blown ashore by bad weather, and afterwards a quarrel broke out between the chaplains over the seating arrangements at dinner, resulting in Botolf declaring he would 'never eat [a] meal's meat more in this hall'.[12] He announced his intention to ask Arthur for a licence to go away and study in Louvain University, which Arthur agreed to consider. The following morning, Botolf approached Honor on her way to church and asked her to influence Arthur to gain his permission. However, he decided to depart anyway, without the licence being granted. Having promised Corbet and Philpot gold rings made from ten crowns given to him by the Pope, he left Calais for Gravelines, taking Woller with him.

Letters written by Botolf from Gravelines show him making his final arrangements, selling off various items he had left behind. To Arthur, he sent a bill of sale for his clothing, bedding and books, and a pair of shears, which he had sold to Corbet and Philpot.[13] To Corbet, he apologised for his swift departure and asked for clothes and other items to be sent on the following night, and that Philpot should meet him at four p.m. at the Checker (Exchequer) at Gravelines.[14] He also asked Corbet to send him a shirt he had lent Woller, a length of kersey, his blue Lisle livery coat, his books, ring, scabbard, gowns and a knife and bodkin (dagger). He requested that Corbet try to obtain the permission that Arthur had not yet granted, thinking it easy to dupe him into signing a licence: 'no doubt if you make the writing ready to his hand he will sign and seal it', but that 'if you suspect anything take my Lady's advice'. This did not reflect well upon Honor,[15] as even 'without feigning', he would 'never have other master and mistress but them'.[16] One of the papers Arthur appears to have signed was to authorise the Captain of Gravelines to issue Botolf with a passport enabling him to travel freely in Flanders. Again, it may have been this laxity that would count against Arthur.

Philpot went to Botolf at Gravelines, meeting him outside the convent gates and walking about the walls, which they considered a secret place to talk. It was there that Botolf elaborated on his plan: Philpot and a small group of men were to overwhelm the night watchmen at the Lantern Gate, while Botolf scaled the walls with a small army of 500, and broke the gates open. 'As many as will resist', Botolf promised, 'shall be destroyed without mercy'.[17] Later, Botolf set off for Ghent with a John Browne, who was Corbet's servant, to whom he fed all sort of misinformation, including that Philpot had been slain. Botolf had had some letters directed to the English Embassy in Ghent, which was then under the control of Sir Thomas Wyatt. Perhaps tipped off by Francis the Post, from Calais, who had encountered Botolf on the road, Wyatt read the letters and found them suspicious, so dispatched them to England. In the meantime, though, Philpot had got cold feet and confessed the plot to Arthur or the commissioners on 2 or 3 April, in the hopes of saving himself. The various plotters were arrested and interrogations began on April 11. Arthur's name does not appear among those asking the questions.

Six days later, on 17 April, Arthur was recalled to England. Henry's letter was not accusatory in tone, requesting that as Arthur was 'principal minister' in Calais, the king was 'desirous to hear your advice' so that he might 'declare our mind and pleasure unto yourself on that behalf'. Nevertheless, he was commanded to depart immediately, leaving the keys and charge of Calais in the hands of the Earl of Sussex.[18] Just days earlier, Henry had written to the commissioners still in Calais, headed by Sussex, containing their opinion of 'the infection of the multitude by the teaching of Damplip', and thanking them for their 'diligence about Philpot'.[19] Botolf was to be lured back to Calais with the false promise of a new position, in a letter that Philpot was forced to write.[20]

Arthur prepared to make his farewells, with no idea that this was anything other than a similar trip to those he had made in recent years. The emphasis upon his competency and Honor's faith was concerning, but he hoped to have a good opportunity to speak plainly with his nephew and finally put an end to all doubts. He would have promised to write to Honor, his 'own sweetheart' and promised to return as soon as he could. Perhaps she went down to the harbour to wave off his ship. She had no idea she would never see him again.

Eighteen

Defeat
April–May 1540

Both Honor and Arthur had taken Henry's reassurances at face value and suspected that the real cause of his summons to England was to elevate Arthur to an Earldom. Honor had pleasant matters to consider at home also, as on 24 April, she received a letter from Monsieur de Riou, brother of Honor's dear correspondent with whom Anne Basset had formerly dwelled. It contained a formal offer of marriage for Mary from Gabriel de Montmorency, Seigneur de Bours since the death of his father in 1537, an offer which no doubt would have delighted Honor. It would not have taken her by surprise, given the letters and exchange of gifts between the young pair, and the two visits Gabriel had made to Calais so far that year. Word did reach Honor that Arthur had experienced some illness soon after his arrival in England, though, as her acquaintance Lamberde du Flos responded from Boulogne, 'I perceive by your letter that you have had news that your husband is ill, for which I am sorry'.[1]

However, Arthur was well enough to attend the annual Order of the Garter ceremony at Windsor on 23 April, in the presence of King Henry and the leading dignitaries of the court.[2] Among them were the Dukes of Norfolk and Suffolk, both known to Honor, along with Baron Sandys of Guisnes and Arthur's old friend, Sir William Kingston, Keeper of the Tower of London. Arthur also sat in the third and final session of Henry's seventh parliament on eight occasions, perhaps dressed in borrowed robes, as his parliamentary gown was left behind in Calais. These sessions were regular, on 27 and 29 April, then 1, 3, 4, 8, 10 and 11 May,[3] accounting for every session until the parliament went on its Whitsun break. The matter under discussion was the Order of the Knights of St John, or the Knights Hospitaller, a Catholic order recently driven out of Rhodes.[4]

At Westminster, Arthur would have paid his respects to Thomas Cromwell, who had been created Earl of Essex and Great Chamberlain at Westminster on 18 April, still appearing very much a man on the rise. This is misleading though, as Henry was on the verge of turning against Cromwell, influenced by the Duke of Norfolk, and was about to bring down his overmighty subject. Cromwell may not yet have been aware of the strength of feeling against him, but he was treading a fine line, having been the architect of the Cleves marriage from which he had not been able to save Henry. The atmosphere in parliament must have been tense. Welsh chronicler, Elis Gruffydd, comments that Arthur was shunned by his peers, as 'none of the Great men of the council looked at him save askance, for they saw that he was besmutted in some way or other'.[5] No other evidence supports this statement, which has more of a ring of truth when applied to the imminent treatment of Cromwell in June, but it may have been the case. It is possible that Arthur felt some unease, but he kept attending the sessions, as was his duty. He also reputedly wrote letters to Honor during this time, which might have shed light upon his state of mind, but none of these survive.

On 1 May, great jousts were held, with Arthur's stepson, John Dudley, participating along with Edward Seymour, Anthony Kingston, George Carew and Cromwell's son Gregory, behind white velvet barriers that kept back the court. A tournament followed on the third, and riding at the barriers on the fifth, with open house kept at Durham House, the Dudley's house near the Savoy, on the Thames, where the king and queen and 'all the lords' were feasted.[6] If Arthur was present, which he probably was, he would have had a chance to see Anne of Cleves again, far less happy now than when she had passed through Calais four months earlier. Ominously, though, Arthur was scheduled to attend the garter feast at Windsor Castle on 9 May, but he was recorded as not being present, 'for approved reasons'.[7] This may have been due to illness, or to something far more sinister brewing.

Behind the scenes, it appears that Arthur was involved in discussions, or was being questioned about, affairs in Calais. At the same time, those involved in the Botolf plot were being interrogated before being sent to the Fleet prison. A week after missing the garter feast, he was summoned to Greenwich, where the court was celebrating Whitsun, or Pentecost. Here, while the feasting and celebrations unfolded, on Whit Tuesday, 17 May, Arthur made a declaration, which is likely to have been his best formal, written statement in response to his critics. Sadly, this appears to have not survived. The next day, 18 May, according to Elis Gruffydd, Arthur was interviewed by the Dukes of Norfolk and Suffolk, and Cromwell, in the presence of Henry. Gruffydd adds that 'such witnesses spoke against him [Lisle] that he was unable to go against them, for he went down on his knees and appealed to the king to help him in righteousness'. Henry told his uncle that he would hear the matter himself, and after Arthur asked for his mercy, turned his back and 'went to his room without letting him answer either good or bad'.[8] Some of Gruffydd's account is doubtful, reliant upon Calais gossip, but the image of Arthur kneeling before a cold and distant king, begging for mercy, is certainly full of pathos.

Documents held 'touching the Lord Lisle' in the State Letters and Papers Collection shed light on what is likely to have transpired in the interviews with Arthur at Greenwich over Whitsun. These include a complaint made by William Stevens, a Calais Vinteyne (wine merchant) who had been dismissed from the Lisles' service; communication between the Lisles and Damplip; correspondence arising over the Botolf case, including those written at Arthur's command; a fairly innocuous letter Arthur had written to Emperor Charles about horses; Clement Philpot's declaration; Arthur's issue of a passport to Botolf; money given by the Lisles to Botolf; the lack of security at Calais, in allowing strangers free access to the town; the moral fibre of the Council of Calais[9] and more. Questions were also raised, resulting from the report, about the state of the town. Reputedly, 300 houses or more were vacant, 'and many fallen down for lack of inhabitants', and the promised new walls, funded by merchants of the Staple, had yet to transpire. Comments were also made about the types and number of individuals that were being given salaries, according to the detailed list of the investigation, which recommended that 'no officer taking fee for his office shall stand in wages; That no merchant or other having benefice of the Staple shall have wages; That no burgess that hath competent living stand in wages; That no man holding open shop, except bowyers, fletchers, armourers, smiths, and gunmakers, stand in wages; That no minter stand in wages while occupied in the King's mint; That no man who has once been put out for stirring to anything tending to misgovernance, such as congregations or fellowships, shall ever take wages within the town or be suffered to dwell therein; That no common debater or brawler stand in wages'.[10] The clear implication was that Arthur had been too willing to employ individuals lacking in good character, or to be efficient with his spending. Muriel St Clare Bryne, editor of the abridged Lisle letters, has no doubt that Arthur was scapegoated by Cromwell, in an attempt to deflect attention from himself, less than a month before his own arrest.

On the night of 19 May, the fourth anniversary of the execution of Anne Boleyn, Arthur was arrested. The English sources, including Edward Hall, are strangely silent on this, but a letter from French Ambassador, Charles de Marillac, gives the bare details:

Two days ago, at 10 o'clock at night, lord Lisle, deputy of Calais, uncle of this King, was led prisoner to the Tower, where previously three of his servants had been sent, and similarly to-day a chaplain of his who came in a ship from Flanders. Has not yet learnt the cause; although it is commonly said he is accused of secret intelligence with Cardinal Pole, who was his near relation, and of certain practices to deliver the town of Calais to Pole. However, the said lord Lisle is in a very narrow place, from which no one escapes unless by a miracle. There had already been brought to the same place 10 or 12 'mortes payes' of Calais, who charged the said Deputy with words contrary to honour and fealty... all accusations here are called treason.[11]

The shock for Arthur must have been palpable, even after the events of the previous days. Initially, he was placed under the care of his long-term friend Sir William Kingston, which must have offered some comfort. Kingston's wife Mary had been a good friend and correspondent to Honor over the years, and it is hard to imagine that she did not write to her now, conveying this terrible news. Having expected a letter confirming his elevation to an Earldom, Honor must have struggled to comprehend this turn of events. If Mary had not been able to write in time, Honor would have learned of Arthur's arrest from the two pursuivants who arrived in Calais on 20 May, bringing letters for the Earl of Sussex, commanding the arrest of two of the Lisles' servants.

That evening, Honor's nephew-in-law, Robert Radcliffe, Earl of Sussex, accompanied by Sir Edward Ringley, Sir John Gage and Thomas Fowler, knocked upon the door of the Staple. A brief conversation ensued, as it was explained to Honor that these men whom she knew well had orders to search the house. Honor probably asked questions about her husband and the accusations against him, about the nature of the men's enquiries, and the purpose of the information they were collecting. Did she get any answers? What was the manner of these men towards her, some of whom she would have entertained in those very rooms they were now searching? Did their personal relationship with her ensure their civility, or even their apologies, to a hostess they had respected, and towards her young daughters, or did the force of Henry's law make them brusque and uncivil? Did they fear their own implication in Arthur's failings? With Arthur in the Tower, she had little recourse against any mistreatment. At some point, Honor was confined to a room within the Staple and her daughters were removed to 'various places through the town'.[12] Hopefully this took place before the men began their work.

The inventory made of every room in the Staple shows how thoroughly Sussex went about the king's business, at what was already being described as 'the house *late* held by Lord Lisle in this town'.[13] In the service rooms, they made records of the number of table cloths in the ewery (there were 18), the number of leather cans in the pantry (10), the spits in the storehouse (2) and a moulding bowl in the still room. The contents of each garderobe and spare room was listed, with 66 pairs of sheets in the groom's chamber, the mother of pearl handles in the buttery, along with fish racks and wicker screens, then hangings, a Turkey carpet, a trestle, two benches and a table with a foot in the room designated as the nursery, which Honor had hoped to use three years earlier.[14] In her bedchamber, they counted her tapestries, listed her bedlinen and cushions, opened her chests and coffers to reveal the satin and velvet within, went into the room shared by Honor's daughters, with its red hangings, great bedstead and tin basins.

As a worse indignity, Honor had to leave behind the entire wardrobe and collection of jewellery that her letters reveal she was so proud of. For the woman who had been so particular about the correct type of cloth of silver, her lengths of velvet and the setting of her jewels, she was powerless to stop the men pulling out her personal effects for examination, rifling through her nightgowns and petticoats, laying hands upon her beads and cramp rings. In the chapel, where recently Frances and John Basset had been wed, no doubt they paid special attention to the cloth of gold, with its crimson panels.

But Sussex, Ringley and the others were not just recording the content of Honor's household. They were disbanding it. Henry FitzAlan, Lord Maltravers, had already been appointed Lieutenant in Arthur's place. Before Honor's eyes, the contents of her home were being designated to others, with Maltravers taking possession of the items in the chapel, save for the cloths that went to Thomas Scriven, Mayor of Calais, and a Mr Bennet, as well as vestments embroidered with stars and angels, and the chapel organ was sent to a Mr Portar.

Maltravers claimed the contents of the chaundry, spicery, ewery, buttery, pantry, cellar, kitchen, bakehouse, laundry and vault, clearly with an eye to him moving into the property. The wheat was given to William London, keeper of the Staple Inn, the fish divided between Sussex, Maltravers and Ringley, while some was left to feed Honor. Ringley also got some prunes and raisins from the spicery. The great Bible from Honor's chamber, perhaps the French version or the English one she had asked Husee for, was given to an Oliver Skinner, who also received various clothing items, a roll of silk went to a Thomas Meladye, the harness for Arthur's horse went to Ringley, and an archer's harness to Bayly's widow. From the stables, Sussex claimed a bay gelding and grey donkey, a velvet harness and saddle. Maltravers took a black donkey and grey gelding, while Ringley got two carts and horses and the rest, including a grey and white gelding, two velvet harnesses belonging to Honor, and another from Naples, went to George Gainsford. The wife of one Kinderdale, perhaps a Calais resident, received thirteen hens from Honor's poultry, while her great cages of quails, which had proved so popular with Queen Jane, were taken by Sussex.[15]

At this point, Honor may have also feared being summoned to England and sent to the Tower. She remembered well the fates of those innocents sent there in May 1536, but could have clung to hope concerning the releases of Thomas Wyatt and Richard Page. The day after the inventory of the Staple was complete, on 30 May, Marillac was reporting on the rumours that this may happen: 'since the imprisonment of Lord Lisle about 15 days ago ... it is commonly said that Lisle's wife has been sent for with some of the most prominent men of the town; but of this there is no appearance except the common bruit'.[16] A few days later, Marillac commented that George Carew, Captain of Rysebank Castle, had been questioned by Cromwell, after which he took a fever, so 'everyone thought he had been imprisoned, until, being cured, he came out of his lodging'.[17]

Honor and her daughters were also questioned about the nature of Mary's relationship with Gabriel de Montmorency. So far as Honor publicly admitted, there had been a proposal, but under duress, Mary admitted that she had contracted a secret marriage with Gabriel in the Staple on the evening of Palm Sunday. This might have been before a priest, or simply an exchange of vows, but any match between a Frenchman and the daughter of the Lord Deputy of Calais was problematic. Apparently, Mary had tried to throw some incriminating letters down the jakes (toilet) of the house in order to conceal evidence of her union, but some were found by the investigators. Under examination she admitted she had told her mother about the marriage, but did not know if Honor had told Arthur.[18] On 5 June, Sussex and Gage wrote to Cromwell that he had 'further examined Lady Lisle, her two daughters and Mary Hussey upon the matters of Lord and Lady Lisle, especially the letters cast into the jakes'. The entirety of the investigation centred upon Mary's marriage, with little to nothing concerning Arthur, and Sussex confiscated eight letters Arthur had written her since his departure to England, two letters from Anne Basset, letters from the jakes, and the one from Arthur to the Emperor.[19]

Honor was committed to the care of Francis Hall, 'a sad man and has a sober honest wife'(*sic*), along with a gentlewoman, chamberer and groom. Hall was a spear of Calais, who had previously asked Arthur to be godfather to his child.[20] John and Frances Basset went to England, and apparently Bridget Basset, 'to whom there is no matter laid', was in Calais, and would remain in the house 'til they hear what is to be done for her keeping'. Sussex also noted that the wages of the Lisles' 'poor servants who have served [them] so long' had not been paid that half year, so offered them the king's reward of barely a quarter's wages, which they accepted.[21] Two of the Lisles' servants, Jasper Castle and Symond Trildill, received 16s 8d each, while thirty-six other men were granted 13s 4d. A further seven men were recompensed at 10s, and five more at lesser amounts. A lackey received 4s 8d and the two kitchen lads each got 3s 4d. Two women, Mrs Durdaunt and Mrs Joyes, were recompensed with 10s and the laundress got 6s 8d – totally £32 9s 2d. Overall, the Lisle household had sustained fifty-six servants.[22]

The Lisles' servant, Thomas Larke, a Calais Vintner, was examined about letters exchanged by them before and since Arthur's absence. His answers make clear that he was also Honor's scribe, saying he had 'written several letters' for her since Arthur's departure, and named her other correspondents, including those relating to John Basset's inheritance and her properties in Devon and Cornwall. He had also read Arthur's letters to Honor, remembering that in every case, Arthur had 'desired his wife to be of good cheer' and telling her 'that the King was his gracious lord' and that Cromwell was 'his very friend'. He explained the question of Arthur's letter to the Emperor, which had roused suspicion, but was actually regarding horses owned by a man-at-arms in Calais, which had been detained in St Omer.[23]

Additionally, Maltravers reported something which may have been misguided bravado but sounded damning:

> *Yesterday Sir Edward Ringeley asked William Starkie, late yeoman of the chamber to lord Lisle, 'what he knew by the said lord Lisle'. He replied that the worst point that ever he knew was that while certain Frenchmen were lodging with him at the Staple Hall, after supper he opened the chest wherein the keys lie and showed them to the French men, saying, 'These be the keys of all the gates of this town'. Doubted what might be his meaning therein, and therefore informs the King.[24]*

Another, anonymous complaint written to Arthur at some point in 1538–9 gives a behind-the scenes glimpse of what may have turned some of the Lisles' former friends against them and the rumours and complaints that had dogged them for the last few years:

> *The last time I was with you at Calais, I came purposely to see the welfare of your Lordship and my Lady, and welcome you home out of England according to my duty, setting my own business apart. I expected better thanks than I had, for my Lady insinuated that I and my wife had thought scorn that she should do her service. This we never said or thought. I prayed her ladyship at that time, as I do now your Lordship, to have the matter tried before our faces. It grieved me most of all that your Lordship should think of us so. My Lady told me that she was well pleased she met me in another man's house, otherwise I should have known her mind further. I answered I hoped I had not offended her Ladyship to rail with me, but this I said unadvisedly. If my Lady report that I told her the same time that she should scold with me, I will make good by the Sacrament, no such words ever came out of my mouth.*[25]

Gathering accounts for his 1577 history, Raphael Holinshed repeats the popular rumour that Arthur's guilt stemmed from him being 'privy to a faction which some of his men had consented unto for the betraying of Calais to the French'. This was the most serious charge laid to Arthur, of which he appears to have been completely innocent, and opposed to in all his doings since his early days in service to the Crown. One thing that Arthur's life certainly demonstrates is his lifelong loyalty to Henry.

On 2 July, King Henry wrote to Sussex and Gage, thanking them for their diligence in Calais, 'where they were sent to appease the sedition likely to arise from diversity of opinion in religion'. He announced the formal transfer of the town to Maltravers 'in place of Lord Lisle, who, for his offences, still remains in ward'.[26] There was a glimmer of hope, though, as ten days after Arthur's death, Henry stated that he did not think his uncle's errors had been made out of malice,[27] but clearly there was the implication that he had erred. The king was determined to deal with the case himself, removing it from the hands of Cromwell and the council. In this, Arthur was far more fortunate that others who had been investigated in recent years, and those who would soon to be facing fresh charges. As yet, no charges were brought against Arthur, leaving all those concerned in limbo.

The days passed. Arthur was in the Tower, Honor in custody with Francis Hall, Philippa and Mary bestowed elsewhere in the town. The Staple was stripped of their personal effects and occupied by Lord Maltravers. Through religious differences, the failure to control Calais, Botolf and Damplip and the reports of their enemies, the once loved and trusted servants of Arthur's nephew had been utterly destroyed. What was Honor guilty of? Pride, superstition, force of character perhaps, but hardly the wickedness claimed by her detractors. Living, or rather continuing to exist, under such circumstances, it would be no surprise if Honor 'fell distraught of mind' as her detractor, John Foxe, later claimed.

Nineteen

A Question of Life or Death
1540–2

Eight days after the Lisles' household at the Staple was disbanded, Thomas Cromwell was arrested. Henry's most able minister, who had masterminded the dissolution of the monasteries and pursued religious reform, was unable to release the king from his undesired marriage to Anne of Cleves. Less than two months after he had been elevated to Earl of Essex, the net closed in around Cromwell at a council meeting in Westminster. Dramatic accounts describe him being stripped of the trappings of his offices, with the Duke of Norfolk pulling his St George's Collar from off his shoulders, telling him that traitors should not wear it, and the Earl of Southampton untying the Order of the Garter. Cromwell reputedly replied: 'this, then, is my reward for faithful service!' Arthur might have said the same. He would have been aware of the arrival of another such high-profile prisoner at the Tower on June 10.

A letter from Thomas Cranmer to Henry regarding Cromwell's arrest indicates the atmosphere of uncertainty at court. Expressing his 'amazement and grief', at the guilt of a man who 'cared for no man's displeasure' and was so 'vigilant to detect treason' in his service of the king, Cranmer was very sorrowful, because 'whom shall the King trust hereafter?'[1] Ironically, Cranmer had written a very similar letter about Anne Boleyn's guilt four years earlier. Since her trial, Henry's suspicions and accusations had intensified, drawing in the supposed Exeter plotters, the leaders of the Pilgrimage of Grace, and many others who would join Arthur in the Tower in 1540–1. Marillac rejoiced in Cromwell's fall, seeing him as the instrument of much suffering: 'who alone has been the cause of all the suspicions conceived against not only his friends, but his best servants',[2] which certainly would have included Arthur. The French man hoped that the absence of this 'wicked and unhappy instrument' would be to the 'common welfare of Church, nobles and people'. His correspondent, Anne de Montmorency, echoed the idea that Cromwell had set Henry 'against his good friends and allies and loyal servants'.[3]

From the Tower, Cromwell sent a letter very similar to that which Arthur might have composed, had he committed his sentiments to paper: 'I never in all my life thought to displease your Majesty; much less to do or say that thing which of itself is so high and abominable offence. Your Grace knows my accusers, God forgive them ... For your Majesty has been most bountiful to me, and more like a father than a master. I ask you mercy where I have offended... Acknowledges himself a miserable sinner towards God and the King, but never wilfully...Written with the quaking hand and most sorrowful heart of your most sorrowful subject, and most humble servant and prisoner, this Saturday at your Tower'.[4] In the meantime, Cromwell was interrogated by the Duke of Norfolk regarding the Cleves marriage, with Henry prolonging his life in the hopes that he would find the means of dissolving it, so that he might marry another of Norfolk's nieces, Catherine Howard.

Whilst maintaining outward appearances in his marriage to Anne of Cleves, Henry had kept his distance since conceiving a personal dislike of her appearance. It did not take long before his attention wandered to his new wife's household, in which Anne Basset served as a maid, giving rise to rumours that she might become his second wife. Although the Countess of Rutland attended Anne, when Honor had written on behalf of her daughter Katherine, she was told 'the king does not wish more maids to be taken in until some of those now with the Queen are preferred'.[5] Fortunately for the Basset girls, Henry's interest focused upon Catherine Howard, a teenager making her first court appearance who was flattered by his attentions. It was Honor's friend, and Katherine Basset's hostess, Eleanor, Countess of Rutland, who disabused Anne of Cleves over the state of her marriage, informing her that there must be more than a goodnight kiss in order for it to be consummated. Investigations were made into the match at length, with members of the court questioned, before Anne was asked to leave for Richmond on 24 July. On 6 August, she was informed that her marriage was invalid and that she would receive a settlement in line with her new status as the king's sister. After her initial shock, she was wise enough to accept it.

It is difficult to know how much information reached Honor, imprisoned in her room, overseen by Francis Hall. In the past, she had received regular updates from her correspondents about English affairs, especially the rise and fall of favourites and how the king fared. If she heard about Cromwell's fall and the rejection of Anne of Cleves, she may have taken it as indicative of the king's aggressive stance towards his enemies, and his ruthless desire to achieve his wishes. She may have heard of Gregory Botolf's impending release from prison at the end of June, with the proviso that 'if anyone could lay anything to his charge within eight days, he should be heard', otherwise Botolf was at liberty.[6] Francis Hall, Honor's keeper, may have heard this, listening out for information relating to the Lisles and Calais, and formerly having been devoted to his master and mistress. He certainly would have heard of Cromwell's execution, at the Tower on 28 July, and Henry's marriage to Catherine Howard the same day. This would have made her old friend Sir Edmund Howard Henry's new father-in-law, except he had died the previous year. Perhaps Hall informed Honor, or perhaps he chose not to, considering that it might alarm her about a similar sentence being passed for Arthur. Perhaps he received instructions not to pass letters on to the prisoner. Still confined within the Tower walls, Arthur could not avoid knowing that 'Thomas Cromwell, cloth carder', was beheaded on Tower Hill, and his head set upon a spike on London Bridge. A week later, Clement Philpot and Edmund Brindholme, formerly Arthur's chaplain, were hanged at Tyburn for their part in the Botolf conspiracy. The fear of sharing such a fate must have haunted Arthur every single day.

For a time, all was quiet. The summer months passed into autumn as Arthur, Honor and her daughters could do little but wait. By the time November arrived, Francis Hall was struggling to keep Honor in addition to his own family, writing to the Privy Council that he 'has had the Lady Lisle and three of her folk twenty-seven weeks and cannot, without help, longer maintain them'.[7] The council discussed the matter on 13 December, and granted Hall 26s 8d a week 'for [the] diet of Lady Lisle, one priest, and three persons, and the priest's wages', and paid for his expenses up to that point.[8] When the council met again, at Hampton Court in January, instructions issued for the payment of Hall included four additional women, which may have been Philippa and Mary Basset and their waiting women.[9] At least it is clear from this that Honor had company of her own, a priest to comfort her and the three waiting women who had initially accompanied her.

The council also set about investigating and settling the Lisles' debts. Sir Edward Ringley had managed to speak to all his creditors by February, save for John Maister of Sandwich and Hugh Gyles of Calais, and informed Henry that a 'good round sum' was owed to a goldsmith of Paris.[10] By the time March arrived, Arthur had been incarcerated for over nine months. Having expected to only be away for a brief period when he left Calais the previous April, he was running out of clothes. Again, the Privy Council discussed his needs, and instructed the king's tailor, John Malte, to make Arthur 'a large gown of damask furred with black cony' (rabbit) and nine other items. At the same time, clothes were also made for Arthur's imprisoned aunt Lady Salisbury, including 'a furred night gown, furred petticoat and worsted kirtle'.[11] By this point, Margaret Pole was aged 67 and had been incarcerated without trial for almost two and a half years.

In April 1541, Honor received the tragic news of the death of her eldest son, John Basset. When the news of Arthur's arrest reached England, John had hurried back to Calais and brought Frances and their two daughters back with him in June 1540. Now Frances was pregnant again, but John had fallen ill with some unknown malady. At the age of only 23, he made his will, 'whole and perfect of mind and memory but sick of my body'. He died three days later. Frances was his sole executrix, to whom he left all his goods, chattels and lands for the duration of her life. Eventually, the inheritance that Honor had been chasing for John passed to his posthumous son, born that October, whom Frances named Arthur after her father.

The year 1541 marked something of a cull among Henry's officials and relatives. While Arthur awaited his fate, he was joined by two other men who had held important positions of governance outside England. Sir John Wallop had been Lieutenant of the Calais Castle since before the Lisles arrived and ambassador to Paris since February 1540. He had formerly dwelled in Calais with his wife Elizabeth and had responded with enthusiasm to the news of Honor's pregnancy, hoping that the same may come to pass for him. In December, William Sandys, Baron Sandys, Captain of Guisnes, who had survived its swampy, malarial conditions, died at The Vyne, his imposing home in Hampshire that had once entertained Henry and Anne Boleyn. Wallop applied for the Guisnes role but just three weeks later, he was passed over in favour of William Howard, the new queen's relation, and cast into disgrace. Marillac wrote that Wallop was 'lodged in the Tower, accused of treason, and with him the Master Porter of Calais, so that it is presumed to be for the same cause for which the deputy, Lord Lisle, was arrested'.[12] It must have seemed to Arthur that fresh charges were to be brought against him, but nothing tangible materialised to accuse Wallop, save for vague statements about transgressions and forgetfulness; he was then 50 years of age. Questioned by the council, he made assertions similar to Arthur's – that he never had 'any evil mind or malicious purpose, but only ... wilfulness ... which he confessed had been in him' and he had 'meddled above his capacity and whereof he had no commission'.

Henry judged him to be 'a man unlearned' who did not intend to cloak his transgressions, and he was ultimately pardoned for his good service.[13]

The Countess of Salisbury did not receive such leniency. On the morning of 27 May, Margaret was informed that she was to be executed imminently. No charges were brought against her and she continued to deny any wrongdoing. The sentence was carried out at once, reputedly in a botched and agonising way, and the Plantagenet matriarch, Arthur's cousin and peer, was no more. Her death must have caused him distress and alarm. In addition to the lack of trial, it was not clear what had prompted this suddenly after such a long incarceration. It also set a fresh precedent for the removal of the king's relatives, with little regard for age, good character or royal blood.

At the end of June, Leonard Grey, Viscount Grane, Deputy of Ireland between 1536 and 1540, was also arrested and sent to the Tower. There was also a Basset connection. Honor's two stepdaughters from her first marriage, Anne and Thomasine, had lived in the household of Giles Daubeney, with the expectation of marriage to his son (later Lord Bridgewater) and inheritance of their mother's lands, which did not take place. This was the source of the inheritance that was due to John. After Giles' death, his widow Elizabeth, remarried to Grey. Reputedly, Grey had been involved in several massacres during his time in Ireland and was accused of murder, which he initially denied, as well as entertaining 'arrant traitors and rank papists'.[14] He was executed on 28 July, a year to the day after Cromwell. Alarmingly, though, it was thought his fate might hasten Arthur's. This was not just idle gossip repeated by a foreign ambassador; this time, newly appointed Clerk of the Parliamentarians, William Paget, wrote to Wriothesley, Earl of Southampton, that Grey 'shall be arraigned, and with him, the common saying is the Lord Lisle'. In the Star Chamber, he had found the councillors busy discussing another case, that of Thomas Fiennes, Lord Dacre, who was also convicted of murder and hanged at Tyburn at the end of June, but it meant the subject of 'Lord Lisle came not forth today'.[15] However, Paget added ominously, 'for the other prisoners in the Tower, if it is not this week, it will be the next, like poor lord Lisle, deputy of Calais'.[16]

Marillac recorded these deaths amid a swathe of others. A Master Neville, 'a gentleman well known in this Court, and of mediocre wit … for not revealing the conspiracy lately made in the North which one of the conspirators had disclosed to him'. Three men in the North of England, including two priests, were hung, drawn and quartered for treason; two archers of the guard died for robbery, another was condemned to lose his hand and pardoned at the last minute. Margaret's grandson, Henry Pole, was still incarcerated in the Tower, expecting death any day, although he would remain for the rest of his natural life. Against this backdrop of bloodshed and fear, Marillac also heard the rumour in June that the Lisles had been dreading: 'it is said also that Lord Lisle, Deputy of Calais … [is] in great danger of dying this week or the next',[17] although the following month, the ambassador was proved wrong, hearing that Arthur would 'be kept alive and has more freedom than formerly'. At this point, it was being rumoured that Arthur would 'remain prisoner for life in the Tower, where he is a little more at large than he was'. Marillac reported that 'some lords of this court have heard their master say the said Deputy offended more through simplicity and ignorance than malice'.[18] This contrasts with the view that was held in Europe, expressed in Strasbourg, that Arthur 'was imprisoned when Cromwell was condemned, and where he still awaits the King's pardon. At Calais he was a most grievous persecutor of the Gospel'.[19] It may have been seen as ominous, too, that accounts were made of Arthur's possessions and lands at this time, assessing how much each estate was worth, including his homelands in Devon, Frithelstock Priory, which Henry had granted him, and the Basset lands 'now in viscount Lisle's in right of his wife, Lady Honor': Umberleigh in Devon and Tehidy in Cornwall.[20] There certainly was a climate of suspicion, accusation and execution in the summer of 1541, fuelled by Henry's paranoia and failed communications. Arthur had survived over a year in the Tower, and Honor in her single room in Calais, but they knew they could take nothing for granted.

In mid-November, the Privy Council catered for Arthur and Honor again, about a year after Francis Hall's first request for assistance. Richard Pollard was charged to deliver £220 16s 4d to Hall 'out of receipts of Lord Lisle's lands, for expenses of the lady [blank] his wife'.[21] Richard Pollard was also charged to pay £14 10s for Arthur's board, but this was delivered to Sir Edmund Walsingham, the new Lieutenant of the Tower, as Arthur's friend, Sir William Kingston, had died the previous year.[22] At least Walsingham was known to Arthur, having been at the Field of Cloth of Gold in 1520, then also becoming a sewer in Henry's household.

The same month, information emerged about the private behaviour of new queen, Catherine Howard, before and after her marriage. Following investigation, Henry learned that Catherine had conducted relationships before marrying him, which was not a crime, but she had been mistaken not to disclose this, allowing him to believe she had come to his bed a virgin. Worse, though, through the summer progress of 1541, she had been privately meeting with Thomas Culpeper, with the assistance of her lady in waiting, Jane Rochford, formerly wife to George Boleyn. Catherine was arrested on 23 November and sent to Syon Abbey, while Lady Rochford went to the Tower. Again, Arthur is likely to have been aware of her presence and the rumours of her interrogations that led her to lose her mind.

In early December, it appears that Katherine Basset got into trouble at court for gossiping about Catherine Howard. Katherine's guardian, the Countess of Rutland, was the leading lady in Anne of Cleves' household, so her young ward was often with her, serving the German queen in the first half of 1540. This had established ties of loyalty, so that Katherine disapproved of Henry putting her aside and marrying Catherine Howard, whom she would have known. She was less than discreet, though, and an account in the State Letters and Papers shows that she was briefly arrested and questioned, along with a woman named Jane Rattsey, for interpreting Catherine Howard's fall as a sign of divine disapproval:

> *Jane Rattsey, examined of her words to Eliz. [sic] Bassett: 'What if God worketh this work to make the lady Anne of Cleves queen again?' says it was an idle saying suggested by Bassett's praising the lady Anne and dispraising the Queen that now is. Never spoke at any other time of the lady Anne, and she thinks the King's divorce from her good. Examined why she said, 'What a man is the King! How many wives will he have?' She said it upon the sudden tidings declared to her by Bassett, when she was sorry for the change and knew not so much as she knows now.*[23]

The misnaming of Katherine as Elizabeth is a little confusing here, although it has been accepted by many historians as a straightforward mistake. Anne Basset was also in Anne of Cleves' household, but had a warmer relationship with Henry, so is unlikely to have spoken of him critically and openly in such a way. If Katherine was indiscreet, and examined as a result, she was soon released. At least one family member was out of danger.

In December, Culpeper and Catherine's former lover, Francis Dereham, were executed at Tyburn, and their heads placed upon spikes above London Bridge. If Francis Hall or his wife were passing on news to Honor, she would have heard of the death of a young man with whom she had corresponded about innocent things such as spaniels, hawks and bracelets. Honor had probably never seen Catherine Howard, but Culpeper's death confirmed

Henry's utter ruthlessness in removing those who had betrayed him. Or those he perceived had betrayed him, as Dereham's crime had been to keep quiet about knowing Catherine in her younger days. Catherine and Lady Rochford were beheaded the following February.

1542 arrived without celebration for Honor or Arthur. No doubt Honor's greatest comfort was the presence of her chaplain after such a hard year, lacking in hope, full of loss. A Damocles' sword had hung constantly above her head, as she awaited the next piece of bad news, fearing the ultimate fate for her husband. Then, finally, there came a glimmer of hope. On 17 January, Marillac reported that 'the deputy of Calais, lord de Lisles [*sic*] who was made prisoner in the Tower two years ago, is going to have his pardon. The Order of the Garter is said to have been sent back to him, and indeed he has liberty within the Tower, where he used to have but one narrow chamber'.[24] Apocryphal stories from Gruffudd recount how Henry passed the Tower in a barge, travelling from York Place to Greenwich, whereupon Arthur 'raised his hands high, and shouted hoarsely from the Tower'. Hearing him, the king 'sent his secretary to the Tower to the Lord to show him the King had given him his pardon' and that he was to be released a few days later, with his possessions and offices restored.[25] Thomas Wriothesley was sent to deliver Arthur a ring from Henry, a 'rich diamond, for a token from him, and to tell him to be of good cheer'.[26] Holinshed claims that 'after due trial it was known that he was nothing guilty to the matter', but Arthur was never put on trial, rather, this means an examination of the evidence of the Privy or Royal Council.

Wriothesley's visit to Arthur was intended to reassure him and bring him hope of his freedom. Ironically, the 'such immoderate joy' that Arthur felt as the result of this news had the opposite effect: 'his heart being oppressed therewith, he died the night following through too much rejoicing'.[27] Just as Arthur was on the verge of being released and reunited with his wife, he suffered a fatal heart attack, dying on 3 March 1542. Marillac reported: 'Lord Lisle, formerly deputy of Calais, being out of trouble and his Order, honour and goods restored, died a few days afterwards'.[28] Arthur was buried in the Chapel of St Peter ad Vincula, in the grounds of the Tower of London, where Anne Boleyn lay, and where Catherine Howard had been placed only weeks before. Henry paid the costs of his funeral.

Twenty

Full Circle
1542–1566

Ninety miles to the west of Bideford, close by the mining village of Illogan, lies the great estate of Tehidy. High on the north Cornish coastland, it overlooks white sandy beaches that stretch out to wide waters where the Celtic Sea meets Atlantic currents. Today, the extensive countryside is open to the public, and the nearby holiday park attracts visitors to its peaceful, beautiful surroundings. A number of houses have stood on the site, from when the Bassets first acquired it in the twelfth century, rebuilt in 1498, through to the Palladian mansion of 1734, destroyed in a fire in 1919. It was restored on a smaller scale by 1922, operating as a hospital, before being sold off in the 1990s and converted into flats.

When Honor arrived at Tehidy in March 1542, it was a remote, quite place. The belts of woodland surrounding the house were filled with ash and oak, beech and chestnut trees, and the grounds were bright with bluebells and daffodils. The house that was to become her home for the remainder of her life had belonged to her first husband, Sir John Basset, bestowed upon her as part of her marriage jointure, a welcome retreat from all that she had suffered. It still bore the memories of her former life; the marks of conflicts that had become history as the Tudor dynasty emerged. This was the house that rebels had dismantled in 1497, out of revenge for John's loyalty to the Crown during the uprising in favour of Perkin Warbeck, and which John had carefully rebuilt in 1501. In recent years, Honor's brother-in-law, Thomas St Aubyn, second husband of her sister Mary, had watched over the house for her, sending her gifts of puffins caught on the rocky shoreline. Above the main door, the Basset coat of arms allowed her to retreat into the comfort and respectability of her former life, in a landscape that felt like home.

The events of March 1542 had turned on a knife's edge. Just as the Lisles were set to be reunited, to gather their family together and live out their days, perhaps at Soberton, Honor received the heartbreaking news of Arthur's death. She was not old by modern standards, at the age of forty-nine, but effectively, life as she knew it was now over. In the hours and days following, she processed that there would be no more marriage, no more visits to court, no more gifts sent to the king or queen, no more purchases of silver cloth or diamonds set in Bruges. The Privy Council wrote to Lord Maltravers in Calais instructing him to set Honor and her daughters at liberty, and to restore their clothes and jewellery. A clerk named Harry Simpson was given £100 for the payment of Honor's debts and her transportation to England.[1] Among Honor's returned clothing, she would have found something suitable for mourning: she had black satin lined with buckram, black velvet lined with white taffeta turned up with powered ermines, black velvet furred with miniver, or ermine, or lamb, and a black enamelled chain. Along with Philippa, Mary and Bridget, she walked through the streets of Calais for the last time, past the landmarks that had defined her life there; the marketplace, the church, the walls and the homes of various friends she had visited. Passing through the Lantern Gate, they took a ship to England, and crossed the choppy waters to Dover. The last time she had sight of the town had been upon her happy return home three years before, full of excitement at the impending reunion with her husband. Now, with her daughters, she made the long journey west to the tip of Cornwall.

Arthur's stepson, John Dudley, inherited the title of Lord Lisle, which had been entailed upon Arthur for the duration of his life, through his first wife. He was invested around the time of Honor's departure, on Sunday 12 March, at Westminster Palace and dined afterwards with the Lord Great Chamberlain, the Earl of Sussex, who had disbanded her household.[2] In time, Dudley would become Earl of Warwick, Duke of Northumberland and mastermind the succession of Lady Jane Grey that led to his downfall and execution. One of his sons, Robert Dudley, would become Elizabeth I's favourite.

Two years after Honor left Calais, Henry declared war on the French after Francis I gave assistance to the Scots. Calais was used as the base for the invasion, by which a huge fleet under the command of the Duke of Suffolk, laid siege to Boulogne. Through the last ten days of July and into August, the town's sea defences came under bombardment, until only the castle was isolated, surrendering on 13 September. The victory was short-lived, though. At the end of the month, a French army arrived, outnumbering the English, who retreated to Calais. The drama played out in the home of

Honor's friends, the Marshal of France since 1542, Oudart du Bies, his wife Jeanne and daughters Madeleine and Ysabeau. Later, Oudart was put on trial for supposedly deserting Boulogne, and sentenced to death, but he was eventually pardoned after a period of incarceration. Another casualty of the war with France was Henry's splendid ship, the *Mary Rose*, based in Portsmouth. Fifteen years earlier, Arthur had overseen repairs to it, and provisioned its sailors; now it sank in the Solent under French fire, taking with it Captain Roger Grenville, Honor's great-nephew and George Carew, Lieutenant of Calais' Rysbank Fort.

In Cornwall, Honor's daughters made marriages among the local gentry, many of whose families were known to her from her childhood. At some point in the mid-1540s, Philippa became the wife of James Pitts of Atherington,[3] a nearby parish that Honor had gained as part of her marriage settlement. The church of St Mary's Atherington, now houses the tomb of John Basset that Honor had ordered to be made for him, which was relocated in 1818 after the chapel at Umberleigh fell into disrepair. Around 1548, Philippa bore a son named Arthur. Mary Basset married John Wollacombe of Overcombe, on the south coast of Devon, and bore him eleven children, including a short-lived daughter named Honor. Frances Basset, John's widow, remarried to Thomas Monke of Potheridge, ten miles south of Bideford. Honor's other stepdaughters also found husbands, but in the east of the country, with Elizabeth becoming the wife of Sir Francis Jobson, MP for Colchester, and Bridget marrying a William Carden of Kent.

In 1543, Henry VIII married for the sixth and final time to Katherine Parr. Still at court, Anne Basset secured a position in the new queen's household and remained there until she outlived Henry in 1547. After that, she reappears as a lady-in-waiting to Henry's eldest daughter Mary, during which time she married Sir Walter Hungerford in 1554 at Richmond Palace. Mary bore two children and died in 1557, in her late thirties, perhaps as the result of childbirth. Katherine Basset remained with the Countess of Rutland until her marriage to Sir Henry Ashley of Kent, bearing at least one son.

Honor's two surviving sons had very different lives. The younger boy, James, entered the service of Bishop Stephen Gardiner, whom he served loyally all through Edward and Mary's reigns, despite Gardiner's fall in 1551. James visited the bishop during his time in the Tower, even sharing part of his confinement, before he was restored to favour under Elizabeth. James married Mary Roper, the granddaughter of Thomas More, and became a Gentleman of the Privy Chamber. Mary I's husband, Philip of

Spain, stood as godfather to James' first-born son, Philip Basset. Honor's middle son, George, lived at the Basset property of Umberleigh until his nephew Arthur, son of John, came of age. He married Jacquet, the daughter of John Coffin of Porthledge and had three children. They left Umberleigh in 1561/2 and moved to live with Honor at Tehidy.

In 1558, Calais fell to the French. When Mary I supported a Spanish invasion of France, as part of the next phase of the Italian Wars, France retaliated by laying siege to the town. Thomas Wentworth was then Lord Deputy, unable to withstand the three-part attack from 30,000 men. The English residents of the town were accompanied to boats the following day and sent back across the Channel. Mary I was devastated by the news, supposedly telling her ladies-in-waiting that when she was dead, they would cut her open and find Calais written upon her heart. Honor might have said the same.

Honor died in 1566 and was buried in Illogan Church on 30 April.[4] She was 73. The last twenty-four years of her life passed in a long, drawn-out silence after the frequency and detail of her letters. Like many maturer women who had outlived their men and experienced loss, such as former queen Elizabeth Woodville and Arthur's paternal grandmother Cecily Neville, she opted for a secluded life of devotion and contemplation. It is unlikely that she still wrote to London for velvets and furs, but perhaps the Honor who loved animals used to walk in the woods around Tehidy with pet dogs at her heels, and sit quietly to remember her loved ones in the estate chapel.

***

Honor's story encompassed intense highs and crashing lows. She had accomplished far more than was expected from a girl from her origins in Bideford, whose sisters made local marriages, and who might have remained forever in the West Country. The turning point in her life was meeting Arthur, which propelled her into the heart of the Tudor court at the moment when Anne Boleyn rose to power. As a result, Honor was witness to some of the most dramatic and transformative events of the sixteenth century, from Anne's coronation to the dismantling of centuries of Catholic practices. As a woman of her times, Honor had to find a fine balance between accepting these changes and reconciling them with her conscience. She rode high on the Boleyn wave initially, exchanging gifts and hospitality with both Anne and George, but her life in Calais put her at one remove from the intrigues that brought about their downfall.

If the fall of Anne Boleyn did not make Honor fear for her own future, Henry's series of accusations and executions in the following years must have been terrifying to behold. The king's increasing suspicion and paranoia, and his determination to rid himself of rivals and enemies saw the deaths of those formerly close to him, such as Thomas Cromwell, who had played such a significant role in Honor's life; Margaret Pole, Lady Salisbury and her Plantagenet family; Catherine Howard and Honor's correspondent Thomas Culpeper, to name the most prominent. The accusations against Arthur must be considered in this context, as well as that of the dissolution of the monasteries and continuing redefinition of heresy. As the earlier deaths of Thomas More and John Fisher prove, Henry was adamant to remove anyone who would not accept his new, self-appointed position as Supreme Head of the Church of England or who failed to conform to the changing, uncertain rules about religious practice.

The accusations against Arthur were building for several years prior to his arrest. The position he inherited in Calais was something of a poison chalice, coming at a time of the Staplers' debt, economic and material decline, and shifting relations with France. A number of criticisms about Arthur's management of Calais were ignited by instances of insurrection, with the arrival of reformist preachers and instances of resistance to change, as well as his good relations with local French dignitaries. This was unfortunate timing for Arthur. The final straw, though, came when his actions appeared to threaten the safety of Calais, with the Botolf plot and Arthur's lax security about French visitors to the town. These elements coincided with an intense period of Henry's suspicion, culminating in Arthur's arrest. As it happened though, Henry was eventually able to see that while his uncle might have been guilty of mismanagement, it was not done through malice. However, Arthur was also luckier than some, as Cromwell's case reveals. Ultimately, if Henry had wanted to execute Arthur, he would have done so.

The thorny question remains: what was Honor's contribution to her husband's arrest? Was she really the 'wicked' Lady Honor who persecuted reformists, as John Foxe later claimed, or was she simply concerned with the business of being Arthur's wife, unaware of the complexities of the situation, finding it difficult to adjust to the changes made to her lifetime's faith? The truth probably lies somewhere in between. Nothing about Honor's story suggests wickedness, and fortunately, Foxe's agenda is so transparent as to easily dismiss his more extreme claims. However, it appears that Honor was considered on several occasions to have overstepped the line, and interfered in Arthur's work, with advice, comments or suggestions, that were unacceptable certainly to men such as Cromwell. But the Lisles had a close marriage, confiding and dependent upon each other; Arthur would have been aware of Honor's opinions and feelings without requiring much verbal communication. It would have been impossible in such a loving union for him to have overlooked these, and they may have subtly influenced him. No doubt, there were also times that his wife spoke her mind.

It is in the question of religion that Honor may have unwillingly caused additional trouble. Of the two of them, it was her who was known for the 'superstitious' practices that can be found throughout her letters: pilgrimages, prayers for the dead, connections with monastic establishments, images, relics. As these ancient methods were called into question in the late 1530s, many English subjects struggled to accept what was, for them, a threat to their immortal souls. From the publicised executions of high-profile figures, to localised rebellions, and the cases of individuals questioned and punished for heresy, Honor was certainly not alone. Henry expected an entire country to abandon the beliefs that had been held by previous generations and the rites of passage that comforted them in their darkest hours. It was Honor's misfortune that she adapted slowly, cushioned by the High Catholicism of France, and that her marriage to a man questioned for his inability to enforce the new laws brought her name to prominence. Ultimately, it was religious change that caused the Lisles' downfall.

This does not mean in any sense that what happened to Arthur was Honor's fault. Had circumstances been different, she would have passed unnoticed. Had Damplip never come to Calais, or Gregory Botolf never entered the Lisles' service; had the residents of Calais accepted change more readily, or added pressure not come from European war, Honor and Arthur might have lived out their years in the town. Honor's life happened to coincide with circumstances that brought her to imprisonment in 1540. Many of these influences were out of her control, coming from wider tides of change throughout Europe. Yet she was not entirely a passive figure amid all this. There is a good chance that she contributed to Arthur's financial mismanagement by upholding the lifestyle that is seen in her letters. Her orders for clothing, jewels, saddles, wine and spices continued despite John Husee's embarrassed pleas for her creditors to be paid. Her ongoing engagement with the trappings of the Catholic Church appear to have been well-known enough to give her a reputation that was unhelpful at the least. Even her correspondent, Anthoinette de Saveuses, was cautious about sending gifts to England from a religious house.

Of course, all this is coloured by hindsight. Can Honor really be accused, in the late 1530s, of not foreseeing what lay ahead? She was living a lifestyle commensurate with her position, and was certainly not the only nobleman's wife to accrue debts in maintaining her appearance or table. Status and security in the sixteenth century often depended upon looking the part, and Honor was the first lady of Calais, the gateway to England, entertaining royalty and foreign dignitaries. She had to put on the show that Henry expected, for which her precedent was his visit in 1532. Additionally, she was worshiping in the manner she had been raised all her life, and like many others, was torn between her beliefs and her loyalty to the king, which had every appearance of imperilling her soul. Calais itself was at one remove from the realities of court life; Honor was not present to witness the fall of Anne Boleyn, or the execution of the Carthusian monks, or the destruction of Thomas Becket's shrine. At a distance, it is easy to believe ourselves safe from harm, that such things will never happen to us.

The forces that brought the Lisles down were bigger than any gown Honor bought, or any pilgrimage she undertook. She might have been a little wiser, perhaps, a little more frugal, but then so might we all. Honor fulfilled the role that was expected of her in challenging times, and she was the victim of political and religious forces determined to seek out enemies. Ultimately, while Arthur may have spent two years in the Tower, his death was of natural causes. He did not go to the block, watched by jeering crowds, or suffer the attainder that would strip his loved ones of dignity and assets. Honor was able to retire in peace and watch her grandchildren grow up. It might have been a difficult old age, filled with regrets and memories, but Honor Plantagenet was one of the great Tudor survivors.

Notes

Introduction

1. Foxe, John, *History of the Acts and Monuments of the Church.* London, 1563.
2. Granville, Roger, *The History of the Granville Family.* W. Pollard and Co, Exeter, 1895.
3. Ibid.
4. Sandeman, G.A.C., *Calais Under English Rule.* Oxford, 1908.
5. Byrne, Muriel St Clare (ed.), *Lisle Letters,* 6 Vols. University of Chicago Press, 1981.

ONE: Heritage, Birth and Childhood, 1493–1513

1. Watkins, John, *An Essay Towards a History of Bideford.* E. Grigg, Exeter, 1792.
2. Twelmow, J.A. (ed.), *Calendar of Papal Registers relating to Great Britain and Ireland*, Volume 11, 1455–1463. HMSO, London, 1921; (499; 1459), pp.525–549.
3. Watkins, *An Essay Towards a History of Bideford.*
4. *London Quarterly Review,* Volume C1 January–April 1857. Leonard Scott, New York, 1857.
5. Isabel's date of death is listed as 2 February, or before 2 February 1494, on various genealogical and family research sites, including Geni, Find a Grave, Ancestry, My Heritage, Genealogi Online, Werelate and Geneanet, but it is impossible to verify using primary sources.
6. Granville, Roger, *The History of the Granville Family.* W. Pollard, Exeter, 1895.

7. Contemporary spellings of Grenville from the State Letters and Papers of Henry VIII include Granville, Greynfeld, Grenefeld, Graynvile, Grenvile, Greneville and Granyfeld.

8. Campell, William, Rev. (ed.), *Materials for a History of the Reign of Henry VII*, Volume 1. Longman and Trubner, London; Parker, Oxford; Macmillan, Cambridge; A C Black, Edinburgh; A Thom, Dublin, 1873.

9. Ibid.

10. Myers, A.R. (ed.), *Liber Niger Domus Regie Angliae Edward IV*. Manchester, 1959.

11. Hall, Edward, *Hall's Chronicle*. J. Johnson, 1809.

12. Leland, John, *The Itinerary of John Leland in or about the years 1535– 43,* Lucy Toulmin Smith (ed.). George Bell & Sons, London, 1907.

13. Ibid.

14. Watkins, *An Essay Towards a History of Bideford*.

15. Byrne, *Lisle Letters*.

16. de la Tour Landry, Geoffroy. *The Book of the Knight of La Tour-Landry*. William Caxton, London, 1484.

17. Vives, Juan Luis, *The Education of a Christian Woman*. 1523

18. Byrne, *Lisle Letters*.

19. SLP Volume 1, Appendix: Commissions of the Peace and Miscellaneous, J. S. Brewer (ed.). HMSO, London 1876, pp.1533–1537.

20. Ibid., (52), pp.425–435.

21. Ibid., 1509–1514, February 1513 (4377), pp.739–759.

22. See Appendix 1 for the complete will.

23. Ibid.

24. Granville, Roger, Rev. *The History of the Granville Family*. William Pollard, Exeter, 1895.

TWO: Lady Basset, 1513-1529

1. *Calendar of State Papers Milan,* Volume I, Allen B Hinds (ed.). London, 1912, (552), pp.310–341.

2. Rose, Susan, *England's Medieval Navy 1066–1509*. Seaforth Publishing, 2013.

3. www.englandsimmigrants.com/

4. Ibid.

5. Ibid.

6. The exception being Honor's great-great-grandfather John, who married Margaret Burghersh from Ewelme, Oxfordshire, in around 1391.
7. SLP Volume 1, 1509–1514, J. S. Brewer (ed.). HMSO, London 1867, (632, part 26), pp.347–359.
8. Ibid., Appendix: Commissions for the Peace and Miscellaneous (33), pp.1533–1557.
9. www.cothaymanor.co.uk/gardens/.
10. Lysons, Daniel and Lysons, Samuel, *Magna Britannia,* Volume VI. Devonshire, Thomas Cadell, London, 1822.
11. Risdon, Tristram, *The Chorographical Description or Survey of the County of Devon* (*c.*1630). Rees and Curtis, Plymouth, 1811.
12. Landry, *The Book of the Knight of La Tour-Landry.*
13. Byrne, *Lisle Letters,* Volume I. University of Chicago Press, 1981, p.308.
14. SLP Volume 2, 1515–1518, (625), pp.162–174.
15. Ibid., (3485), pp.1102–1114.
16. Ibid., (3783), pp.1183–1198.
17. SLP Volume 3, 1519–1523, (703), pp.231–249.
18. The record does not specify whether this is John Arundell of Trerice or of Lanherne, but it is more likely to have been Trerice.
19. *Rutland Papers: Original Documents Illustrative of the Courts and Times of Henry VII and Henry VIII.* Camden Society, J.B. Nichols (ed.), 1842.
20. Ibid.
21. Licence, Amy, *1520: The Field of the Cloth of Gold.* Amberley, 2020.
22. SLP Volume 3, 1519–1523, (1081), pp.382–398.
23. Ibid., (1379), pp.541–553.
24. Ibid., (2415), pp.1001–1120.
25. Ibid., (3504), pp.1453–1472.
26. Ibid., (3583), pp.1472–1492.
27. SLP Volume 4, 1524–30, J.S. Brewer (ed.). HMSO, London 1875, (819), pp.356–372.
28. Ibid., (2672), pp.1166–1184.
29. Ibid., (137, part 18), pp.41–58.
30. Ibid., (547), pp.232–251.
31. Ibid., (3008, part 23), pp.1333–1352.
32. Byrne, *Lisle Letters,* p.314.
33. SLP Volume 4, (5510, part 21), pp.2427–2437.

34. SLP Volume 6, (1449), pp.578–591.
35. SLP Volume 7, (566), pp.217–236.
36. Ibid., (1009), pp.380–385.

THREE: Lady Lisle, 1529–32

1. SLP Volume 4, (15), pp.5510–6075.
2. SLP Volume 2, pp.1458–63.
3. Ibid., pp.1481–90, footnote 6.
4. *Victoria County History of Hampshire*, Volume 3. William Page (ed.), London, 1908.
5. SLP Volume 3, (812), pp.274–285.
6. SLP Volume 4, (1021), pp.443–459.
7. Ibid., (1990), pp.892–903.
8. Ibid., (2751), pp.1212–1232.
9. Ibid., (3717), pp.1431–1446.
10. SLP Volume 6, June 1533, pp.262–275.
11. *Victoria County History of Hampshire,* Volume 3. William Page (ed.), London, 1908.
12. SLP Volume 4, (6456), pp.2883–2902.
13. SLP Volume 6, (14; 15), pp.262–275.
14. SLP Volume 11, (1344), pp.520–541.
15. Hall, *Hall's Chronicle.*
16. Ibid.
17. SLP Volume 5, (24), pp.10–22.
18. SLP Volume 5, pp.747–762.
19. Ibid., Treasurer of the Chamber's Accounts.
20. SLP Volume 5, pp.747–762.
21. Ibid., (961), pp.440–459.

FOUR: Calais and Ceremony, 1532–3

1. Hall, *Hall's Chronicle.*
2. SLP Volume 5, pp.763–777, appendix 33.
3. Ibid.
4. SLP Volume 5, (1555), pp.650–669.
5. Hall, *Hall's Chronicle.*

6. Calton, Robert, *Annals and Legends of Calais*. J.R. Smith, 1852.
7. SLP Volume 5, pp.747–62.
8. Ibid.
9. Ibid.
10. Ibid.
11. Ibid.
12. Ibid.
13. Ibid.
14. Calton, *Annals and Legends of Calais*.
15. Harleian MS 283, p.31.
16. Hall, *Hall's Chronicle*.
17. Ibid.
18. Ibid.
19. SLP Volume 5, pp.747-64.
20. Hall, *Hall's Chronicle*.
21. SLP Volume 5, pp.747–64.
22. Ibid., (1570), pp.650–669.
23. Ibid.

FIVE: The New Constable's Wife, 1533

1. Bernard, G.W., 'Thomas Cromwell and Calais'. Southampton University Website, August, 2007.
2. SLP Volume 6, (238), pp.45–56.
3. Ibid.
4. *Testament Vetusta.*
5. Ibid.
6. SLP Volume 6, (239), pp.99–115.
7. Ibid., (243).
8. Ibid., (584), pp.262–275.
9. Ibid., (584).
10. Hall, *Hall's Chronicle*.
11. Ibid.

SIX: The Calais Inheritance: People and Places, 1533

1. Calton, *Annals and Legends of Calais*.
2. SLP Volume 6, (277), pp.121–144.

3. Ibid.

4. SLP Volume 5, (336), pp.140–145.

5. Ibid.

6. Ibid.

7. Ibid.

8. SLP Volume 7, (652), pp.247–259.

9. Calton, *Annals and Legends of Calais.*

10. SLP Volume 6, (1181), pp.481–496.

11. Calton, *Annals and Legends of Calais.*

12. Ibid.

13. SLP Volume 6, (1026), pp.432–449.

14. SLP Volume 12, (555), pp.209–228.

15. SLP Volume 13, (841), pp.308–353.

16. Wood, Mary Anne Everett, *Letters of Royal and Illustrious Ladies,* Volume 3. Henry Colburn, London, 1846.

17. Levin, Carole; Bertolet, Anna Riehl; and Carney, Jo Elridge, *A Biographical Encyclopaedia of Early Modern Englishwomen.* Routledge, 2017.

18. SLP Volume 6, (948), pp.404–418.

19. SLP Volume 7, (733), pp.277–294.

20. Ibid., (1523), pp.569–576.

21. Ibid., (1362), pp.516–529.

22. SLP Volume 6, (719), pp.313–334.

23. Ibid., (263), pp.284–295.

24. Ibid., (1134), pp.466–477.

SEVEN: Finding Solutions, 1533-4

1. SLP Volume 6, (678), pp.306–313.

2. Ibid., (706), pp.313–334.

3. Ibid., (1027), pp.432–449.

4. SLP Volume 7, (5), pp.1–4.

5. SLP Volume 6, (1028), pp.432–449.

6. Ibid., (1064), pp.449–466.

7. Ibid., (834), pp.352–370.

8. Ibid., (930), pp.404–418.

9. Byrne, *Lisle Letters*, pp.62–5.

10. James, Susan E., *The Feminine Dynamic in English Art 1485–1603: Women as Consumers, Patrons and Painters.* Taylor and Francis, 2017.

11. Byrne, *Lisle Letters*, p.83
12. SLP Volume 6, (665), pp.295–305.
13. Byrne, *Lisle* Letters, p.86.
14. SLP Volume 7, (1053), pp.407–412.
15. Ibid., (1150), pp.1450–1453.
16. Ibid., (1154), pp.481–496.
17. Ibid., (931), pp.404–418.
18. Ibid., (1146), pp.477–481.
19. SLP Volume 7, pp.277–294.
20. Ibid., pp.311–317.
21. Ibid., (1112), pp.421–433.
22. Ibid., (443), pp.183–88.
23. Ibid., (1243), pp.478–482.
24. Ibid.
25. Ibid., (683), pp.306–313.
26. Ibid., (609), pp.236–241.
27. Ibid., (566), pp.236–241.
28. Ibid., (780), pp.352–370.
29. SLP Volume 6, (959), pp.404–418.
30. SLP Volume 7, (105), pp.38–61.
31. Ibid., (811), pp.305–310.
32. SLP Volume 6, (1434), pp.539–545.
33. Ibid., (1512), pp.565–569.
34. Ibid., (555), pp.217–236.

EIGHT: Court News, 1534–5

1. SLP Volume 7, (24), pp.12–16.
2. Ibid.
3. Ibid., (37), pp.16–30.
4. Ibid.
5. Ibid., (228), pp.85–91.
6. Ibid., (324), pp.126–135.
7. Ibid., (304, 324), pp.126–135.
8. Ibid., (522), pp.199–210.
9. Byrne, *Lisle Letters*, p.118.
10. SLP Volume 7, (1004,), pp.418–432.
11. Byrne 126

12. SLP Volume 7 pp.12–16 5
13. Byrne, *Lisle Letters*, p.129.
14. Ibid., p.41.
15. Ibid.
16. SLP Volume 7, (509), pp.199–210.
17. Ibid.
18. Ibid., (556), pp.217–210.
19. Ibid., (613), pp.236–241.
20. Ibid.
21. Ibid., (505), pp.199–210.
22. Ibid., (436), pp.177–183.
23. Ibid., (780), pp.294–305.
24. Ibid., (823), pp.311–317.
25. Ibid., (876), pp.322–325.
26. Ibid., (845), pp.311–317.
27. Ibid., (824), pp.311–317.
28. Ibid., (620), pp.241–247.
29. Ibid., (627).
30. Byrne, *Lisle Letters*, p.182.
31. Ibid.
32. SLP Volume 7, (461), pp.188–199.
33. Ibid., (501), pp.199–210.
34. Ibid.
35. Ibid., (349), pp.140–145.
36. SLP Volume 8, (434), pp.161–187.
37. SLP Volume 7, (766, 774), pp.294–305.
38. Ibid., (1190), pp.457–462.

NINE: Embroidery and Spices, 1534–5

1. SLP Volume 7, (25), pp.12–16.
2. Ibid., (428), pp.177–183.
3. Byrne, *Lisle Letters*, p.105.
4. SLP Volume 7, (503), pp.199–210.
5. Ibid., (978), pp.373–377.
6. Ibid., (987), pp.377–380.
7. Ibid., (989).
8. Ibid., (1015), pp.385–401.

9. Ibid., (1582), pp.589–599.
10. Ibid., (979), pp.373–377.
11. Ibid., (1461), pp.545–550.
12. SLP Volume 8, (378), pp.149–161.
13. Ibid., (545), pp.202–218.
14. Ibid., (657), pp.242–262.
15. Ibid., (416), pp.149–61.
16. Byrne, *Lisle Letters*, p.135.
17. SLP Volume 7, (1164), pp.453–457.
18. SLP Volume 8, (191), pp.68–85.
19. Ibid., (274), pp.114–126.
20. SLP Volume 7, (1163), pp.453–457.
21. SLP Volume 9, (679), pp.218–231.
22. Ibid., (857), pp.271–288.
23. Ibid., (857, 858).
24. Byrne, *Lisle Letters*, p.135.
25. SLP Volume 7, (307), pp.126–135.
26. Byrne, *Lisle Letters*, p.250–1.
27. Ibid., p.251.
28. SLP Volume 7, 1275, pp.487–493.
29. Byrne, *Lisle Letters*, p.138–9.
30. Ibid., p.255.
31. Ibid., p.146.
32. SLP Volume 8, (702), pp.262–277.
33. Ibid., (703).
34. Ibid., (709).
35. SLP Volume 9, (768), pp.248–262.
36. Ibid., (70), pp.19–40.
37. Ibid., (715), pp.231–248.
38. SLP Volume 7, (37), pp.16–30.
39. Ibid., (176), pp.68–85.
40. Ibid., (954), pp.363–373.
41. Ibid., (977), pp.373–377.
42. Ibid., (1542), pp.569–567.
43. Ibid., (909), pp.326–357.
44. SLP Volume 9, (266), pp.81–96.
45. Ibid., (377), pp.114–133.
46. Byrne, *Lisle Letters*, p.107.
47. Ibid.

48. SLP Volume 8, (1080), pp.419–421.
49. Ibid., (422), pp.161–187.
50. SLP Volume 9, (928), pp.356–379.
51. Ibid., (612), pp.195–212.
52. Byrne, *Lisle Letters*, p.196.
53. SLP Volume 7, (588), pp.217–236.
54. SLP Volume 8, (419), pp.161–187.
55. Ibid., (1248), pp.478–482.
56. Ibid., (353), pp.124–149.
57. Ibid., (423), pp.161–187.
58. Ibid., (544), pp.202–218.
59. Ibid., (1084), pp. 423–434.
60. SLP Volume 7, (228), pp.85–91.
61. Ibid., (92), pp.30–36.
62. Ibid., (1404), pp.475–478.
63. Byrne, *Lisle Letters*, p.105.
64. SLP Volume 8, (706), pp.262–277.
65. Ibid., (353), pp.124–149.
66. SLP Volume 9, (924), pp.310–318.
67. Ibid., (1004), pp.340–350.
68. SLP Volume 10, (136), pp.38–47.
69. Ibid., (33), pp.12–26.
70. SLP Volume 8, (1192), pp.462–475.
71. SLP Volume 9, (738), pp.248–262.
72. SLP Volume 8, (1448), pp.539–545.
73. SLP Volume 9, (625), pp.195-218.
74. SLP Volume 8, (530), pp.188–202.
75. Ibid., (670), pp.242–262.
76. Ibid., (1017), pp.379–402.
77. SLP Volume 9, (584), pp.181–195.
78. SLP Volume 8, (443), pp.161–187.
79. Ibid., (444).
80. Ibid., (489), pp.188–202.

TEN: Heresies and Reform, Summer 1535

1. SLP Volume 9, (996), pp.318–340.
2. SLP Volume 8, (324), pp.539–545.

3. SLP Volume 9, (531), pp.202–218.
4. Ibid., (530).
5. Duffy, Eamon, *Stripping the Altars.* Yale University Press, 1992.
6. Sandeman, G.A.C., *Calais Under English Rule.* Oxford, 1908,
7. SLP Volume 8, (458), pp.161–187.
8. Calton, *Annals and Legends of Calais.*
9. SLP Volume 8, (437), pp.161, 187.
10. Ibid., (435).
11. https://discovery.nationalarchives.gov.uk/details/record?catid=4248327&catln=6.
12. SLP Volume 8, (829), pp.305–325.
13. Ibid., (607), pp.218–241.
14. Ibid.
15. Ibid.
16. Ibid., (791), pp.287–305.
17. Ibid.
18. Ibid., (568), pp.202–218.
19. Ibid., (663), pp.242–262.
20. Ibid., (771), pp.287–305.
21. Ibid.
22. Ibid.
23. SLP Volume 9, (812), pp.271–288.
24. Ibid.
25. SLP Volume 8, (888), pp.345–356.
26. Ibid., (921), pp.356–379.
27. Ibid., (605), pp.218–241.
28. Ibid., (884), pp.345–356.
29. SLP Volume 9, (890), pp.288–310.
30. SLP Volume 8, (794), pp.287–305.
31. Ibid., (902), pp.345–356.
32. Ibid., (997), pp.379–402.
33. Ibid.
34. Ibid., (931), pp.356–379.

ELEVEN: The Lisles at Home, Early 1536

1. Dating according to Bryne.
2. SLP Volume 15, (852, 853), pp.412–436.

3. Ibid.

4. Ibid.

5. Ibid.

6. Turpyn, Richard, *The Chronicle of Calais*. John Gough Nichols, 1846.

7. SLP Volume 15, (852, 853), pp.412–436.

8. Ibid.

9. SLP Volume 11, Miscellaneous 7.

10. SLP Volume 15, (853), pp.412–436.

11. Byrne, *Lisle Letters*, p.108.

12. SLP Volume 15, (853), pp.412–436.

13. SLP Volume 10, (68), pp.12–26.

14. Ibid., (454), pp.182–195.

15. Ibid.

16. Ibid., (455).

17. Ibid., (465), pp.182–195.

18. Ibid., (502), pp.205–217.

19. Parish, Helen, '"Multe etiam alie reliquie quorum scripta desunt": the migration of relics in Reformation England', *Reading Medieval Studies*, 45, (2019), pp.133–150.

20. Ibid.

21. SLP Volume 10, (292), pp.114–129.

22. Ibid., (337), pp.130–138.

23. Ibid., (465), pp.182–195.

24. Ibid., (466).

25. Ibid., (467).

26. Ibid., (543), pp.205–217.

27. Ibid., (544)

28. Ibid., (193), pp.64–81.

29. Ibid., pp.126–135, grants.

30. Ibid., (69).

31. Ibid., (122), pp.38–47.

32. Ibid., (332), pp.108–126.

33. Ibid., (377), pp.126–135.

34. Ibid., (336).

35. Ibid., (487), pp.195–205.

36. Ibid., (499).

37. Ibid., (608), pp.240–259.

38. Ibid., (445), pp.161–181.

39. Ibid., (673), pp.275–287.

40. Ibid., (445), pp.161–181.
41. Ibid., (210), pp.64–81.
42. SLP Volume 11, (1264), pp.514–520.
43. SLP Volume 10, (325), pp.108–126.
44. Ibid., (631), pp.240–259.
45. Ibid., (134), pp.38–47.
46. Ibid., (425), pp.161–181.
47. Ibid., (446).
48. Ibid., (486), pp.195–205.
49. Ibid., (493).
50. Ibid.
51. Ibid., (539), pp.205–217.
52. Ibid., (465), pp.182–195.
53. SLP Volume 12, (376), pp.154–198.
54. Ibid., Miscellaneous 7.

TWELVE: Thunder Round the Throne, 1536

1. Wood, Mary Anne Everett, *Letters of Royal and Illustrious Ladies*, Volume 3. Henry Colburn, London, 1846.
2. SLP Volume 10, (650), pp.259–274.
3. Ibid., (669).
4. Ibid.
5. Ibid., (673), pp.275–287.
6. Ibid., (675).
7. Ibid., (708), pp.287–310.
8. Ibid., (738), pp.310–329.
9. Ibid., (747).
10. Ibid., (748).
11. Ibid., (789), pp.329–349.
12. Ibid., (789).
13. Byrne, *Lisle Letters*, p.214.
14. Ibid., pp.214, 215.
15. Turpyn, *The Chronicle of Calais*.
16. Ibid.
17. SLP Volume 10, (837), pp.329–349.
18. Ibid., (845).
19. Ibid., (855), pp.349–371.

20. Ibid., (865).
21. Ibid., (953), pp.391–401.
22. Ibid., (866), pp.349–371.
23. SLP Volume 11, (107), pp.46–54.
24. SLP Volume 10, (918), pp.371–391.
25. Ibid., (952), pp.391–401.
26. Ibid., (1000), pp.402–420.
27. SLP Volume 11, (108), pp.46–54.
28. Ibid., (264), pp.103–114.
29. Ibid., pp.263–283, grants 3.
30. Ibid., (943), pp.391–401.
31. Ibid., (994), pp.402–420.
32. Ibid., (964), pp.391–401.
33. Byrne, *Lisle Letters*, p.262.
34. Ibid., p.26.3
35. SLP Volume 10, (1165), pp.470–91.

THIRTEEN: Pregnancies, 1537

1. SLP Volume 11, (1191), pp.468–491.
2. Ibid., (1202).
3. Ibid., (1360), pp.541–547.
4. SLP Volume 12, (637), pp.295–305.
5. SLP Volume 11, (1181), pp.468–491.
6. Byrne, *Lisle Letters*, p.299.
7. SLP Volume 12, (272), pp.111–121.
8. SLP Volume 11, (1256), pp.514–520.
9. Ibid., (1274).
10. Ibid., (1256), pp.492–513.
11. Ibid., (1282), pp.520–541.
12. SLP Volume 12, (23), pp.1–16.
13. SLP Volume 11, (1320), pp.520–541.
14. Ibid., (1303).
15. SLP Volume 12, (61), pp.16–30.
16. SLP Volume 11, (1342), pp.520–541.
17. Ibid., Miscellaneous 8.
18. SLP Volume 12, (196), pp.78–112.
19. Ibid., (241).

20. Ibid., (329), pp.144–154.
21. Ibid., (354), pp.154–198.
22. Ibid.
23. Bryne, *Lisle Letters*, p.308.
24. SLP Volume 12, (450), pp.210–255.
25. Ibid., (547), pp.254–267.
26. Ibid., (634), pp.281–292.
27. Ibid., (586), pp.268–281.
28. Bryne, *Lisle Letters*, p.299.
29. Ibid., p.209.
30. SLP Volume 12, (555), pp.254–267.
31. Bryne, *Lisle Letters*, p.264.
32. Ibid., p.265.
33. Ibid.
34. Ibid., p.267.
35. Ibid., p.268.
36. Ibid., p.269.
37. Ibid., pp.269–270.
38. SLP Volume 15, (39), Addenda, pp.510–568.
39. SLP Volume 12, (467), no. 2, pp.181–191.
40. Bryne, *Lisle Letters*, p.310.
41. Ibid., p.311.
42. SLP Volume 12, (654), no. 2, pp.228–245.
43. SLP Volume 15, (36), Addenda, pp.510–568.
44. SLP Volume 13, (539), pp.193–207.
45. Ibid.
46. SLP Volume 12, (615), no. 2, pp.209–228.
47. SLP Volume 15, (809), pp.376–412.
48. SLP Volume 12, (711), no. 2, pp.245–262,
49. Ibid., (900), pp.309–324.
50. Ibid., (731), pp.263–283.
51. Ibid., (658, 686), pp.245–262.
52. Byrne, *Lisle Letters*, p.271.
53. SLP Volume 2, (861), no. 2, pp.295–309.
54. Byrne, *Lisle Letters*, p.272.
55. Ibid., p.271.
56. SLP Volume 12, (923), no. 2, pp.324–335.
57. SLP Volume 13, (92), pp.20–40.
58. Ibid., (696), pp.260–276.

59. Ibid., (179), pp.50–60.
60. Ibid., (277), pp.76–88.
61. Ibid.
62. Ibid., pp.50–60.
63. Ibid., (163).
64. Ibid., (457), pp.157–176.
65. Ibid., (732), pp.277–291.

FOURTEEN: Shrines and Sacraments, 1538

1. SLP Volume 13, part 1, (342), pp.108–123.
2. Ibid., (836), pp.301–311.
3. Ibid., (884), pp.311–333.
4. Ibid., (514), pp.193–207; (564, 580), pp.207–223.
5. Ibid., (996), pp.354–372.
6. Ibid.
7. Ibid., (936), pp.345–354.
8. Ibid.
9. Ibid.
10. Ibid., (1031), pp.372–383.
11. Sandeman, *Calais Under English Rule.*
12. Ibid.
13. SLP Volume 13, part 1, (510), pp.176–192.
14. Byrne, *Lisle Letters*, p.387.
15. Foxe, *History of the Acts and Monuments of the Church.*
16. SLP Volume 14, (1219), pp.545–554.
17. Ibid., (1086), pp.494–502.
18. SLP Volume 13, part 1, (1386), pp.492–507.
19. Ibid., (1291), pp.464–491.
20. Bernard, 'Thomas Cromwell and Calais'.
21. Ibid.
22. Duffy, *Stripping the Altars.*
23. SLP Volume 13, part 1, (1387), pp.513–525.
24. Ibid., (1388).
25. Ibid., (491), pp.464–491.
26. Ibid.
27. Ibid.

28. Ibid., (1464), pp.540–561.
29. SLP Volume 13, part 2, (277), pp.75–101.
30. Foxe, *History of the Acts and Monuments of the Church.*
31. SLP Volume 13, part 2, (523), pp.194–211.
32. Ibid., (248), pp.75–101.
33. Ibid., (897), pp.369–378.
34. Ibid., (390), pp.141–154.
35. Ibid., (296), pp.116–126.
36. Ibid., (302).
37. Ibid., (317).
38. Butler, Derek, *The Quest for Becket's Bones.* Yale University Press, 1995.
39. Ibid.
40. SLP Volume 15, (809), pp.376–412.
41. Aston, Margaret, *Broken Idols of the English Reformation.* Cambridge, 2015.
42. SLP Volume 13, part 2, (623), pp.239–253.
43. Ibid.

FIFTEEN: Mine Own Sweetheart, November 1538

1. SLP Volume 13, part 2, (788), pp.296–308.
2. Ibid., (1065), pp.438–55.
3. Ibid., (773), pp.296–308.
4. Ibid., (774).
5. Ibid.
6. The Agas Map of London: https://mapoflondon.uvic.ca/map.htm.
7. SLP Volume 13, part 2, (780), pp.296–308.
8. Ibid., (833), pp.308–353.
9. Ibid.
10. Ibid., (884), pp.369–378.
11. Ibid., (841), pp.308–353.
12. Ibid., (841).
13. Ibid., (798).
14. Ibid., (850), pp.353–369.
15. Ibid.
16. Ibid.
17. Ibid., (848).

18. Ibid., (862).
19. Ibid., (878), pp.353–369.
20. Ibid., (870), pp.353–369.
21. Ibid., (871).
22. National Archives Prob 11/27/582.
23. SLP Volume 13, part 2, (894), pp.369–378.
24. Ibid., (884).
25. Ibid., (942), pp.378–409.
26. Ibid.
27. Ibid., (981), pp.409–426.
28. Ibid., (942), pp.378–409.
29. Ibid., (898), pp.369–378.
30. Ibid., (906).
31. Ibid., (931).
32. Ibid., (936).
33. Ibid., (977), pp.409–426.
34. Ibid., (981).
35. Ibid., (991).
36. Ibid., (1165), pp.475–496.
37. Ibid., (1180).

SIXTEEN: The Gathering Storm, 1539

1. SLP Volume 14, part 1, (20), pp.1–11.
2. Ibid., (130), pp.117–128.
3. Ibid., (316).
4. Ibid., (310).
5. Ibid., (330), pp.129–143.
6. Ibid., (382), pp.143–166.
7. Ibid., (465), pp.177–195.
8. Ibid., (527), pp.195–206.
9. Ibid., (577), pp.206–226.
10. Byrne, *Lisle Letters*, p.360.
11. SLP Volume 15, (856), pp.359–399.
12. Byrne, *Lisle Letters*, p.320.
13. SLP Volume 14, part 1, (856), pp.386–399.
14. Ibid., (368), pp.129–143.
15. Ibid., (766), pp.359–374.

16. Byrne, *Lisle Letters*, p.416.
17. SLP Volume 14, part 1, (353), pp.387–399.
18. Ibid., (930), pp.436–414.
19. Ibid., (966), pp.442–449.
20. Ibid., (973), pp.449–469.
21. Ibid., (452), pp.177–195.
22. Ibid., (305), pp.117–128.
23. Ibid., (398), pp.143–166.
24. Ibid., (306), pp.117–128.
25. Ibid., (432), pp.166–177.
26. Ibid., (307), pp.117–128.
27. Ibid., (29), pp.11–22.
28. Ibid., (1180), pp.502–506.
29. Ibid., (974), pp.449–462.
30. Byrne, *Lisle Letters*, p.463.
31. SLP Volume 14, part 1, (1042), pp. 470–488.
32. Foxe, *History of the Acts and Monuments of the Church.*
33. Ibid.
34. Ibid.
35. Byrne, *Lisle Letters*, p.462.
36. SLP Volume 14, part 1, (1042), pp.470–488.
37. Ibid., (1060), pp.488–494.
38. Ibid.
39. Ibid.
40. Ibid., (1088), pp.494–502.
41. SLP Volume 14, part 2, (228), pp.62–102.
42. Byrne, *Lisle Letters*, p.418.
43. SLP Volume 14, part 2, (493), pp.170–176.
44. Ibid., (347), pp.122–128.
45. Turpyn, Richard, *Chronicle of Calais*. John Gough Nichols, 1846.
46. Ibid.
47. SLP Volume 14, part 2, (761), pp.274–303.
48. Ibid., (761), pp.226–233.
49. Ibid., (673), pp.262–274.
50. Ibid., (664), pp.233–243.
51. Turpyn, *Chronicle of Calais.*
52. Byrne, *Lisle Letters*, p.359.
53. Ibid.

SEVENTEEN: World About to Fall, March and April 1540

1. Bernard, 'Thomas Cromwell and Calais'.
2. SLP Volume 15, pp.150–181, note 30.
3. Ibid.
4. Ibid., (316), pp.118–132.
5. Ibid., (471), pp.181–209.
6. Ibid., (608), pp.251–300.
7. Ibid.
8. Ibid.
9. Ibid., (609).
10. Ibid.
11. Ibid.
12. Byrne, *Lisle Letters*, p.482.
13. SLP Volume 15, (363), pp.133–150.
14. Ibid., p.364.
15. Ibid., p.363.
16. Ibid.
17. Byrne, *Lisle Letters*, p.486.
18. SLP Volume 15, (536), pp.209–251.
19. Ibid., (537).
20. Ibid.

EIGHTEEN: Defeat, April–May 1540

1. SLP Volume 15, (571), pp.251–300.
2. Ibid., (560).
3. Byrne, *Lisle Letters*, p.496.
4. Hall, *Hall's Chronicle*.
5. Byrne, *Lisle Letters*, p.496.
6. Hall, *Hall's Chronicle*.
7. SLP Volume 15, (560), pp.251–300.
8. Byrne, *Lisle Letters*, pp.497–8.
9. Ibid., (727, 728), pp.325–349.
10. Ibid., (729).
11. Ibid., (697), pp.325–349.
12. Byrne, *Lisle Letters*, p.500.

13. SLP Volume 15, (852), pp.412–436.
14. Ibid.
15. Ibid., (853).
16. Ibid., (736), pp.349–364.
17. Ibid., (767).
18. Ibid., (750).
19. Ibid.
20. Byrne, *Lisle Letters*, p.225.
21. SLP Volume 15, (749), pp.349–364.
22. Ibid.
23. Ibid., (751).
24. Ibid., (919), pp.355–481.
25. SLP Volume 15, Miscellaneous, pp.510–568.
26. Ibid., (833), pp.412–436.
27. Watkins, Sarah-Beth, *Arthur Plantagenet: Henry VIII's Illegitimate Uncle*. Pen and Sword, 2022.

NINETEEN: A Question of Life or Death, 1540–2

1. SLP Volume 15, (770), pp.364–376.
2. Ibid., (785).
3. Ibid., (786).
4. Ibid., (776).
5. Ibid., (215), pp.70–82.
6. Ibid., (812), pp.376–412.
7. SLP Volume 16, (298), pp.123–145.
8. Ibid., (325), pp.152–156.
9. Ibid., (452), pp.219–229.
10. Ibid., (567), pp.267–281.
11. Ibid., (581), pp.282–289.
12. Ibid., (606).
13. Archbold, William Arthur Jobson (1899), 'Wallop, John (d.1551)', in Lee, Sidney (ed.), *Dictionary of National Biography*, Volume 59. London: Smith, Elder & Co., pp.152–155.
14. SLP Volume 16, (830), pp.395–404.
15. Ibid., pp.376–412.
16. Ibid.
17. Ibid., (903), pp.437–443.

18. Ibid., (1011), pp.477–485.
19. Ibid., (1204), pp.553–560.
20. Ibid., (1218), pp.560–577.
21. Ibid., (1347), pp.613–629.
22. Ibid., (1361).
23. Ibid., (1407), pp.644–660.
24. SLP Volume 17, (34), pp.10–19.
25. Byrne, *Lisle Letters*, Volume 6, p.180.
26. Ibid.
27. Holinshed, Raphael, *Holinshed's Chronicles*. John Harrison, London, 1577.
28. SLP Volume 17, (145), pp.62–71.

TWENTY: Full Circle, 1542–1566

1. SLP Volume 17, (155), pp.62–71.
2. Ibid., (163).
3. Byrne, *Lisle Letters*, p.514.
4. Ibid.

Select Bibliography

Archbold, William Arthur Jobson (1899), 'Wallop, John (d.1551)', in Lee, Sidney (ed.), Dictionary of National Biography, Volume 59. London: Smith, Elder & Co., pp.152–155.

Aston, Margaret, *Broken Idols of the English Reformation*. Cambridge, 2015.

Bernard, G.W., 'Thomas Cromwell and Calais'. Southampton University website, 1–111, August 2007.

Bush, M.L., 'The Lisle-Seymour Land Disputes: A Study of Power and Influence in the 1530s', *The Historical Journal*, Volume 9, No.3. (1966), pp.255–274.

Butler, Derek, *The Quest for Becket's Bones*. Yale University Press, 1995.

Byrne, Muriel St Clare, *Lisle Letters* (Abridged Version). Penguin, 1985.

Calendar of State Papers Milan, Volume I, Allen B Hinds (ed). London.

Calton, Robert, *Annals and Legends of Calais*. J.R. Smith, 1852.

Camden, William, *Camden's Britannica*. F. Collins and A and J Churchill, Paternoster Row, London, 1695.

Campell, William, Rev. (ed.), *Materials for a History of the Reign of Henry VII*, Volume 2. Longman and Trubner, London; Parker, Oxford; Macmillan, Cambridge; A.C. Black, Edinburgh; A. Thom, Dublin, 1877.

Clark, James. G., *The Dissolution of the Monasteries*. Yale University Press, 2021.

de la Tour Landry, Geoffroy, *The Book of the Knight of La Tour-Landry*. William Caxton, London, 1484.

Domesday Book, A Complete Translation, Ann Williams, Geoffrey Haward Martin, (eds.). Penguin, 2003.

Duffy, Eamon, *Stripping the Altars*. Yale University Press, 1992.

Foxe, John, *History of the Acts and Monuments of the Church*. London, 1563.

Granville, Roger, Rev., *The History of the Granville Family*. William Pollard, Exeter, 1895.

Grummitt, David (ed.), *The English Experience in France c.1450–1588.* Routledge, 2002.

Hall, Edward, *Hall's Chronicle.* J. Johnson, 1809.

Holinshed, Raphael, *Holinshed's Chronicles.* John Harrison, London, 1577.

James, Susan E., *The Feminine Dynamic in English Art 1485–1603: Women as Consumers, Patrons and Painters.* Taylor and Francis, 2017.

Leland, John, *The Itinerary of John Leland in or about the years 1535–43*, Lucy Toulmin Smith (ed.). George Bell & Sons, London, 1907.

Letters and Papers, Foreign and Domestic, Henry VIII, Volumes 1–17, Various editors. HMSO, London.

Levin, Carole; Bertolet, Anna Riehl and Carney, Jo Elridge, *A Biographical Encyclopaedia of Early Modern Englishwomen.* Routledge, 2017.

Licence, Amy, *1520: The Field of the Cloth of Gold.* Amberley, 2020.

Licence, Amy, *Anne Boleyn: Adultery, Heresy, Desire.* Amberley, 2017.

Lysons, Daniel and Lysons, Samuel, *Magna Britannia,* Volume VI, Devonshire. Thomas Cadell, London, 1822.

MacCulloch, Diarmaid, *Thomas Cromwell: A Life.* Penguin, 2018.

Parish, Helen, '"Multe etiam alie reliquie quorum scripta desunt": the migration of relics in Reformation England', *Reading Medieval Studies*, 45, (2019), pp.133–150.

Risdon, Tristram, *The Chorographical Description or Survey of the County of Devon* (c.1630). Rees and Curtis, Plymouth, 1811.

Rose, Susan, *Calais: An English Town in France 1347–1558.* Woodbridge, 2008.

Rose, Susan, *England's Medieval Navy 1066–1509.* Seaforth Publishing, 2013.

Rutland Papers: Original Documents Illustrative of the Courts and Times of Henry VII and Henry VIII. Camden Society, J. B. Nichols, 1842.

Sandeman, G.A.C., *Calais Under English Rule.* Oxford, 1908.

Turpyn, Richard, *The Chronicle of Calais.* John Gough Nichols, 1846.

Victoria County History, Volume 3, William Page (ed.). London, 1908.

Vives, Juan Luis, *The Education of a Christian Woman.* 1523.

Watkins, John, *An Essay Towards a History of Bideford.* E. Grigg, Exeter, 1792.

Watkins, Sarah-Beth, *Arthur Plantagenet: Henry VIII's Illegitimate Uncle.* Pen and Sword, 2022.

Wood, Mary Anne Everett, *Letters of Royal and Illustrious Ladies,* Volume 3. Henry Colburn, London, 1846.

Index

Acknowledgements

I would like to give many thanks to the team at Pen and Sword for their ongoing support and the specific work done on this book: Jonathan Wright, Sarah-Beth Watkins, Sarah Hodder, Laura Hirst and Paul Wilkinson. I'm very grateful for the generosity of my fellow historians in giving up their time to read an advanced copy of this book and offering me their kind words: Alison Weir, Philippa Gregory, Nathen Amin, Owen Emmerson and Gareth Russell. Also, many friends in the historical community have encouraged me and offered their thoughts, especially Anne Marie Bouchard, Sharon Bennett Connolly, Adrienne Dillard, Kristie Dean and many others. Thanks to Michael Prowse and Katherine Walker for their advice and thoughts and many thanks to Joe Pellett; I couldn't have asked for a better colleague and friend. A huge thanks to my wonderful, inspiring students, who never tire of listening to my historical anecdotes! Thank you as always to my family, to my mother and my godmother Susan, and to my husband and sons.